FIELD HOCKEY

THE COACH AND THE PLAYER

Mildred J. Barnes

University of Iowa

FIELD HOCKEY

THE COACH AND THE PLAYER

Allyn and Bacon, Inc.

Boston

To

my Mother and Father

who made it all possible

Library of Congress Catalog Card Number: 69-17421

Printed in the United States of America

Third printing . . . October, 1971

PREFACE

Several years of playing and coaching have convinced me that field hockey is a fine sport. Opportunities to meet new people, to make new friends, to compete with highly skilled players, and to participate in a truly amateur sport are available to anyone who picks up a hockey stick and accepts the challenge of the game. Because of the advantages, benefits, and values that accrue from playing, the need to prepare a sufficient number of qualified teachers to assist players is great. The purpose of this book is to identify for the teacher and the player the basic principles for performing techniques and team play correctly. These principles are based on mechanics, mathematics, kinesiology, and psychology. If this book inspires even a few players or coaches to experience the satisfactions gained from playing or coaching, the author will have achieved her purpose.

An analysis of the techniques used in the game and drills for their development are provided. Attack play and defense play are described in terms of action in the attacking end of the field, in the midfield area, and in the defensive end of the field. Suggestions are given for introducing hockey at the beginning level and for raising the standard of play to a competitive level. Techniques for practicing segments of attack and defense play are described.

A special feature of the text is the contribution made by various United States Team players. Alison Hersey, Mary Ann Harris, and Diane Crowley Treese (former All England player) wrote Chapter V on Position Play by Forwards, and Adele Boyd, Jenepher Shillingford, and Marilyn O'Neill in collaboration with Vonnie Gros wrote Chapter VII on Position Play by Defense. The authors identify the qualities and stickwork necessary for each position and the responsibilities of each player in the attacking end of the field, in midfield, and in the defensive end of the field. The coach of the United States Team, Libby Williams, offers valuable suggestions in Chapter XI for coaching at high school, college, and association levels.

An ample quantity of photographs appears throughout the book.

United States players are shown in a sequential analysis of techniques and game tactics.

The author wishes to express thanks to the players, coaches, umpires, and friends who, over the years, have made the game of field hockey so enjoyable for her. Continued appreciation is given to my students who have demonstrated the effectiveness of the principles herein described.

Special thanks is expressed to Caroline Haussermann who encouraged the development of the book, wrote Chapter I, and who, in general, was extremely helpful.

The author is particularly indebted to the United States players previously mentioned who have written so competently for this book. Deep appreciation is also expressed to the United States players who gave their time so that photographs could be taken.

The author is especially grateful to Elenore Pepper, a United States player for many years, who was able to capture the highlights of expert play in her photographs which appear throughout the book.

Thanks also is given to Mary Bottaro for forwarding information on United States Teams, to Dean Martin for her suggestions in the preparation of the manuscript, and to Laird Addis, who so capably typed the manuscript.

Acknowledgement is also given to Marion Broer, who provided the technical data on shooting angles and to the American Association for Health, Physical Education and Recreation for permission to reprint portions of various resource materials.

FOREWORD

THE ALLYN AND BACON SPORTS EDUCATION SERIES

Today, sports are playing a major role in the life of practically every American: the educated and non-educated, the advantaged and disadvantaged, the handicapped and non-handicapped. Our fast-growing involvement in sports is manifested principally in two different ways: through *participation* as players, coaches or officials and through *observation* as spectators at sports events—on the scene or through television, radio, and movies.

The increased interest in sports is the result of several trends. Many people have more leisure time because laborers, office personnel and people in the professions work fewer and fewer hours per week.

Another trend is the increased emphasis on physical fitness. Automation, labor saving devices, and the mechanization of many industries are responsible for reducing the amount of physical activity among people today. As a result, many people need to become active in order to be physically fit. It is interesting to note, however, that today's advocates of physical fitness recommend sports participation rather than formal exercise or calisthenics. Sports are more in keeping with the culture and philosophy of our country. The *President's Council on Physical Fitness and Sports* stresses the need for such activity to bring about physical fitness.

Interest in sports is also being promoted by the increase in television and radio broadcasts. Sports such as hockey, gymnastics, and soccer—currently not familiar to the general public—are, and will continue to be, presented and explained. Broadcasts of team sports, such as football, basketball, and baseball, as well as of the lifetime sports, including tennis and golf, will be expanded. There will be more programs on which sport skills will be analyzed and strategy will be discussed by knowledgeable commentators using techniques such as stop action and instant video replay.

An important result of this increased emphasis on sports in American life is the need for improved literature—literature not only to guide the participant and coach in our rapidly developing sports and recreation programs, but also to inform the spectator about the strategy, tactics, and techniques involved.

The *Allyn and Bacon Sports Education Series* has been created in response to this need. Each book is designed to provide an in-depth treatment of a selected sport for students majoring in physical education and for people in other fields who would like to coach. Young men and women who are beginning their coaching careers, as well as experienced coaches, will find great value in the books. It will be noted that reference is made to *both* men and women: even though some of the volumes will be used exclusively either by men or by women, most of the books are designed for use by both. The books also provide a source of information to spectators. They can become more knowledgeable about and appreciative of the basic and finer aspects of sports.

The authors have been carefully selected. They include experienced coaches of high school, college, and professional teams, outstanding sportsmen, and physical educators from teacher's colleges and universities. Some books represent the combined effort of two authors, each with a different background and each contributing particular strengths to the text. For other books, a single author has been selected, whose background offers a breadth of knowledge and experience in the sport being covered.

Among our co-authors are Bob Cousy, an outstanding college coach and former professional player, and Frank Power, a successful high school coach. They wrote the volume on basketball. The result of this collaboration is a combination of drills, techniques, and coaching tips that will be helpful to both high school and college students of the game.

Professor Mildred Barnes of the University of Iowa and Professor Kitty Kjeldsen of the University of Massachusetts, leading experts on women's physical education activities, developed books in field hockey and woman's basketball and gymnastics.

Jack Barnaby, the successful tennis coach of Harvard University, authored the book on tennis. Mr. Barnaby has also taught boys and girls during the summer months for many years and thus combines a background of teaching and coaching.

This Sports Series will enable readers to experience the thrills of the sport from the point of view of participants and coaches, to learn some of the reasons for success and causes of failure, and to receive basic information about teaching and coaching techniques.

Each volume in the series reflects the philosophy of the authors, but a common theme runs through all: the desire to instill in the reader knowledge and appreciation of sports and physical activity which will carry over throughout his life as a participant or a spectator.

The general topics within each volume include a background of the sport, skill drills, practice sessions, rules of the game, and specific coaching techniques and strategy. Pictures, drawings, and diagrams are used throughout each book to clarify and illustrate the discussion. Some books include related references and sources for audio-visual aids, such as films, film strips, and loop films.

The reader, whether beginner or experienced in sports, will gain much from each book in this in-depth *Allyn and Bacon Sports Education Series.*

Arthur G. Miller
Department of Physical Education
Boston University

CONTENTS

FIELD HOCKEY SYMBOLS

KEY TO DIAGRAMS

↑↓ Direction team is attacking

F, D Forward, defense players

CF Player on one team

(CH) Player on opposing team

x Any player

o An opponent

→ Path of player

⊢ - → Path of ball

⌇⌇⌇ Dribble

• Ball

FORMATIONS FOR DRILLS

Pairs	Two opponents			
Partners	Two teammates	F →	or D →	F →
		F →		
Columns	x x x x x →			
	x x x x x →			
Lines	x x x x x			
	↓			
	↑			
	x x x x x			
Shuttle	x x x x x →	← x x x x x		

Scattered,
Informal,
Individually

x   x x
  x x   x x x
    x   x   x
x   x   x x
  x   x x   x

I

SIDELIGHTS AND FRINGE BENEFITS

by Caroline Haussermann[1]

Anyone with a stick, a ball, a field, and a few friends can play an approximation of field hockey by running from one end of the area to the other and attempting to place the ball in an area called a goal. Even though this game would be fun and involve exercise, there also would be inevitable squabbles over boundaries, rules, and method of play unless there was some formalized structure on which to rely. Therefore, as with other major sports, there are organizations that govern the playing of field hockey throughout the world and in the United States.

INTERNATIONAL HOCKEY

The International Federation of Women's Field Hockey Associations (IFWHA) is the parent organization. IFWHA was founded in 1927, about thirty years after the first organized field hockey was started in the British Isles. It is unique in that IFWHA was founded and is administered by women with a women's philosophy for a game played by women. From the eight charter nations, including the United States, IFWHA has grown to a membership in 1968 of 32 nations representing every continent.

The purpose of the IFWHA is to further sportsmanship and the playing of field hockey for enjoyment and recreation, to develop uniformity of rules, and to provide a workable constitution under which all countries may develop the game and administer Federation business. Every four years, an International Conference is held by the IFWHA in one of the member countries. First held in 1930 at Geneva, the Conference games have been played since in Denmark, the United States, South Africa, England, Australia, Holland, and most recently in Germany in 1967; New Zealand is scheduled as the site for the Conference in 1971. For the hardy player of lasting ability and stamina, these Conferences afford a grand opportunity to tour the world!

There are now 22 nations actively participating in these Conferences. Unlike the Olympics, in which representation is limited to sixteen teams in an elimination type of competition, the Conference games are played with every team meeting six other nations and with no championship awarded. Simultaneously, meetings are held with delegates from each member nation to discuss rules, constitution, and national problems. Players and delegates alike meet for two weeks at a central Conference site to enjoy the common bond of field hockey, a universal game that is now played with uniform rules under one Code of Rules.

HOCKEY IN THE UNITED STATES

Field hockey started in this country in 1901 when Miss Constance Applebee came from England to study at Harvard Summer School. With a group of eager students and teachers, she organized the first game and established herself as "Miss Hockey" in this country. From Harvard, she went to Vassar, and then helped start the new game at Wellesley, Smith, Radcliffe, Mt. Holyoke, and Bryn Mawr. Her influence was felt by many young women. All of those who have played under her throughout the years will long remember her colorful comments and vibrant spirit. To this day, Miss Applebee remains active, alert, interested, objectively critical, and beloved by all hockey enthusiasts.

The interest in and continued growth of the sport can be attributed to the assistance given by coaches from other nations who have spent a considerable amount of time in the United States teaching the fundamentals of the game. The devotion of many retired players and other interested individuals who have contributed innumerable hours for the advancement of the game cannot be overlooked.

By 1922, the game had grown so popular that the USFHA was founded with five local Associations. As a member of the IFWHA, the United States Field Hockey Association, Inc. (USFHA) is a large, strong, growing organization devoted to the promotion of field hockey in the United States for girls and women. Today, field hockey is played from coast to coast in nine major sections. There are thirty-nine local Associations and fourteen Directly Affiliated Clubs in these Sections; within these groups there are more than 215 Active Clubs and 1,000 Schools and Colleges, the latter as Allied members of the USFHA. About 1,000 other schools are playing but are not yet members. The game is known to be played in 47 states, and it is safe to assume that the other three states may play some form of field hockey in their schools.

The current *DGWS Field Hockey-Lacrosse Guide* will supply the reader with the names of individuals who serve as chairmen of USFHA Committees and who are ready to assist schools, colleges, clubs, or associations in the local area. The Coaching Committee will send a visiting coach to any area of the country when an application is received from a group in any local area. Through the Extension Committee, personnel are supplied to staff clinics or workshops. The Extension service is an excellent way of obtaining experts to help raise the standard of play in a community and surrounding area. The transportation expense of these coaches must be met by the local group, either through donations, registration fees, or other means.

Technical materials also are produced by the USFHA. Films are available for rent or sale. Printed materials may be purchased at a nominal fee. The films and materials available are listed in the *Guide*. A used equipment service also is maintained. Schools that are interested in obtaining used equipment or USFHA loan kits can apply to the Chairman of this committee. Applications should be made early because there is a long waiting list for this service. Additional used equipment is needed to maintain this service. Therefore, schools with established programs in hockey should not throw away old equipment. Another school would be delighted to obtain it. Make donations of equipment to the Chairman of the Used Equipment Committee.

Through Allied Membership in the USFHA, the grade and high schools receive coaching assistance, umpiring services, technical material (both written and filmed), reduced rates at all exhibition games, coaching clinics, and the official publication, *The Eagle*. This magazine is published four times yearly for all active and allied members of the USFHA. It contains pertinent articles about field hockey at home and abroad, pictures, coaching hints, techniques, news, and information.

Another publication with which the USFHA is directly linked is the *Field Hockey-Lacrosse Guide* of the Division for Girl's and Women's Sports, published by the AAHPER every two years. Members of the USFHA are appointed by that body to serve along with DGWS appointments as advisors and editors of articles pertinent to field hockey. The rules and the names of all committee members and Sectional and Association Officers are listed in this valuable booklet, which also contains articles of current interest.

Who plays field hockey? What goals can they achieve? The average player is introduced to the game in the 9th grade. She may play a competitive schedule on the varsity, junior varsity, or intramural level. After graduation from high school, she may go to college, where she can continue to play field hockey on her college team. In some instances, the college is part of an All-College Association in the USFHA; in cases where there is no college association, the player may play for a Club on weekends. The non-college player or the college graduate form the nucleus of the Club teams. Age is no barrier in joining a Club once a girl has graduated from high school.

At this point, a player is eligible for selection to a local Association team. When she has made this team, she can go to a Sectional tournament, where her team meets others within that Section. The best players are then selected to a Sectional team—either the first, second, third, and in some cases fourth. All of these Sectional teams go to the National Tournament, which is held on Thanksgiving weekend by rotation in each of the nine Sections. The best 22 players then are selected as members of the United States First and Reserve teams. The girls on these teams represent the finest our country can offer in field hockey players.

The *Field Hockey-Lacrosse Guide* lists the names and addresses of all of the Association and Club presidents throughout the country. By contacting the president in the local area, an interested player can learn how she can become a member of the group and where and when practices and games are held.

Figure 1:1 identifies the member countries of the IFWHA and the clubs and associations in each section of the USFHA. An association is composed of at least three clubs who play a minimum of four games per season. In non-metropolitan areas of the country, there may not be enough players in a local area to form several clubs and an association. Nevertheless, clubs can affiliate directly with the section until three clubs can be formed.

It is interesting to note, however, that players in certain areas of the country have a better chance of becoming a United States team player. The hockey played in some areas of the country is more advanced than in other parts. In the Philadelphia area, for example, field hockey begins in the elementary schools, so that when the youngsters reach high school and college, they possess extensive skill and technical knowledge of the game. In other parts of the country, the students never see a hockey stick until they select a hockey course in college. Until these areas introduce hockey at the secondary school level, they cannot expect to compete on an equal footing with players from the Philadelphia area.

Tables 1 and 2 indicate the number of United States and Reserve players each section has provided for each year the United States teams have been chosen.[2,3]

It is evident that Philadelphia has dominated the United States team since it was first selected. As a matter of fact, Philadelphia has had more than three times as many players (317) named to the United States team as any other section. The Northeast section is a distant

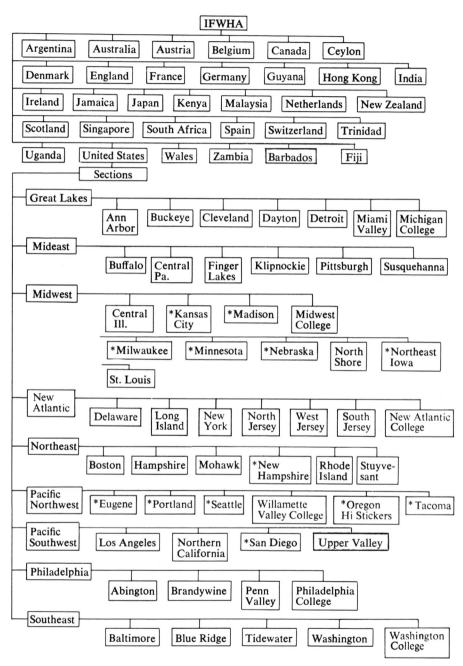

Figure 1:1. Member Countries of the IFWHA and the Clubs (*) and Associations in Each Section of the USFHA (inclusive September, 1969).

Table 1. Number of players by section on each United States Team Years (1924 — 1967)

Sec.	24	25	26	27	28	29	30	31	32	33	34	35	36	37*	38*	39	40	41	42†	43†	44†	45†	46	47	48	49	50	51	52	53	54	55	56	57	58	59	60	61	62	63	64	65	66	67	68	Total
GL										1															1	1	1				1												1	1		7
ME																															1			1	1	1				2	2	2		1		11
MW				2	2	1								5	2	1	1	2																									1			17
NA																	1							1	1	1	1	2	1		1												1			10
NE	2	3	2	1	3	4	2	4	2	3	4	7	6	1	3	1	2						5	1	2	2	3	1	1	1	1		2	4	5	4	1	2	1				1			87
PNW																																														—
PSW																																			1											1
PHIL	9	8	7	8	7	6	9	7	9	8	7	7	12	7	8	7	9	6					6	8	6	6	6	8	7	9	9	9	6	5	4	6	10	9	10	9	9	10	8	7		317
SE																							2	2	2	1			1				1	1	3								1	1	1	16

* U. S. Squad (not Teams) selected
† No team selected

Table 2. Number of players by section on each United States Reserve Team Years (1924 — 1967)

Sec.	24	25	26	27	28	29	30	31	32	33	34	35	36	37†	38†	39	40	41	42†	43†	44†	45†	46	47	48	49	50	51	52	53	54	55	56	57	58	59	60	61	62	63	64	65	66	67	68	Total
GL																									1	1	1	1	1	3	1	1	2	1	1	1				1	2	3	2	4	1	1	30
ME																																	2	2	3	2	3	5	2	3	2	2	3	2	3	26
MW	1	1	3	6	2	2	2	1			1				5	5	2	2												1																34
NA			4																				1	1	4		1	4	2		1		2				1	4	1	2	1		1	1	1	32
NE	1	4	1	2	7	5	7	6	7	6	7	5			3	1	5	2					4	4	3	2	4	1		2	3	6	4	1		2	1	1	1	1	1	1	1	1	1	115
PNW																																														—
PSW																																														—
PHIL	3	2	6	3	2	4	2	3	3	5	4	4			3	4	1	5					5	4	5	2	6	4	4	6	3	5	7	6	5	6	2	4	2	2	3	4	3	5	5	152
SE	5										1	1					1	2					2	2	2	2	2	2	2	3	1	4	1	2										2		39

† No Team selected

6

second with 87 players named, and this number is five times as many as any other section.

Philadelphia and the Northeast Section have dominated the Reserve team. Philadelphia has contributed 152 players, and Northeast has contributed 115 players. The other sections combined have contributed about the same number of players as has Philadelphia or the Northeast section alone.

It is interesting to note, however, that in recent years, Northeast has contributed fewer players to both of the United States teams. Apparently, quality play in that section has diminished, while play in the Great Lakes, Mideast, and New Atlantic sections has improved. All of these sections have a long way to go before they will be ready to challenge the dominance of Philadelphia. The contributions of the Midwest, Pacific Northwest, and Pacific Southwest areas have been negligible or non-existent lately. It may be significant that each of these sections is dominated by clubs rather than associations.

Appendix A identifies those players who have made the United States Team five, ten, fifteen or more years.

TOURS

Since World War II, there has been an increasing number of exchanges of teams between nations. Touring Teams are formed with the current national team players as the nucleus. Players pay their own transportation and receive the hospitality of the country in which they tour.

Since 1948, ten Touring Teams from the United States have visited all parts of the world, and eight foreign teams have visited the United States. This figure does not include the 16 teams that attended the 1963 Conference in Baltimore. A player who is selected to the United States team realizes the ultimate in hockey excitement, because to tour for one's country is an honor and unique pleasure. When foreign teams come to the United States, they play against Sectional, Association teams, as well as against the United States team. In some cases, Club teams have that honor. Such competition is thrilling, but equally as important is the exchange of friendships between national groups and the understanding of other peoples that evolve.

It would be erroneous for the reader to believe that only a select few players may ever reach the point of touring through field hockey. In recent years, there has been an increasing interest in exchange of teams of comparable ability on other than the national level. Local Association teams and special groups have organized and conducted tours; invitations have been extended to other teams from different countries to visit local areas under the sponsorship of the USFHA. In the future, school groups may spend their spring or Christmas vacations as Touring Teams abroad.

Appendix A identifies players who have been on 2 to 4 or on 5 or more United States Touring Teams.

HOCKEY CAMPS

A unique development in field hockey started in the United States is the Hockey Camp. The Mount Pocono Hockey Conference, which was founded and directed by Miss Applebee, has been known to players for two generations. Teams going to the Poconos Hockey Camp in Pennsylvania in late August and early September have received excellent instruction from top American and British coaches.

In 1946, a second camp, Merestead Hockey & Lacrosse Camp, was started by Miss Anne Townsend, Miss May Fogg, and Mrs. Eduarda Boehm in Maine. This camp serves individual players as well as teams. Other camps soon followed, including Valley Farm Hockey Camp in Michigan, directed by Miss Betty Dillahunt; the Sanford Hockey Camp in Delaware; the Glassboro Hockey Camp in New Jersey; the Cran Barry Hockey Camp in California; and most recently, the Poconos Sports Camp in Pennsylvania.

Similar programs are offered in all camps. Sessions last for two or three periods of one week each. Days are spent in drills, learning new techniques, coached games, and competition for players of all ages and ability.

The Day Camp is a less expensive, recent local outgrowth of the overnight hockey camp. Day Camp programs run in the mornings or afternoons for five days and appeal primarily to high school players. One specialized Invitational Day Camp for Advanced players was started in 1966 by Miss Elizabeth Williams in Philadelphia.

The specialized and concentrated training given at all the Hockey and Day Camps leads to the advancement of play standards. All camps are members of the USFHA and are staffed by the best of coaches in an effort to develop the individual skills of the enthusiastic player to the highest possible level.

Eleven people play on a field hockey team. Multiply these eleven by the countless schools and colleges and clubs that play; then by the more than 50 Associations and the nine Sections; add to this number the dedicated workers who keep the organizations running smoothly and efficiently, the umpires who officiate games, the committee members who work in their areas of interest and write their reports. The result is a large and keen group of women, devoted to a challenging team game that is played throughout the world. Girls and women of all ages and at every level of play and organization from the local to the International scene are welcome; the bond of friendship established through competition and service is lasting and rewarding.

FOOTNOTES

1. An assistant professor at the College of William and Mary and the Director of Merestead Hockey and Lacrosse Camp, Caroline Haussermann is well qualified to write on this topic. She played for the Northeast, Philadelphia, and Southeast Sections and was a member of the United States Team in 1957 and the Reserve Team in 1958–1960. She was a member of the United States Touring Team to South Africa (1958), Europe (1959) and to Great Britain (1961). She is a National Umpire.

2. BOTTARO, MARY, *USFHA - Past and Present* (Detroit: 19984 Whitcomb Ave., n.d.), pp. 15–38 and supplement.

3. *DGWS Field Hockey - Lacrosse Guides* (Washington, D.C.: American Association for Health, Physical Education and Recreation, 1201 Sixteenth St., N. W.), all publications.

II

SKILLS AND DRILLS

Like basketball, hockey is a game in which players pass the ball down the field (court) and attempt to score by putting the ball in a goal. Through passing and occasional dodges, the opponents can be made aware of possible evasive tactics, and a team can maneuver to score. In hockey, scoring is accomplished by means of the strokes involved.

The potential of a team as a whole is measured by the skill of each player on the team. Like a chain, a team is as strong as its weakest link. A player with severe deficiencies will be exploited by the opposition.

Ball control in hockey is as important as it is in any other sport. Few teachers tolerate a basketball player who dribbles the ball at chest level or who throws the ball with the hope that a teammate will catch up to it before it goes out of bounds. Standards should not be lower in teaching hockey than they are in other sports. Players should not get away with dribbling the ball six feet in front of them or be permitted to lace it and chase it. Hockey is a game that requires skill and forethought as much as other team sports. Players must know what strokes to use and how to use them, and what to do with the ball and how to do it.

There are fifteen strokes to learn. Beginners will attempt and master only a few. As players progress, they will become accomplished in an increasing number of strokes. Ultimately, players who continue the game will master all of them. Some of the strokes are used constantly, others are used infrequently, and others are used only in an emergency.

Pertinent to a discussion on ball control are the mechanical principles involved in throwing, catching, and the use of an implement in striking the ball. Basically, the principles related to throwing are applied to passing skills, and those related to catching are used in fielding. The principles discussed in the following passages are applicable to every pass and to fielding a ball that approaches from any direction. If students have difficulty in performing strokes, the teacher may wish to refer to this section for possible errors in application. Although players develop their own style in executing skills, the appropriate mechanical principles must be applied for repeated success. Correction of individual performance should be based on the principles involved.

11

MECHANICAL PRINCIPLES RELATED TO PASSING

Hockey sticks are constructed so that the ball must be played primarily on the right side of the body. All players must grip and hit the ball as though they are right-handed. Left-handed sticks are illegal.

Force

Maximum force is obtained by using many parts of the body and by contracting the muscles rapidly in sequential order. To obtain force, rotation of the body is desired. By taking a forward-backward stride with the left foot forward (hockey players are right-handed) and by turning the left shoulder forward, the hips and shoulders are rotated similarly as in an overarm or underarm throw. The momentum created as the body rotates forward with rapid muscular contraction should be continuous as the weight transfers onto the bent forward leg. The body should follow through in the direction of the pass so that momentum is not lessened at the time of the hit. Although what the player does with the stick following the hit does not exert any influence on the ball, it does ensure that the momentum is continued through the hit rather than decreased before impact.

Wrist snap as the ball is contacted provides speed at the end of the stick, and therefore increases the distance that the ball will go. Running also increases the possible force because the inertia of the moving body is transferred to the stick. Short steps help a player retain her balance as she hits the ball on the run.

Increasing the backswing strengthens the force of a hit. A short backswing can provide the necessary power to hit a hockey ball; maximum force is seldom needed. A hockey player also is limited to a shoulder-level backswing for safety reasons. A player should not feel restricted by the short backswing if she applies other principles to produce force.

In hockey, the problem of hitting is not to hit the ball hard but to hit at the most desirable speed. The only time the ball is hit with maximum effort is on a wing-to-wing pass, and perhaps on a muddy field to get the ball from inner to inner. Players often have to be encouraged to give sympathetic passes rather than to hit the ball harder. The faster a player's muscles contract, the faster her stick will move. Therefore, she can obtain a less than maximal effort by executing the same movement pattern more slowly. The player also can regulate the speed of the pass by not rotating her shoulders and hips or by rotating them to a lesser degree (common for the push pass) and by contracting opposing muscles to help deceive the real intent of the hit (done to fake a hit in one direction and then hit in another). A player's ability to hit a ball at different rates of speed is a sign of a mature hockey player.

Another factor is important before the topic of force is completed. A counterforce that is equal to the force made by the body as it prepares to hit the hockey ball is exerted against the ground. Because of this action-reaction law, a firm surface is required for players to retain proper balance. Many hockey players therefore select canvas or leather shoes with cleats to give them added traction. Good traction is especially important when players are practicing on wet or dewy fields. Because a wet surface cannot provide necessary counterforce, players will slip and stick action will be less controlled, leading toward dangerous play. Students who do not have cleated shoes and who must practice on wet surfaces should be limited to the push pass. The action-reaction force is less for the push pass than for the drive; therefore, play can be more controlled and less dangerous.

Direction

The basic movement pattern used in hockey is the underhand throw as the ball is projected along the ground. The ball is hit in the direction the force is applied. If a player wants to hit the ball to the left, she must turn the stick in that direction.

The underhand throw is made by swinging the arm in an arc. There is only one point along this arc that the ball can be released and travel along the intended path. By transferring the weight onto the forward foot as the ball is hit, the arc is flattened and direction is improved. Players may witness this phenomenon with a simple demonstration. A player stands with her feet together and simply swings her arm in an underhand arc. The rest of the class observes the continuous arc that is followed. The player takes a step and transfers her weight to her forward foot as she makes the arc. Immediately the class should notice that the arc is flattened at the bottom.

The flattened arc is caused by the transfer of weight, which moves the shoulder forward and lets the hand travel along a straighter line than is possible with the feet together. For a more dramatic demonstration, let the player follow the same directions with the stick in her hands. This second demonstration shows the importance of teaching the transfer of weight and hitting the ball with bent legs. If teachers could convince students of the propriety of this action, fewer fouls for sticks would occur and dangerous play would be almost eliminated.

Direction is especially significant on long hits because errors become magnified as the ball travels further. An error of a few inches on a hit from a wing to an inner can increase to an error of several feet if the ball is permitted to go through to the other wing. Control as well as direction are more difficult when many body parts are used to gain force. Therefore, short passes usually are preferred to longer ones.

Pointing the forward foot toward the receiver will help turn the hips the desired degree and thus aid direction. The backward and forward swing should be pendular to keep the swing on line. A pendular swing can prevent the outside-in and inside-out swings that put sideward spin on the ball, thus decreasing the distance and altering the direction.

MECHANICAL PRINCIPLES RELATED
TO FIELDING AND STRIKING

The direction that the ball will rebound as it is fielded depends on the angle from which it comes and the position of the stick as the ball contacts it. The angle that the ball rebounds is equal to the angle of approach, unless the stick alters that angle. If a ball approaches from directly in front of a player, it will rebound directly forward if the stick faces it. However, if the stick is angled to the right, the ball will be deflected in that direction. The same principle follows if a ball is hit directly from the right. If the stick faces that direction, the ball will be deflected back along the same path.

In hockey, the manipulation of the stick to face the proper direction is important. A ball rarely approaches from directly in front, where it is easy to redirect it forward. The ball usually approaches from a right to left angle or from a left to right angle at varying degrees, or from in front of or behind the receiver. Generally, in hockey a player wants to control (deflect) the ball forward so that she can proceed toward goal. If a ball approaches from either the right or the left, the player turns her stick on an angle toward that direction and the ball will deflect straight ahead.

The angle that the stick faces depends on the angle from which the ball has come and on the speed of the ball. The greater the angle and the greater the speed of the ball, the more the stick has to be turned. Failure to angle the stick causes the ball to continue at an angle opposite that from which it approaches.

DRILLS—A FRILL?

A knowledge of the rules of the game and of the mechanical principles involved in playing it is not enough to play good hockey. If the player cannot apply her knowledge, she will be of little help to her team.

Strokes must be practiced repeatedly so that they become automatic. A player who knows her strokes is free to focus her attention on the game. Skills must be mastered in drills before they are performed well in game situations. As precision improves in drills, success will increase in games.

Strokes in themselves are not particularly difficult. The ability to use them at the proper time and in conjunction with the total team effort may be a different story.

Practice in itself will not result in perfection; directed practice is necessary. Most experienced teachers can present skills so that students gain a clear concept of what they are trying to do. Most teachers also can select appropriate drills for practicing skills. But this is only the beginning of a teacher's responsibility. A good teacher must be able to analyze and correct errors that students make. To recognize that something is wrong but not know what or why is inadequate. The cause must be recognized and the information relayed to the student in terms of a suggestion that will correct the error. To tell a player that she is obstructing an opponent on a circular tackle is meaningless. To tell her that her body is between the opponent and the ball also is of little help unless it is followed with a cue such as, "get ahead of your opponent," or "turn your left shoulder forward." The suggestion must be in terms of *how* to correct the fault rather than *what* the error is.

Students prefer to play the game rather than to practice. Therefore, drills must be developed that are game-like, interesting, and fun. Students need a lot of practice to develop ball control. Ideally, there should be one ball for every student or for every 2 students. If not enough balls are available, old tennis balls can be weighted with rags and re-sealed, to augment the regular supply of balls.

Add variety to drills. Spice them up in any way possible, providing the original objective of the drill is retained. Use targets to develop accuracy. Targets can be old towels, Indian clubs, flags, cartons, or tin cans. What fun to hear a resounding noise tell everyone that a drive was accurate! Target sizes can be adjusted to the ability of the players. Make the size challenging, but of a size that some degree of success is possible. For more experienced players, the size of the targets can be decreased. Even within a beginning class, smaller targets may be used to challenge the more skillful students.

Drills also provide students with immediate knowledge of their performance. Each student can judge her own progress in relation to that of the rest of the class. This self-testing device may stimulate some students to work harder.

Drills should be organized so that students are running. Emphasis should be placed on the player positioning herself in relation to the ball rather than on moving the ball to suit her position. Drills must be introduced that incorporate *all* of the elements of the game. To expect a student in a game to know how to field a ball from behind and make the necessary adjustments if she is marked closely is asking a lot, if previously the player has only experienced fielding a ball hit from in front. Each player must have ample opportunity to practice her stick-work under gamelike conditions. She must undergo a slow process from the first introduction of a technique until she has practiced under many and varied circumstances so that she can perform the technique during the complexities of a game.

III

THE STROKES

GRIP

A hockey stick is flat on one side and rounded on the other. Only the flat side of the stick may be used to propel the ball. The stick must be constructed to be used primarily on the right side of the body. Therefore, left-handed sticks are illegal, and all players must grip and hit the ball as if they were right handed. This is not detrimental to the left-handed player since, by the nature of the grip, the left hand is the working hand for most of the strokes.

The player holds the stick in her right hand with the flat side of the stick facing left. She places her left hand at the top of the grip and shakes hands with it. Maintaining this grip, she turns the stick so that the flat side of the stick faces forward and is perpendicular to the ground. The right hand is placed on the stick a few inches below the left hand.

Figure 3:1

Fingers of both hands are wrapped around the stick. The lower the right hand is placed, the more control the player has over her stick; the higher the hand is placed, the more natural is the running position of the body. Therefore, skilled players prefer to place the right hand relatively close to the left hand so that the head can be held higher, giving good vision of teammates and opponents.

While students become accustomed to the grip, they should be watched. A check should be made to see that the palm of the right hand faces forward and that the fingers do not grip down the stick, thus hampering the execution of strokes. Many players find the grip of the left hand unnatural and tend to slide the hand around the stick so that the fingernails face forward. These players must be urged continually to get the back of the left hand facing forward. If the left hand is in the wrong position, the player will be unable to control the stick or perform many of the strokes. Early detection of an improper grip is important, because most strokes depend on a proper grip for execution.

CARRYING POSITION OF THE STICK

In any team game there are times when a particular player is not involved in playing the ball and other times when she must prepare to play it. When the ball is at a distance, most players find it easiest to run if the stick is carried horizontally across the body with the toe of the stick up. The arms are flexed comfortably, the right hand grips loosely and slides further down the stick, and the stick is in a position that does not hamper the rotating, driving motion of the legs.

As the ball approaches a player, she can easily extend her right arm to place the blade of the stick lower. As she prepares to field the ball, she can flex slightly more from the waist to bring the stick to the ground. It seems natural for a player to carry the stick horizontally across her body while running freely, but if players prefer to carry the stick in fielding position constantly, this may be a more natural position for them.

FOOTWORK

Hockey is a running game. Good running involves the ability to run with speed attended by control; to accelerate; to veer to the left and to the right; and to pivot quickly, accelerate, and run in the opposite direction.

Improvement in footwork is accompanied by increased mobility and ability to manipulate the ball. As players learn to move their feet into the proper position, they can dodge or pass in any direction. The choice of strokes is not limited and the stroke can be executed quickly and accurately.

Players must recognize that the ball is never out of position. Their own feet are in the wrong position. If the ball is not where they would like it for execution of a particular stroke, they do not move the ball into position, but rather they move their feet. As soon as players demonstrate their understanding of this principle, their individual skills will improve.

Short strides are desirable when a player is playing the ball or when she prepares to receive it. Swerving and changing direction can be done quickly. Long strides cover more ground and are used when a player is a considerable distance from the ball.

Some players tend to take a hop or a skip prior to hitting the ball. Such action should not be accepted since it advertises the intention of the player and slows her forward momentum. After a hop or a skip, a player must accelerate to keep up with the ball. This takes too much energy.

Drills

Balls should be omitted from the following drills, but players should carry their stick.

1. Run forward, backward, left and right on signal. Keep the stick close to the ground and ready to field a ball.
2. Run forward, accelerate, return to normal speed; repeat.
3. Run forward, swerve to the left, twisting the hips and shoulders around so that the left shoulder and hip are forward (in preparation for the circular tackle, pass to the right and reception from the right); repeat.
4. Run forward, pivot, and run in the opposite direction looking over the right shoulder. Repeat, looking over the left shoulder.
5. Run left, run straight forward (to receive or intercept passes); repeat to the right.
6. Run forward, run backward, accelerate forward (to promote forwards staying on line with the ball on sides when a pass is made behind them or when a player fails to field it cleanly).

DRIBBLING

Once the grip and basic footwork have been learned, students should see what they can do with a ball. Dribbling is presented so that students may learn control. Even though the ball is dribbled forward in a game, students should practice dribbling in every direction so that they gain complete control. By dribbling, a player maintains possession of the ball and progresses downfield with it.

The basic grip is taken. The left arm flexes so that the left elbow is almost as high as the left shoulder and the forearm becomes an extension of the stick. The left wrist is flexed so that the stick is placed perpendicularly to the ground and slightly in front of the right foot. The position of the left arm brings the left shoulder slightly forward, providing greater reach. This places the stick away from the feet and causes the body's weight to move forward, placing the body in a favorable running position.

Figure 3:2

By flexing and extending her left wrist, the player can tap or nudge (not hit) the ball forward. She should tap the ball only as hard as is necessary to keep the ball in front of the feet. The faster a player runs, the harder the ball is tapped. By taking short running strides, a player can tap the ball more gently and keep it under better control. The ball should be tapped frequently and when the player's weight is on her forward foot. The right hand does not give any force to the stroke; it merely guides the stick.

The most common fault of beginners is tucking the left elbow in close to the waist. This causes the stick to be angled to the right and generally forces the right hand to become the propelling force. As a result, players fail to control the ball as they hit and chase it.

A coach can see if a player is dribbling correctly by looking at her from the right side. Her left elbow should be clearly visible, and her left forearm should be away from the body. Inability to see either of these indicates poor dribbling form.

Loose dribble

In the loose dribble, a player taps the ball several feet ahead of her and runs after it. All too often, players are permitted to get away with using this dribble. The loose dribble should be used in only two instances. When a free forward (usually a wing) is far ahead of her teammates, she should use the loose dribble. By dribbling loosely, she can run faster and maintain her advantage. The other occasion occurs when a player is trying to deceive an opponent. By using the loose dribble, she attempts to draw her opponent so that she may dodge her or pass to her non-stick side.

There is danger involved in using the loose dribble. A player may appear unexpectedly from the side or rear to hinder the dribbler or to take the ball from her. Also, an unexpected opportunity for a pass may appear, and without constant control of the ball, the momentary advantage cannot be realized. The loose dribble has limited value, which should be emphasized.

Drills

The following drills are suggested for the normal dribble. Some of them can be adapted for practicing the loose dribble.

1. Scattered. Scoop the ball up and hold the stick horizontally in front of the body, hands well spread; tap the ball continuously for as long as possible—much the same as one would do with a racket and tennis ball. (Improves hand-eye coordination.)
2. Scattered. Walk and tap the ball forward by using the left hand only; as soon as the concept is grasped, increase speed to a run.
3. Scattered. Dribble freely up and down the field.
4. Indicate a starting and stopping point (between the goal and denter lines). Designate the minimum number of taps that must be made within that distance. Emphasize normal running speed.
5. Same formation as No. 4 above. Ask students, "How many times can you tap the ball between points?"
6. Scattered. Dribble forward and make a turn to the right and return to the starting position. Whenever a return to place is desired, encourage the turn to the right; use the same motion necessary for the circular tackle, drive to the right, and

reception from the right. The footwork learned early will limit the number of obstruction fouls later. Emphasize continuous tapping, a small circle with the ball and a large circle with the feet, turning hips and shoulders so that the left shoulder is ahead of the right.

7. Columns of four players with five Indian clubs (or players serving as posts). Each player in turn dribbles forward around each club, starting to the left of the first club, right of the second, and so forth. Start players to the left of the first club so that the turn back around the last club will be made to the right. (If an even number of clubs is used, start players to the right of the first one.) Encourage players to move their feet and body to the side but to keep the ball in as straight a line as possible.

8. Scattered. Make circles; each student turns clockwise continuously; as skill improves, players try to make as small a circle as possible. Emphasize same items as in No. 6. Do not continue too long as players get dizzy.

9. Large circles with 10-12 students per circle. All players simultaneously dribble clockwise around the large circle; on signal, each student makes a small circle as described in No. 8 above and then all continue around the large circle. Signal periodically.

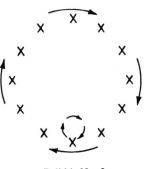

Dribble No. 9

10. Players dribble between the 25 and center lines. After dribbling several yards, each player stops (and stops the forward momentum of the ball), starts quickly, dribbles, and stops, about three times between the lines.

11. Same as No. 10, except a signal is given for each stop. Ball control is improved because players must have the ball near their stick to react on signal.

12. Scattered. Players run backward and pull the ball toward themselves, but never permit the ball to get entangled in their feet. Later, have players dribble forward and backward on signal.

13. Scattered. Players sidestep and dribble several times to the left and back to the right. Emphasize that the ball should remain in front of the player's body; short taps are required to keep the ball controlled. For the dribble to the right, the left shoulder and elbow are far forward.

14. Scattered. Combine dribbling forward, backward, to the left, and to the right.

15. Scattered. Establish a confined space (size depending upon number of players). Dribble in any direction but avoid collisions; use all types of dribbles—forward, backward, left, and right.

16. Scattered. Allow space for players to move forward and to the left. Dribble forward a few yards and pull the ball to the left; immediately sidestep so that the ball is never left of the feet; thrust the left shoulder and left elbow forward and continue dribbling forward; repeat several times. This maneuver is a preparation for the dodge to the left. Increase the difficulty by signalling for the pull to the left.

17. Scattered. Allow space for players to move to the right. Players dribble forward a few yards and then tap the ball slightly to the right; repeat. The tap to the right should be little more than another dribble.

18. Scattered, or use the alleys only. Zig-zag dribble. Dribble forward, pull the ball left, dribble forward, push the ball right; repeat. Confine players so that they progress straight down the field.

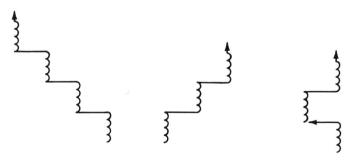

Dribble No. 16   Dribble No. 17   Dribble No. 18

19. Scattered. Zig-zag adaptation. Dribble forward, pull to the left, push to the right immediately, dribble forward; repeat. Permit no reverse sticks. Players must move their feet to the left and back to the right. Train players to move in a straight path down the field; use the alley for the drill.

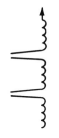

Dribble No. 19

20. Scattered. Players change speed as they dribble forward. Run fast, sprint, and return to normal speed while keeping the ball under control.

DRIVE

The drive should be a part of every player's skill repertoire. It is used for long and short passes, flat and through passes, centering passes, clearing passes by the defense, free hits, and for shots toward goal.

The drive is executed as the left foot bears the weight. (Skilled players can execute the drive off either foot.) The left foot points toward the direction of the pass, and the shoulders and hips also turn toward that direction. This turning helps move the hips out of the way so that a pendular swing can be made. The left arm should initiate the path of the stick, and the right arm guides the stick and helps supply the necessary force. With the right hand merely sustaining the action, it is not as likely to pull or push the stick off its pendular course.

As the backswing is taken, the hands slide together to provide a longer lever and more possible speed at the end of the stick. Straight arms, firm wrists, and a transfer of weight also increase the force. In addition, the weight transfer insures greater accuracy by flattening the arc, and it places the head over the ball, and thus eliminates topping and hitting behind the ball. Weight back on the heels and the resultant undercutting and high flying sticks are eliminated if weight transfer during the drive is emphasized. The follow through is made in the direction of the pass, with the flat side of the stick facing upward; the player continues to run forward. A ball driven correctly has overspin (increasing the distance it will travel) imparted as the back of the ball is contacted on the upswing.

To many players, the term "drive" means hitting the ball as hard as possible; unfortunately some of them never learn otherwise. How silly it is to hit the ball hard when a player stands only a few feet away. To drive the ball short distances, players need to contract muscles slowly so that less speed is imparted. A player's momentum as she runs while hitting the ball accounts for some of the ball's speed. The inability of players to drive the ball at varying speeds is unforgivable.

The most common error occurring with the drive is the failure to transfer the weight. If more teachers were concerned with this action, rather than with whether the hands are together on the stick, better driving habits could be developed. Occasionally, students stop and turn both feet, as though they were driving a golf ball. This poor technique indicates that students are permitted to practice from a stationary position. Another common error is failure to keep the head over the ball when hitting. If players would get their head over the ball, they could reduce the number of poor drives.

Left drive

Hitting the ball to the left is easy because the hips and shoulders are turned slightly. To hit a flat pass, the ball should be opposite the left foot; to angle the pass, the ball should be further toward the right side of the body. The flat pass is useful to all players except the left wing and left half and should be mastered by the right wing and right half.

Figure 3:3

Figure 3:3 continued

Straight drive

A considerable amount of body rotation is necessary to execute the straight drive. For this reason, it is hard to understand why some teachers teach the straight drive first. The player must turn her left shoulder to point forward and swing her hips to the left so that a pendular swing is possible. Players frequently overrun the ball and are unable to transfer their weight. Defense players use this pass and forwards find it invaluable in shooting.

Right drive

The right drive, which is the most difficult drive, is done by overrunning the ball and turning the left shoulder and hip to face the intended direction of the pass. The feet should be positioned so that a transfer of weight is possible with the forward swing of the stick. Because hip rotation is difficult when the right foot is forward, it is advisable for beginners to attempt the drive only with the left foot forward. The right drive should be perfected by the left wing and left half and is invaluable to all other players except the right wing and right half.

Figure 3:4

Drills

Precede all drills by players dribbling at normal speed followed by the drive. Never practice from a stationary position.

1. Scattered. Drive in any direction; recover own ball and continue. (Specify a direction for the drive, if desired.)
2. Columns. Drive at targets. Place flags at desired width to designate target area. Make the area large enough to provide success; decrease the size for advanced players.
3. Columns. Drive at the goal to practice the straight drive; block off part of the goal as skill improves.
4. Columns. Place a row of No. 10 or gallon cans to serve as a resounding target for players' aim. This is a "fun" drill.
5. Columns. Start the players at a greater distance from the target area; players drive on a signal, the timing of which is varied to force players to drive at different angles toward the target.
6. Columns. Form circles with lime, oilcloth, or plastic on the field 10, 15, 20, or 30 yards from the driving point. Players drive so that the ball stops within the designated circle. Award points for success and use competition between squads. Form concentric circles with different point allotments, if desired. (This drill helps students learn to give sympathetic passes.)

7. Partners. Pass down the field; after passing, sprint to catch up on line with the ball; give a sympathetic pass, but challenge one another to greater speed and improved footwork. Stress: Indian givers are undesirable; if a poor pass is made, the passer pulls away from the ball and lets her partner field it; stay on line with the ball until it is hit and then sprint forward.

8. Partners. How many passes can each twosome make in 100 yards? Encourage normal running speed.

9. Partners, but standing obliquely to one another (may be done in circles of 3, 4, or 5 players). Players move in a circle counterclockwise and use the left drive; move clockwise and practice the right drive.

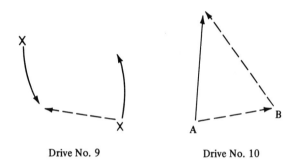

Drive No. 9   Drive No. 10

10. Partners—triangular passing. Player A hits a flat pass to B, who returns a through pass to A; A hits a flat pass to B, and the pattern is repeated. Players A and B exchange positions. Practice from the left and right.

11. Squads; drive for distance. How far can you hit the ball to the left? To the right? Straight ahead?

12. Squads. Each player in turn dribbles and drives straight ahead as far as she can, sprints to drive again, and continues until the ball crosses the goal line. First squad finished wins.

13. Shuttle formation. Dribble forward, drive toward partner, and go to the end of the opposite line. Partner runs forward to field after the ball is hit, dribbles, and drives. Continue.

14. In groups of three or five. Practice passing down the field. Start the ball with a different player each turn.

DRIVE—HANDS APART

Increased use of this stroke has been observed in advanced play. The principles for the drive (previously described) are utilized except that the ball is hit with the hands separated. This means that the position of the hands does not have to be altered following the dribble; thus, the drive can be executed more quickly while concealing the intent longer.

The wrist snap at impact is important to provide the force necessary, since the speed at the end of the stick is lessened because of the shorter lever. As strong wrists and arms are necessary to perform this stroke well, young children should not be expected to use it. It may be desirable to permit only skilled players to drive with the hands in this position. After beginners learn the correct technique for the drive, they can apply the principles with the hands apart.

Drills

The same drills as described for the drive may be used to practice this hybrid stroke.

FIELDING

The ability to dribble and drive is valuable only if the player can control the ball. Almost anyone, with some practice, can get her stick in front of the ball; but it is the player's ability to stop the ball and immediately guide it into position for the ensuing action that is important. Without this guiding action, the ball rebounds out of reach or to an opponent, and efforts are thwarted.

The technique of fielding a hockey ball (at least when it approaches from in front) is analogous to fielding a softball; for this reason, softball players often make good hockey players, particularly defense players because the ball approaches from the same direction. The fielder lines herself up with the ball, goes to meet it, and reaches forward with her

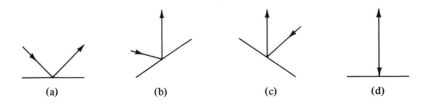

    (a)   (b)   (c)   (d)

Figure 3:5. Receiving from in front. (a) incorrect angle of stick, causing the ball to be deflected to the side; (b), (c), and (d), correct position of stick to deflect the ball forward as it approaches from different angles.

stick on the ground and perpendicular to it. Her hands are separated to provide better control and to shorten the lever so that the ball can be moved more quickly. As the stick "catches" the ball, the player relaxes her wrists and hands to help absorb the force of the ball, and at the same time guides it into position to pass, dribble, dodge, or shoot. Under no circumstances should beginners be permitted to hit the ball before it is stopped. Such action often results in dangerous hitting and purposeless passing.

If it is desirable to deflect the ball slightly forward, the angle of the stick as it "catches" the ball is important. Since the angle of rebound equals the angle of incidence, there is only one angle at which the stick

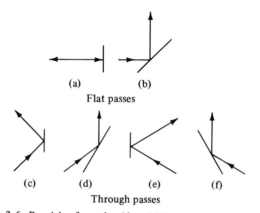

Figure 3:6. Receiving from the sides. (a) incorrect angle of stick and (b) correct angle of stick for receiving a flat pass from this angle; (c) incorrect angle of stick and (d) correct angle of stick for receiving a through pass from the left at this angle; (e) incorrect angle of stick and (f) correct angle of stick for receiving a pass from the right at this angle.

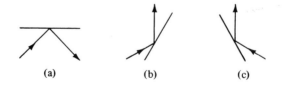

Figure 3:7. Receiving from behind. (a) incorrect angle of stick to deflect the ball forward; (b) and (c) correct angle of stick to deflect the ball forward as it approaches from this angle.

can be placed to deflect the ball directly forward. This factor is extremely important at all levels of play. Unfortunately, many players never learn to make the minor adjustments necessary in stick position for fielding balls from different angles. Figures 3:5, 3:6, and 3:7 show the angle at which the ball approaches, the angle of the stick, and the resultant angle of the rebound from the stick.

Receiving the ball from in front

Fielding a ball from directly in front is not difficult. The player places her weight on her left foot and reaches forward. The left elbow is high, and the forearm becomes an extension of the stick. The stick faces directly forward so that the ball is guided in that direction. If the ball approaches from in front but to the right of the player, little difficulty is encountered when the player moves in that direction as the ball comes toward her stick side. The stick must be angled in order to guide the ball forward, however.

If the ball approaches from the left, the player goes toward it and turns her left shoulder and feet forward. She lets the ball cross in front of her body so that she can field it on her stick side. The stick is placed at an appropriate angle to guide the ball forward. Immediately, the player thrusts her left elbow up and out to place the stick in position to pass or dribble.

Intercepting or receiving a ball from in front is probably the easiest fielding task. Nevertheless, any time the ball approaches at any angle from the left, fielding is more difficult. A beginner's difficulty with reception from the left is often magnified because she continues running toward the ball (and the sideline) rather than turning her feet forward toward the attacking goal line. Failure to turn her feet causes the player to stop the ball on the left side of her body, with her feet also facing that direction. Her only subsequent play is to hit the ball to the left. This fails to clear the ball to her forwards and may provide the opponents with another scoring attempt.

Receiving the ball from the sides

A forward receives a pass from another forward from either the left or right. When receiving the ball from the left side, the player allows the ball to cross in front of her body to field it on her stick side. She angles the stick as necessary and quickly moves her top arm into position to dribble or pass (Figure 3:8). During the fielding process, her left

Figure 3:8

elbow is low and pointed toward the ground but must be elevated to guide the ball forward.

To receive a ball from the right, the player must exercise a strong twist of her trunk to bring her left shoulder forward and turn her hips so that her stick may face the oncoming ball. The angle of the stick depends on the angle of the hit (Figure 3:9).

Because a player has a limited reach on her left side, balls hit in that direction must be angled closer to the receiver than those hit to the right. The reception is easiest when the ball comes toward the center of the body. A ball sent far ahead causes a player to sprint in order to get around the ball. If she still cannot reach the ball, she is forced to use the reverse stick to attempt to field it. Since the toe of the stick provides little room for error, the player would prefer a more empathetic teammate.

Figure 3:9

Receiving the ball from behind

Except for the wings, forwards may receive the ball from either left or right and must adjust their positioning accordingly. To avoid an obstruction foul, the forwards face the goal they are attacking and look over the shoulder nearer the ball. They place their stick on the ground to serve as a target, but the final decision for pass placement rests with the defense player who has a clear view of the adversaries. Due to the position of the opponents, the defense player may choose to hit directly to the forward or into the space ahead of her. Each hit necessitates a different means of fielding.

To await a ball coming from the rear and to the right, a player looks over her right shoulder. She twists around from the waist to place her stick at the desired angle. If the pass is ahead, she sprints forward, angles her stick as necessary, fields, and controls the ball. If her opponent is covering the space, her teammate will pass the ball directly toward her, in which case she pivots off her left (forward) foot, cuts to meet the pass, controls it, and carries on (Figure 3:10).

Figure 3:10

A forward looks over her left shoulder with her stick angled forward while waiting for a ball from the left (Figure 3:11). If it is a through pass, the player runs forward, swerves her body to the left of the ball to field it on her stick side. If the ball is hit directly to her, she pushes off from her right (forward) foot and takes the weight back onto the left leg. The right leg crosses over and the player follows with a step left. This circling around behind the ball permits it to cross over so that it may be fielded on the right side of the body. Accompanying the footwork must be a strong twist of the torso to prevent obstruction.

Figure 3:11

Drills

Any drill that utilizes two or more players involves fielding. Whether fielding improves as a result of drills depends upon the teacher's demands and emphasis. Drills suggested for improving passing also are appropriate for improving fielding. In addition, other drills are presented below.

Fielding from in front.

1. Shuttle formation. Run forward, receive a rolled ball, and dribble to the end of the opposite line. Repeat, receiving a ball that is hit.

2. Partners. One player stands diagonally forward and to the right. She rolls the ball and her partner runs forward to receive it. Exchange places. Repeat from the other side.

3. Shuttle formation with one line 8-10 yards to the left of the other. All players in one line with the ball. The first player drives the ball to the right and the opponent runs to her right toward the ball, intercepts (fields) it, and dribbles to the end of the opposite line. Continue. Repeat to receive from the left.

4. Groups of three—two attack players, one defense player. A passes to B, and C runs forward to intercept. Exchange places. Later have B pass to A.

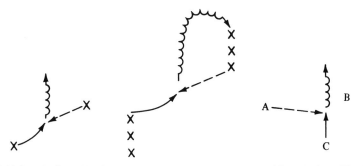

Field from in front No. 2   Field from in front No. 3   Field from in front No. 4

Fielding from the sides.

1. Column with leader to the left and on line with the first player in the column. Leader rolls the ball diagonally ahead to first player who receives it, dribbles, turns to the right, and continues to the end of the line. Change the leader to the right of the line.

2. Same formation and directions as for No. 1 except the leader rolls a flat pass. Repeat from the right side.

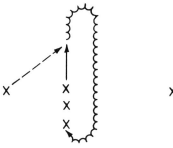
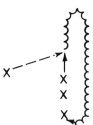

Field from sides No. 1   Field from sides No. 2

3. Same formation and directions as in No. 1 except the leader may roll the ball on any angle. Repeat from the right side.

4. Repeat Nos. 1-3 above with a hit ball.

5. Groups of three—two attack players and one defense player. B passes to A but aims it toward C (be certain to inform students that normally a flat pass to A would be advisable with C in that position, but the purpose of the drill is not one of practicing good passing techniques but rather to improve fielding). A cuts in for the ball and takes it with her. Limit C to a stationary position at first, and then permit her to take one or two steps. Change positions. Also change direction of the pass so that A passes to B.

6. A column in each alley. Each player in turn swerves out to the sideline in position to receive a pass (no balls are used, however) then swerves into the alley to receive a pass from the other direction.

7. Same formation as for No. 6 except have 6-10 players evenly spaced down the field along the sideline. Each player is supplied with an ample number of balls. The first player (A) in the column starts dribbling and passes to B; B catches the ball (in her hands) and rolls it back. A fields it and passes to C. Continue down the field. The second person in the column may start as soon as A passes to C; if the ball is passed poorly, one of the extra balls is pressed into service.

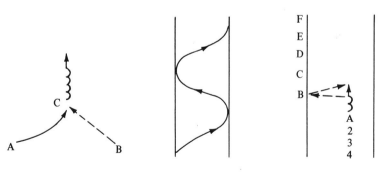

Field from sides No. 5   Field from sides No. 6   Field from sides No. 7

8. Partners—a wing and any other player. The partner hits the ball to the wing, who attempts to save the ball before it goes across the sideline. The right wing extends her stick as far forward as necessary; the left wing tries to sprint around the ball or, if necessary, uses her reverse stick.

Fielding from the rear

1. Partners—one attack and one defense player on the same team. The defense player dribbles forward as the attack player runs ahead. The attack player receives the pass, dribbles a few times, stops, and turns around. Continue in the opposite direction. Repeat from the other side.
2. Groups of three—one attack player, one defense player backing her up, and an opposing defense player. A starts with the ball and C marks B closely; A passes to the space, and B cuts to the non-stick side of C to field it. Repeat from the left and change positions.
3. Same formation as No. 2, except C is covering the space; A passes to B, who fields the ball and dribbles a few steps. Later, B may attempt to dodge C or to pass to a teammate. Repeat from the other side and change positions.

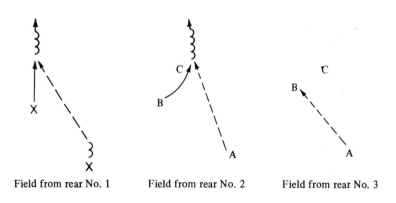

Field from rear No. 1   Field from rear No. 2   Field from rear No. 3

4. Same formation as No. 2 except let C take any position she wishes and A and B must adjust accordingly. Repeat from the left and change positions.

Hand stop

Generally, when a ball is raised in the air legally, it can be fielded with adept movement of the stick. At other times, the ball is lifted so high that play would be dangerous if a player attempted to field the ball in this manner. If the ball is shoulder level or higher, a hand stop is preferable and the only legal method. Following the catch, the ball must be dropped perpendicularly. Dropping the ball poses no problem when the ball is caught in front or to the right of the body. The catch on the left, however, tempts the player to transfer the ball across her body before dropping it. Such action is in violation of the rules, as the player is called for advancing.

The hand stop also may be used to field corner hits. One player stops the ball for another player to hit it immediately. It is questionable whether lack of success or lack of courage has contributed to the disuse of this plan in recent years.

TACKLES

Unlike its namesake in football, a tackle is a means by which the ball is taken from an opponent. Thievery is quite ethical, and the removal of the ball from an adversary makes defense play exciting and challenging. But the theft of the ball cannot always be accomplished. Two players of comparable ability should have equal success. Therefore, if the tackler gains the ball fifty per cent of the time, her task has been performed adequately. Even if the robbery is foiled by a good opponent, the tackler may force the dribbler to pass before she is ready. An erratic pass may result, and a teammate may intercept. A tackler should be praised when she forces an erratic pass.

Three tackles are commonly used. The choice of tackle depends on the relative position of the two players. Each tackle requires precise timing. The tackler carefully observes the tempo of the opponent's dribble and the relation of the ball to her stick.

Straight Tackle

As its name implies, the straight tackle is made as a player faces an opponent. It is useful for all players. Defense players often employ it to stop an opponent who is dribbling. Forwards use it to tackle their opponent when they intercept a pass.

The tackle is simple if the opponent dribbles loosely; the tackler judges when the ball is off her foe's stick and interjects her own. But usually dribblers are not so obliging, and the intervention becomes more difficult. The tackler moves to either side to keep in line with the ball, and at the same time sweeps her stick along the ground to threaten the dribbler. The tackler advances toward the dribbler cautiously. She knows that if she rushes forward, she is easy prey for a dodge. As the dribbler takes her stick back from the ball, the tackler places her weight on her

left foot (preferably) and reaches forward to field the ball. As her
tackle is made, her forward momentum is stopped so that if necessary
she can pivot quickly to pursue her opponent. The position of her hands,
arms, and body are identical to that for fielding a ball approaching from
in front. As the ball is trapped and guided forward, the opponents pass
right shoulders and no contact results (Figure 3:12). A tackle made
with the left foot forward is advantageous because it helps to bring the
left shoulder and hip forward. This position permits greater rotation
and helps the tackler to avoid a collision. When the feet cannot be so
arranged, special effort must be made to avoid colliding.

Figure 3:12

Not many players enjoy dribbling into a tackle. Players with good ball control will attempt to dodge or pass before being tackled. A coy tackler can hamper her opponent's timing. By thrusting her stick forward and quickly shifting her weight back, the tackler may be able to intercept the pass or attempted dodge. Other moves with the feet and stick can be developed for the same purpose.

Drills. Most of the following drills are done in pairs, but they may be modified to other formations, if desirable. After the tackler gains ball, she controls it for a few paces, turns around, and becomes the dribbler for the next turn.

1. Easy running; dribble loosely; allow the tackler to take the ball. Increase to normal speed.
2. Dribble with the ball well controlled; tackle.
3. Dribble with the ball under control; tackler employs preliminary feints before tackling.
4. Dribbler changes speeds, accelerating as tackler approaches.
5. Groups of three—two attack players, one defense player. As tackler approaches, dribbler may pass or dodge; the defense player tackles or feints the tackle and intercepts the pass or dodge.

Left Hand Lunge

The left hand lunge is one of the most useful strokes in field hockey. It is used by every player except the left half and left fullback. It is used primarily as a tackle to obtain the ball when tackling back on the stick side of an opponent. Attack players employ the left hand lunge when tackling back after they have lost the ball. The right half and right back use the lunge exclusively when tackling back so that they can remain on the goal side of their opponent. They also use it to prevent the ball from going over the end line. The center half also uses the lunge when tackling back on the stick side of the center.

The lunge is not used only for tackling purposes. It is invaluable for attack players when an errant pass from the left is too far ahead. By reaching with the lunge stroke, the ball can be fielded. The right wing should become adept with the stroke to save the ball from going over the sideline. If a ball is hit too far ahead for a player to control it, she may pass it by means of a lunge before an opponent has time to intercede. The player also may lunge to deflect the ball slightly sideward to start what might be a loose left dodge.

The lunge can be done with either one or two hands; the one hand lunge is more common. Apparently, players are often not close to the ball and therefore must rely on the extra reach gained by the one hand lunge. The stroke is started with the stick in the normal carrying position. The stick is thrust forward, down, and left, with the right hand providing the force. The weight of the body is taken on a bent left leg, and the player reaches as far forward and left as she can with the stick brushing along the ground until it contacts the ball. The right arm immediately extends backward to assist in balancing the body. While keeping her stick on the ball, the tackler runs forward, turns, and points her feet toward her own goal. At the same time, she replaces her right hand on her stick; her position now is identical to that for a straight tackle (Figure 3:13). If the opponent has not overrun the ball by this

Figure 3:13

time, a gentle upward lift will free the ball for a pass. When a lunge is unsuccessful, the tackler tries again after she returns the stick to her right hand.

Deflecting the ball can replace a tackle if the opponent is dribbling loosely. The tackler lunges to deflect the ball to the left (to the non-stick side of the dribbler) and hastily removes her stick so that her opponent is not tripped. As the dribbler overruns the ball, the tackler recovers quickly and passes.

The difficulty beginners encounter with the lunge is twofold: they tend to provide the initial impetus with the left hand, causing the toe of the stick to go up instead of down (the reason for returning the stick to the right hand before trying another lunge); and they tend to attempt the lunge when they are too close to the opponent. In doing so, they exert unnecessary energy to catch up to the foe. Then their extended arm provides too great a reach, or they lunge with a bent left elbow, which effects little force. If they are too close to the opponent, they should adjust and use the two-hand lunge with its accompanying limited reach. Better still, they should learn to perform the one hand lunge from the proper distance.

Drills. If the lunge is unsuccessful, let the same player try again; if successful, the tackler should control the ball. Players may turn around and proceed in the opposite direction.

1. Informal, no balls. Lunge forward—to recognize the length of the reach.
2. Informal. Place a ball forward and to the left; players lunge, run to get behind the ball, and dribble.
3. Pairs. One player dribbles, opponent lunges.
4. Pairs. One player dribbles and tries to dodge the opponent, who attempts a straight tackle; if she misses she pursues with a lunge.
5. Pairs. One player dribbles loosely; the tackler lunges but deflects the ball to the side, recovers, and controls it.
6. Partners. The player on the left hits a right drive ahead of her partner, who must lunge to reach and control it.
7. Groups of three—two attack players and one opposing defense player. The attack player on the left hits a right drive to her partner; the defense player moves forward to intercept, but the other attack player deflects the ball and dodges past the defense player. Rotate positions. Encourage a pass far enough ahead to

make the lunge a suitable stroke (the ball may be rolled for greater accuracy).

8. Same description as for No. 7, except that the attack player lunges to return a pass to her teammate (instead of dodging).

Circular Tackle

The circular tackle is the most difficult of all tackles; it requires extensive finesse for its execution. The circular tackle is used to tackle back on the non-stick side of an opponent. It is employed by the center half and exclusively by the left half and left fullback so that they can stay goal side of their opponents. It also should be used by the left wing as she tackles back on her opposing right half.

Because the approach is made from the left of the enemy, the tackler must circle around in front of her in order to avoid obstructing. The name of the tackle derives from this action. The starting position for the tackle is the same as for fielding a ball hit from the right. The tackler must overtake her adversary or delay the tackle; if the opponent is ready to shoot and hesitation might be costly, a jab can be made. (The jab will be discussed later.) The left shoulder and the left hip lead as the trunk rotates. The left elbow is high and away from the body, causing the right shoulder to drop considerably. After the dribbler is overtaken, the first tap of the ball is made as the left foot is forward to assist in the trunk rotation. The body continues in the circular pattern as the head remains over the ball, which is propelled by a series of short taps forward and around the opponent. The body makes a relatively large semicircle, and the ball makes a considerably smaller one. As soon as the ball is out of reach of the opponent, the tackler passes without delay, since she is extremely vulnerable to a lunge (Figure 3:14).

Figure 3:14

Figure 3:14 continued

It is infrequent that a dribbler accommodates a tackler by continuing to dribble at the same pace. A tackler can appear unexpectedly and lunge on a dribbler, but a player trying a circular tackle cannot because she is in full view of the dribbler. The dribbler usually passes before the circular tackle can be completed. The pass by the dribbler can be frustrating to the left half and left back; but if they have succeeded in harrying their opponent, their attempt at a circular tackle may be successful. The left half and left back can further harass the dribbler with a left jab that nudges the ball away from her. They are then in a position to recover the ball after she overruns it.

Drills.

1. Scattered. Dribble forward, turn to the right, and return to the starting position.
2. Scattered. Tap the ball continuously while moving clockwise. Emphasize: head over the ball and feet describing a larger circle than the ball.
3. Players evenly spaced along the left sideline (use the right alley line also if needed). Each player places a ball several yards in front of her and two yards to her right. She runs forward and executes the circular tackle, keeping the ball within the alley.
4. Pairs in the alley. One player dribbles; the other performs the tackle within the boundaries of the alley.
5. Two columns one yard apart, the left column about two yards ahead and facing the opposite direction. A ball is placed five yards in front of the columns. Explain that this drill is to assimilate the action of the attack player (left column) as she

awaits a pass coming from her rear and to the left. The ball is
poorly hit and she must go back after it before it is intercepted.
On signal, therefore, she pivots, runs back, does a circular
tackle to field properly, and takes the ball on with her in the
direction she originally was facing. At the same time, the
defense player (right column) tries to reach the ball first and
take it on in the direction she continues to face. Caution: keep
the forwards facing the goal they are attacking before cutting
back for the ball; prohibit them from facing the ball at the
start, an ungamelike procedure that defeats the purpose of the
drill. Note: Adjustments may have to be made in the distance
between columns; drill may be done in the alleys.

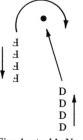

Circular tackle No. 5

PUSH PASS

The push pass commonly used for short distances is the most
accurate pass. Because it requires little force, the arms can supply the
necessary power and can move in relatively slow motion. The pass can
be made with either foot forward; the ball is literally pushed along the

Figure 3:15

ground. The stick is placed perpendicularly behind the ball, and the player tries to keep the ball on her stick as long as possible. On the follow through, the arms are extended as the sweeping action is completed (Figure 3:15).

Since the backswing of the stick is eliminated, the player may disguise her intent to pass until the last instant. The opponent, therefore, cannot be certain if the player will continue to dribble, will pass, or dodge. The push pass places the defense in a less defensible position than does the drive.

Because there is no body rotation, pushing to the right is easier than driving, especially for a flat pass. The other advantage of the push pass is that the direction of the push to the right is not telegraphed to the opponents. Forwards use the pass frequently for these reasons. Defense players find it equally practical when they must reach for the ball or when amid opponents.

Wings and inners sometimes rely on the halves for help near the attacking striking circle. By overrunning the ball slightly and by turning the left shoulder and hip forward, helping the stick to turn to the rear, the ball can be passed backward. This surprise move (when it does not surprise the halves as well) often results in opening the spaces in the circle or in a shot for goal.

Drills

Many of the drills suggested for the drive are appropriate for the push pass. Other suggestions follow:

1. Individually, as needed, no sticks. A player hits at the ball with her hand, then pushes it with her hand. Either a hockey or larger ball can be used to help a player gain the kinesthetic feeling of pushing.
2. Scattered. Push a soccer ball in any prescribed direction. This drill will help increase wrist strength and may provide the correct feeling for the push pass.
3. Scattered. Push at targets; use circles to help players adjust to the power necessary from different distances.
4. Scattered. Push at tin cans or wastebaskets to gain accuracy.
5. Circles of three players. Moving clockwise, the player with the ball passes it to the player in front of her; continue.
6. Partners. Running down the field, pass ahead of partner with a push pass. Exchange places.
7. Same directions as No. 6 except use flat passes; exchange places.

8. Groups of three—two attack players and one defense player facing the dribbler. The attack player on the left dribbles until almost tackled, whereupon she pushes to the right (non-stick side of the tackler). This drill teaches timing for the pass.

9. Three forwards and one goalie. One forward drives for goal; all forwards rush the goal with sticks down and attempt to push a rebound into the goal. (The forwards on each side rush the goal post on their side; the player in the middle goes down the center.) This drill stresses the use of the push on rebounds from the goalie and teaches players to rush as soon as the ball is driven toward goal, not to admire the shot.

10. Groups of three—two attack players, one defense player behind and to the right of the dribbler. The attack player on the right dribbles until the footsteps of the defense player about to try a left hand lunge are heard. She then pushes to the left.

11. Groups of three—two attack players and one defense player behind and to the left of the dribbler. The attack player on the left dribbles until she sees the defense player starting her circular tackle, at which time she pushes to the right.

12. Groups of four. Two players face each other, one in a position for a dribble and the other for a straight tackle with the ball placed between their sticks. On a signal, the opponents attempt to push the ball to a teammate who positions herself for the pass. Note: as the opponents keep pushing the ball to gain the advantage, their teammates may have to reposition for the pass.

FLICK

The flick is a combination of two strokes. It has the accuracy of the push pass and the effectiveness of the scoop. Because the ball is raised, the flick is used for two purposes: to pass the ball over an opponent's stick or to shoot for a goal. The flick is more difficult to receive than a push pass because of the added force and the increased spin. Therefore, players should use the flick for a pass only when it is imperative to raise the ball to evade an opponent.

The flick can be done with either foot forward, but it is easier with the right foot forward and supporting the body's weight. This permits the rest of the body to be behind the ball so that the force may be made in the desired direction. The player pushes forward forcefully to extend her right forearm, and simultaneously pulls with the left arm to thrust the left elbow down between her legs.

In the flick, as in the push pass, the player attempts to keep the ball on her stick as long as possible. The powerful arm movement will cause the player to go into a long, low thrust forward (Figure 3:16). A step onto the left leg prevents the player from falling onto her face. During the lever action, the ball is cupped on the stick instantaneously. This movement, accompanied by the stick contacting the ball in an upward motion, causes the ball to rise and imparts the spin. Strong wrists and precise timing are necessary to perform the stroke well. Once learned, a player can flick the ball in the air twenty-five yards or more. Because it has limited service in a game and is hard to learn, beginners need not attempt the flick.

Figure 3:16

Drills

Some of the drills for the drive and push pass can be adapted for the flick.

1. Pairs. Practice flicking.
2. Groups of three—one attack player, one defensive teammate, and an opposing defense player. The defense player with the ball flicks the ball past the opponent to her teammate. (This drill also provides good practice in fielding a raised ball.)

Flick No. 2

3. Three attack players against a goalie. One attack player flicks the ball toward goal and all three rush and try to flick the rebound into the goal.
4. Three forwards marked (guarded) by opponents in the circle. An extra player rolls or hits the ball to a space behind the defense players. The attack players rush and attempt to flick the ball into the goal.

REVERSE

The reverse stroke should not be taught to beginners. It is better for beginners to move their feet around the ball rather than to move the ball around their feet. Beginners can develop lazy feet and poor footwork if allowed to use the reverse stroke. Unfortunately, many players use the reverse stroke when, with a little more effort, they could get their feet around the ball and thus gain better control. Players should not be allowed to use such lazy behavior. Another disadvantage of the reverse stroke is that it can result in an obstruction foul. As a player reaches to her left across an opponent's body, she may interpose her shoulder between her opponent and the ball. Such a foul can be avoided if a player accelerates and gets her body around the ball, instead of attempting the reverse stroke.

At times, the ball is passed so far ahead that acceleration does not enable a player to catch up to it. To field such a poor pass, the skilled players will use the reverse stroke. The left wing, left inner, left halfback, left back, and right halfback find the stroke useful for fielding hits far ahead on the non-stick side and for saving hits from going over the boundary lines. The reverse stroke is used extensively by the left wing and to a lesser degree by the left inner and center forward for passing to the right and shooting. It is valuable because its direction can be easily camouflaged.

A good eye is necessary for the reverse stroke because only the toe of the stick contacts the ball. The player turns the toe of her stick down by turning the stick with her right hand and letting the stick slide around in her left hand. With the palms facing the ground, both hands then firmly re-grip the stick. The proximity of the hands depends upon how far ahead the ball is. For a greater reach, the hands slide together. Retaining the normal grip and turning the wrists over to get the toe of the stick down should be discouraged, because this action places the

Figure 3:17

Figure 3:17 continued

left wrist in a weak fielding and hitting position. The reach also is limited with the hands in this position because the arms cannot easily be extended to their full length. To pass the ball, a short backswing is taken; the arms and wrist supply the force for the hit (Figure 3:17). A flat pass can be made with either foot being forward, but a through pass can be angled better if the right foot is ahead to aid the hip and shoulder rotation.

Drills

1. Scattered. Each player has a ball and moves laterally to the left and to the right as she pushes the ball left and reverses it back to the right. Players keep their feet moving constantly and keep the ball in front of their body, never hitting it so hard that it goes to the side of the feet. Caution: be sure that players keep moving their feet; this is not a drill to be done for rest or with feet glued to the ground.
2. Partners on line with one another. The player on the right rolls or hits the ball ahead of her partner, who fields it with the

aid of the reverse stick. It might be helpful to place players so that the one on the right can use the corner flag as a target. Exchange positions. (Helpful for forwards in fielding.)

3. Partners with players on an oblique. Players face each other, and one player hits the ball to the non-stick side of her opponent. Change places. (Helpful for defense players in fielding.)

Reverse stroke No. 3

4. Individually or partners. A player dribbles and passes to the right with the reverse stick stroke. Increase to full speed.

DODGES

It is important to remember that the ball travels faster by passing than by dribbling and dodging. Nevertheless, well-executed dodges interspersed with passes keep the defense guessing and help make the attack more aggressive. On some occasions during a game, a player must evade an opponent. For example, when a forward is beyond the rest of her teammates, she must attempt a solo performance by dodging any would-be tacklers. Another instance arises when a defense player is being pressed by opponents. By a quick dodge, she can evade them and pass unhindered to her own forwards. Forwards also may dodge when there is no opening for a pass, or they may dodge simply to surprise an opponent.

The timing of a dodge is critical. If the dodge is attempted too soon, the defender has time to adjust her position to intercept it; if the dodge is started too late, the opponent will tackle. A repertoire of several dodges is important so that the foe cannot anticipate which dodge will be attempted. A player who can perform only one dodge will not pose much of a threat.

When a player attempts a dodge, she must retain full speed during the preparation and the execution. Slowing down proclaims her intention, unless she purposely slows down to dupe the tackler. If so, a rapid acceleration may enable the player to evade the stupefied tackler. Scanning the field for a pass receiver and manipulating the stick to give the preparatory motion for one dodge before starting another also aid deception and enhance the success of the dodge. To be effective, dodges must be performed in a limited space. A dodge that requires more than a few feet provides the tackler time to recover and interfere.

Four dodges are popular: push to the right, pull to the left, scoop, and reverse. The push to the right and the pull to the left are the most common dodges and should be learned first. When they have perfected these, the players can progress to the scoop and reverse. Although some coaches consider the triangular pass as a dodge, it is not discussed in this section because it is not a single player's effort for evasion. The triangular pass requires two players and two passes; therefore, it is presented under strategy for attack play.

Dodging is fun! It is rewarding to outwit an opponent in thought and deed. However, players must be cautioned not to become so enamored with dodges that they use them when a pass would be more appropriate. Dodging is a great asset in maneuvering the ball, but it must be kept in its proper perspective.

Push to the Right (Dodge to the Non-stick Side or Right Dodge)

The easiest dodge to execute is the dodge to the right. It is effective as a dodge for players who are on the right side of the field because their opponents anticipate a pass to the left. The tackler is easy prey for a dodge to her non-stick side because she is drawn to the left for a pass and is playing on the goal side of her opponent. Players on the left side of the field can cut in toward goal more quickly by using the right dodge, but their opponent is generally playing slightly to that side to protect against that move and against a pass to the right.

The attacker may start a right dodge by angling her dribble slightly to the left to lure the opponent in that direction. Just before the tackle, she pushes the ball to the right of the opponent, runs to the left of the opponent (to avoid obstruction), recovers the ball, and continues her dribble. If the player thinks of the push as another dribble, she avoids the ineffective hit and chase dodge. The ball should be tapped just hard enough to go behind the opponent about three to four feet before it is recovered.

Figure 3:18

Drills.

1. Columns. Ask five players to space themselves evenly about ten yards apart, in front of each column. Each player in order dodges each of the "posts." Spacing the posts at this distance makes the dribbler more aware of the need for controlling the ball on the dodge in order to start her next dodge in time.

2. Pairs. One player dodges her partner. Exchange places. At the beginning, insist that the tackler not move; she simply serves as a post. Later, permit the tackler to move her stick; and still later, she may use whatever techniques she desires to make the situation more game-like.

Pull to the Left (Left Dodge)

This dodge is frequently used by players on the left side of the field. They use the left dodge because their opponents play slightly to the right to protect against the pass in that direction and to stay on the goal side of their adversary. The opponents, therefore, are more vulnerable to a dodge to the left even though it is to their stick side. Players on the right side of the field discover that their route toward the goal is shorter if they use this dodge, but unfortunately their defenders position to that side and try not to oblige them.

The left dodge can be started by dribbling slightly to the right to draw the tackler. As the opponent approaches, perfect timing is necessary to avoid her stick. The player pulls the ball laterally to the left as she sidesteps with her left foot. She continues to swerve to the left and accelerates to dart past the enemy. The ball is given a slight tap left so

Figure 3:19

that it is never hit past the left side of the dodger. This dodge must be executed in a small space so that the tackler does not have time to recover. Quick manipulation of the stick is required to turn the stick sideward and then forward. Attention to the position of the left elbow may help some players. For the sideward tap, the left elbow is forced near waist level; but for the acceleration forward, the left elbow is rapidly brought high and forward.

Drills.

1. Columns. In front of each column, place a series of objects (boxes, pinnies, sticks with the blade facing the column, or players) evenly spaced about ten yards apart. Without balls, players run toward each object, veer to the left, and continue. They must be cautioned to approach each object head-on and then veer; some players will veer and remain out to the left. This is an easier maneuver but not a dodge! Repeat the same process, but have players go through the motions of the dodge by manipulating the stick.

2. Scattered. Each player dribbles the ball, pulls it to the left, dribbles forward, and continues toward the other end of the field. Start players on the right side of the field so that they are not lost off the left side.

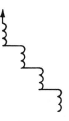

Pull to left No. 2

3. Pairs, in the alley. One player executes the dodge while the other serves as a post. Later, let the post move her stick and ultimately move any way she wishes. Exchange places. Practicing in the alley impresses on the players the need for control.

Scoop

The scoop can be an effective dodge if it is timed properly, even though its intention cannot be disguised. As the scoop is started, a player broadcasts what she intends to do, because her stick is not placed in that position for any other stroke. Nevertheless, the scoop may take the opponent by surprise.

The scoop is a reaching stroke. The player extends the stick in front of her body at about a fifty-degree angle to the ground and places it against the ball with the flat side facing skyward. She grips strongly with her left hand, keeps her left arm motionless, and exerts a slight forward and upward lifting movement with her right hand to lift the ball just a few inches to clear an opponent's stick (Figure 3:20).

If the player starts with her right foot forward, the shaft of the stick is left of her body; thus, she will not be impaled if she misses the scoop. The scoop is easy to accomplish while stationary or while running if the ball is stationary. Its difficulty increases when both player and ball are in motion. If the left hand drops low, making the stick too parallel to the ground, the stick goes under the ball. If the left hand is too high, the ball is merely pushed along the ground.

Figure 3:20

The scoop can be used as a pass when a player is double-teamed or has little space in which to maneuver. It also can be used to score goals. When the ball is just a few yards in front of the goal, the goal-keeper expects the ball to be hit along the ground or close to it. A high scoop may score a goal.

Drills.

1. Scattered. Individually practice scooping the ball forward, left, and right.
2. Scattered. Players place the ball about five yards in front, run forward to scoop in the desired direction.
3. Pairs. One player serves as a tackler while the other uses the scoop. Tell the tackler to remain motionless at first and then permit her to move to make the drill more game-like.
4. Individually. Each player places a ball 4-5 yards in front of her. She runs toward it, scoops it to the right (as for a pass), recovers it and scoops it to the left. Continue.
5. Groups of four—three forwards and one goalie. The ball is placed a few yards from the goal. Each forward in turn attempts to scoop it into the goal. Later add defense players opposing the forwards.

Reverse (Advanced Players Only)

By dribbling to the left and drawing the opponent, a player is free to reverse her stick and pull the ball to the right, away from the opponent's stick side. By moving the ball laterally, the player will not

Figure 3:21

Figure 3:21 continued

obstruct. If the player uses the reverse stroke before she gets too near her adversary, the chances for fouling are reduced (Figure 3:21).

The reverse stroke also is used when a player expects a left hand lunge. Just before the tackle, the dribbler pulls the ball back, and the tackler runs harmlessly by. Some left wings use the reverse stroke indiscriminately to avoid the difficult pass to the right while running full speed. By pulling the ball back, they stop their forward momentum and the right drive is easier to manage. In so doing, however, they find themselves left behind, as their speed is reduced and their teammates continue to sprint forward. Also, teammates may be placed off sides as they get ahead of the ball, or they may be forced to slow their speed to prevent fouling. Because of the disadvantages involved, the reverse dodge has questionable value.

Drills.

1. Individually. Dribble and use the reverse stroke, dribble and repeat the process.
2. Pairs. One attempts the reverse dodge as the other tackles. Exchange places.

Drills for a combination of dodges. As a player attempts a specific dodge against an opponent, the tackler has the advantage because she knows what will be tried. Therefore, drills that give the initial advantage to the attack player should be used because that is a more gamelike situation. By giving the attack player a choice of dodges, she has a better chance of evading her opponent.

1. Columns with four players standing as posts about eight yards apart in front. Each player in turn dodges each of the posts, starting with a push to the right, followed by a pull to the left, scoop, and reverse.
2. Pairs. One player tackles, and the dribbler uses the dodge of her choice to evade her foe. Exchange places.
3. Groups of four—two attack players vs. two defense players. The two attack players attempt to evade their opponents by dodging and passing. Emphasize the use of dodges and demand that each player use at least two different dodges.

EMERGENCY STROKES (FOR SKILLED PLAYERS ONLY)

The right hand lunge, right cut, and jab should be used only when absolutely necessary. They are used when no other stroke is possible because of the player's position in relation to the ball. Frequent use of the lunge and cut indicates poor positioning.

Right Cut

The left half and left back should become adept at the right cut so that they can hamper their opponent when time does not permit a circular tackle. The right cut is similar to the two hand, left hand lunge. The tackler changes her grip to that used for the reverse stroke, slides her hands together, and starts the stroke as she almost overtakes her opponent. She cuts quickly by extending her arms and tries to tap the ball to the side and out of reach of the dribbler. Her stick must be withdrawn quickly so that the opponent is not tripped. After the opponent overruns the ball, the tackler quickly recovers the ball and passes immediately, as she may be subjected to a left hand lunge. Executing the right cut with the right foot forward provides greater reach and reduces the chance for obstructing (Figure 3:22).

Figure 3:22

As the left back does a cut, she may try to tap the ball to the left half, who may clear it upfield. The left half has no helper, so she must be careful not to deflect the ball over the sideline. A player's ability to control the ball with the toe of the stick is limited; precision placement with the tap is impossible.

Drills.

    1. Scattered, without balls. Attempt the cut.
    2. Scattered. Each player places the ball ahead and to her right. She runs forward, cuts, pauses (to let the opponent pass), and recovers the ball.
    3. Pairs. One dribbles while the other cuts. Exchange places.

4. Groups of three—one attack player and two opponents. The forward dribbles while one defense player attempts to cut the ball to her teammate, who clears the ball upfield. Exchange places.

Right Hand Lunge

The right hand lunge is used only out of desperation. It is a very weak, unreliable stroke, but when used at the appropriate time, it can deter a scoring effort. The right hand lunge is used only when a player cannot overtake her opponent to do a circular tackle, and when she cannot catch up on line with her to do a cut. Because she is so far behind the opponent, the player is forced to use the lunge to try to stop the ball or to try to rush and hamper the dribbler.

The tackler (usually the left half or left back) slides her right hand to within a few inches of the top of the stick, changes to the reverse stick grip, and thrusts her stick forward and to the right, the impetus coming from the right arm. The left arm swings backward for balance. Only the tip of the blade touches the ball, and the stick must be withdrawn quickly to prevent fouling the dribbler. The tackler hopes that the dribbler will overrun the ball so that it may be recovered. The tackler should pass the ball immediately, because the dribbler will tackle back with a left hand lunge.

The similarity of the left hand lunge to the right hand lunge is obvious. The right hand lunge, however, is a weaker stroke because leverage against the ball cannot be maintained. Unlike the left hand lunge, the right hand lunge thrusts the stick across the dribbler's body, placing her in a precarious position. Therefore, with the instantaneous contact the tackler can only hope to stop the forward impetus of the ball or to cause the opponent to become nervous and pass to a teammate. Returning the stick to the proper grip from the right hand lunge takes a few seconds longer than it does for the left hand lunge or cut, because both the grip and the position of both hands must be changed.

Drills. The drills suggested for the right cut can be adapted for the right hand lunge.

Jab

As its name implies, the jab pokes the ball away from an opponent. The jab has three purposes. As a free forward at the edge of the circle takes her backswing, a defender may spoil her shot by poking the ball away from her. A defender on the stick side of the shooter usually will attempt the jab. For this reason, a right jab is common. There may be an instance when the only defender within reach is on the non-stick side, necessitating the left jab. The use of the jab permits the defender to continue marking her own player while jabbing. It also provides a delay for a teammate to recover and help foil the next scoring effort. The jabber may be lucky enough to poke the ball far enough for a teammate's clear.

The jab can be used as an alternative to the right cut. By using the left jab, the right shoulder is forced back so that an obstruction foul is not likely. The tackler may attempt to poke the ball to a teammate or to recover it herself.

Another use of the jab is to poke a free ball away from an opponent so that it can be recovered. Because this is an evasive maneuver, the jab can be classified as a dodge when used for this purpose. On passes that are hit too far ahead, a player can jab the ball away from an onrushing defender who is prepared to intercept it. The player can recover the ball by darting around the startled opponent. When the ball is on the non-stick side, a player may jab it toward a teammate who is in a better position to recover it.

The jab is a one-handed reaching stroke performed with either hand. For greater reach, the hand should be close to the top of the stick and the weight taken on the leg toward the reaching side; that is, the right leg if the jab is to the right. The wrist is taut, and the stick is projected

Figure 3:23

Figure 3:23 continued

forward close to the ground until the arm is extended and the shaft of the stick is nearly parallel to the ground. The end of the stick contacts the ball as it is pushed away.

Drills.

1. Scattered, without balls. Attempt the jab with the right hand forward and to the right. Repeat with the left hand forward and to the left.
2. Scattered. Players place the ball five yards in front, run forward, and jab.
3. Pairs. Players face each other 10-12 yards apart with the ball slightly closer to one of the players. On signal, each player darts forward; the player closer to the ball attempts to jab it away from the opponent, recover it, and dribble a few steps. Exchange places.
4. Groups of three—two forwards vs. one defense player, positioned as shown in the diagram. The attack player on the right runs forward, jabs the ball to her teammate, who dribbles on. The defense player tries to reach the ball before the jab.
5. Groups of three—two forwards vs. one defense player. The player on the left runs forward, jabs to her teammate before her opponent reaches the ball, and her teammate returns a pass to complete a triangular pass.

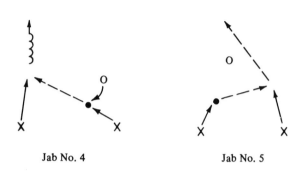

Jab No. 4   Jab No. 5

6. Groups of three—two attack players at the edge of the circle
   and one defender. The defense player marks her opponent and
   jabs, as the free attack player tries to shoot. Practice to the
   right and left.
7. Pairs. One player dribbles and the opponent, to the left and
   behind the dribbler, attempts a jab across her opponent's body
   with her left hand.

CONCLUSION

This chapter has dealt with the mechanics of the game of field
hockey. Without them, an individual's potential as a hockey player is
limited. With a good knowledge of the game's mechanics, a player's
potential is great, provided she has the intelligence to use each technique at appropriate times to outwit her opponent.

IV

THE ATTACK

The best defense is a good offense! Although everyone may not agree with this philosophy, everyone must admit that when a team has possession of the ball, the opponents cannot score! And certainly attacking is more profitable than defending. One must admit, however, that unless the bully is won at the beginning of the game, the ball must be taken from the opponents. But from the moment a team has the ball, the attack is on! Whether the initial "steal" emanates from the goalkeeper, halfback, or fullback makes little difference, provided that each player's thoughts immediately turn to attacking and scoring.

Unfortunately, not many field hockey teams attack with zest and score. They seem to enjoy play in midfield, appear satisfied if they get the ball down to the attacking twenty-five, and give little evidence of dissatisfaction if their effort does not culminate in a goal.

This attitude seems to be more prevalent among hockey players (not good ones, of course) than among athletes in any other team sport. Basketball players expect to score every time they get the ball. When a basketball player has a pass intercepted or passes poorly to a teammate, she is chagrined.

Does failure in hockey provoke a player as much? Or are interceptions in midfield accepted as general procedure? Perhaps a non-aggressive attitude is manifested by hockey players because practice sessions are dominated by play in midfield. Coaches unwittingly may be at fault in promoting this attitude. Unfortunately, many teachers spend so much time teaching players to pass to the wings that they forget about circle play. Then, when players get the ball into the circle, they do not know what to do with it. Coaches would do well to remember that scoring is an important factor in playing field hockey! Teachers should emphasize that defense players as well as attack players help in scoring and that scoring a goal is the main purpose of the game. Frequent practice from the attacking twenty-five into the circle helps players attain this mental attitude. Any other means that a coach can conceive to convince players to score should be used.

Players should be encouraged to take risks during a game for a possible score. They should take advantage of every opportunity to advance the ball toward goal. Once the ball is near the attacking circle, every effort should be made to keep it there until a goal is scored. Even if the ball is lost, the opponents must make several passes before they can advance the ball to the other end of the field. This provides time for recovery; the opponents may make a poor pass, which can be intercepted. Taking a chance to score may be worth the risks involved.

Taking chances is encouraged in softball. For example, when an outfielder throws to the wrong base, a runner is urged to advance an extra base. Taking advantage of such opportunities when the percentages for success are favorable brings many scoring opportunities. Being shut out in a game is not rewarding; neither is a game that ends in a tie. Outscoring the adversaries is more satisfying. Coaches should respect the intelligence of their players and let them use their own initiative in going for free balls or accepting other gambles.

When players understand the importance of scoring, the development of team play to accomplish that purpose must be given attention. In a team game, the attack is a product of the united efforts of all players. It makes no difference who scores, as long as someone does! A team that has individual talent will have little success unless all of the individuals learn to coöperate. Without coöperation and understanding among all players, a team is doomed to mediocrity.

Evaluation of players in terms of game sense and team play is important in selecting players for a starting team. Players with a hard drive, fast reactions, or great speed quickly catch the eye of the instructor. But these qualities must be judged in terms of what the player does with her capacities and how well she fits in with the total team pattern. Some flashy players make poor team players. The player who dribbles beautifully but onto an opponent's stick, the player who dodges when a pass is more appropriate, or the player who drives well but directly to an opponent should be relegated to the role of a substitute until she acquires the necessary game sense for her talent to be a positive influence on the team.

GENERAL CONCEPTS

The player who gets the ball starts the attack for her team. Her teammates immediately change from defense to attack. They try to advance the ball to the attacking end of the field as rapidly as possible and with as few passes as possible. Therefore, when the ball is obtained in the defensive striking circle, it often is passed toward the side of the field away from the other players. If the ball cannot be cleared to the wing, it may be passed to the inner, who in turn can pass it to the wing.

In midfield, the ball can be maneuvered among the inside forwards with occasional passes to the wing. Continuous passing from one side of the field to the other forces the defense to change position constantly, and the attack can take advantage of the opening when a defense player fails to react properly. This pattern of cross-field passes produces positional lapses among the opponents. A good team should master cross-field passes.

Whenever the ball can be maneuvered down the center of the field, valuable time is saved. Maneuvering down the center has the same advantages as a fast break used in basketball. The ball travels a shorter distance, giving the opponents less time to recover proper position. Keeping the ball in the middle of the field allows for passes in either direction. Both of these make correct positioning of the defense difficult. This effective tactic should be used to a greater degree.

As the ball is transported from one end of the field to the other, players should be conscious of spaces—not only the space into which the ball may be passed, but also the space into which they can pull away from another player who has the ball. Spacing players across the full width of the field is essential if a team desires to keep the ball, because crowding decreases the angles for passing. Wings should stay out near the side of the field until the ball is near the striking circle. Passes should be made on the run; players should not have to stop or slow down to look for a space to pass. Whether the ball should be passed square or ahead is a spatial judgment dependent upon the position of the opponents at that instant. Dribbling in one direction and passing in another will help deceive the opponents.

The through pass is most desirable from the attack point of view because it covers ground more quickly (Figure 4:1). In midfield, how-

Figure 4:1

FIELD HOCKEY

Figure 4:1 continued

Figure 4:1 continued

ever, the opponents attempt to prevent the forward pass, so that often the attack may have to use square or flat passes in this area. In the striking circle, the opponents are more likely to mark closely, so a through pass in this area often brings good results. If an opponent can be caught with her weight on her forward foot before passing or dodging, her recovery will be slowed.

Players should remember that forwards on the right side of the field have a greater reach in fielding balls than do players on the left side. Passes to the left should be directed closer to the player than those to the right. Players passing to the left should recognize that they pass to the stick side of their own opponent but to the non-stick side of their teammate's opponent. For this reason, the triangular pass to the left is so valuable. Players on the left side of the field literally run with their left shoulder pointing toward goal, so that their body is rotated in preparation for fielding. Their passes to the right go to the non-stick side of their own opponent, but to the stick side of their teammate's opponent.

PLAY IN THE DEFENSIVE STICKING CIRCLE

Beginning forwards should be encouraged to position themselves at about the twenty-five yard line. Here they tend not to confuse their own defense players and are in position to start up the field as a unit when the ball is cleared. Before long, however, the defense may need some assistance as opposing halves begin to shoot. Then, too, forwards can see an advantage if some of their teammates move closer to the centerline to gain distance on their opponents. The choice of formations depends on the individual abilities of the forwards, the strengths of their opponents, the strengths and weaknesses of their own defense players, the minutes remaining in the game, and the score. Depending on the conditions of the game, a team may use several formations during the course of the contest. The formations can be varied to keep the opponents off balance. The V, the inverted V, the W, diagonal, and M formations offer promise for a breakaway attack (Figure 4:2).

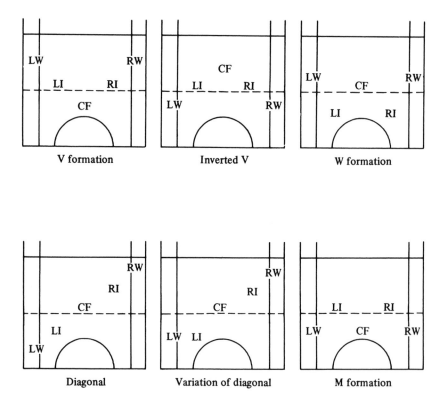

Figure 4:2. Attack formations with play in the defensive striking circle.

V formation

The "V" formation places the wings beyond the twenty-five yard line, well ahead of their opponents. Only the center forward is at the edge of the circle to prevent or interfere with halfback scoring attempts.

This formation is especially useful against inexperienced side halves who do not block the angles so that the defense can clear directly to the wings. Using the V formation pre-supposes that the defense has hard, quick clears and can adjust and pass to the inners if the paths to the wings are blocked. In turn, the inners must pass quickly up to the wings before the halves have time to recover. A team that has relatively strong inners and wings can use a weaker center forward advantageously with this formation.

Inverted V

Relatively weak wings can be deployed to hinder the opposing halves while the inside forwards edge upfield. One inner always will be free and the center forward is well beyond her opponent. Quick passes to the free inner or center can be advantageous. If the ball can be sent immediately to the center, she may have a breakaway with only the covering back to beat.

W formation

Placement of the fleet wings and the center makes them all free for a clearing pass. The inners can serve as a connector between the defense and the wings or center if necessary. A breakaway by any player is possible. A wing either can carry the ball or execute a wing-to-wing pass, which is even more expedient, provided the covering back is not in position to intercept. If play becomes confused and the ball cannot be passed forward immediately, inner-to-inner passes will move the team out of the defensive end.

Diagonal formation

Use of the diagonal assumes that the ball will stay on one side of the striking circle, because reforming the diagonal on the other side when the ball moves across the goal is almost impossible. The diagonal, therefore, is not a standard formation. It is a formation that a team can assume quickly when it is obvious that a teammate will clear the ball to one side. As the clear becomes imminent, players who are near the circle on the opposite side of the field hastily run upfield. The ball usually is cleared to the near inner or wing. She then can swing it across the field, provided that the opposing back is not in position to intercept. The only advantage gained by the variation in the diagonal is that the inner can maneuver somewhat better to position herself for a pass.

M formation

The most defensive formation places only two forwards beyond the twenty-five yard line. The two wings and center are drawn back when their defense is having a difficult time. Either the opposing halves are shooting unmolested or the defense cannot get a good clear out of the circle. One forward can serve as a connector and pass the ball to the free inner, who may have a breakaway with only the covering back to beat.

As players position themselves in one of these formations, they should immediately survey the positioning of the opposing backs and keep watching the changing positioning of the halves. In this way, each player knows exactly which one of her teammates is free; thus, the ball may be sent to her quickly for the breakaway. Scoring is easier when one or two players can outdistance most of the opponents. The player with the ball then has more space in which to maneuver, and there are fewer defense players to impede progress.

If the ball can be passed to a center or inner, the path toward goal is the shortest distance. The inverted V and M formations are favorable for this prospect. In the formations with the wings up the field, the ball travels a greater distance, going diagonally out to the wings. This action gives the opponents more time to recover and, therefore, possibly can negate the advantage gained.

Influence of score and time

When playing against opponents who tire near the end of the first half, a team may wish to use an offensive formation to break through a pregnable defense for a score before time expires. Such a breakthrough is demoralizing for the exhausted team. During the second half, the score and the time remaining can dictate appropriate tactics. If a team is behind, it makes little difference whether they lose by one goal or two. Using an offensive formation is correct procedure midway through the second half. If a team cannot clear the ball from the circle, using the desired formation too early can jeopardize their own defense. An opponent's score at this time can insure victory.

A team that is ahead near the end of the game may wish to play conservatively to assure that the opponents do not score. The M formation serves this purpose. Still, the breakaway threat is a possibility and should be taken advantage of if the opportunity arises.

Changing formations occasionally during the game forces the opponents to be concerned about one more factor; and the more they have to worry about, the more difficult is their position. If the opponents fail to stay alert to formational changes, a team's chance for a breakaway is improved. When the halves begin looking over their shoulders to find their opponents and when they resort to shouting to one another for help, a team knows that its formations have placed the opponents under tension.

Nothing has been said about defensive clears out of the circle. Their accuracy is a necessity for a breakaway to occur. Without a hard, direct hit to the free player, standard offensive tactics must be employed. While the defense players are marking closely, they also must be aware of where their own forwards are positioned.

Beginners must be cautioned not to pass across the goal and to aim the ball toward a teammate. Hitting the ball out of the circle is not enough. All of the defense should be encouraged to acquire good footwork while intercepting passes, particularly from their left, so that the ball can be passed upfield rather than hit toward the sideline. In this way, hits across the goal and across the sideline can be almost eliminated.

Drills

Too often, teachers expect tactics presented to students in a lecture to develop automatically on the practice field. Such is not the case. Reaction to particular situations and precise passing must be practiced. If students do not practice tactics under varying circumstances, how can they be expected to execute them in a game? For this reason, the following drills are suggestions for practice in getting the ball out of the defensive end.

1. Groups of three—goalie, halfback, and wing on the same team. The goalie kicks the ball along the end line to be fielded by the halfback, who passes up to the wing. The half starts in a position as though marking her opponent, and then runs to the side to field the "save" before hitting to the wing.
2. Groups of four—same players as No. 1 plus an opposing halfback. Same directions as No. 1, except the wing is forced to come back for the pass.
3. Groups of three—goalie, inner, and wing on the same team. The goalie kicks the ball out to the inner, who immediately passes on to the wing.
4. Groups of four—same as No. 3 plus an opposing halfback. The inner must place the pass to the wing out of reach of the recovering half.

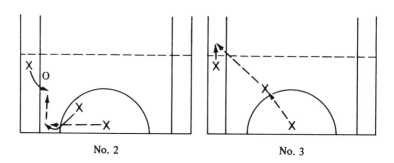

No. 2   No. 3

5. Groups of three—goalie, inner, and center. Directions are the
   same as for No. 3, except the inner passes to the center.
6. Groups of three—fullback, wing, and center on the same team.
   The back passes to the wing, who sends the ball diagonally to
   the center. (Place the ball to the side of the fullback or let the
   wing roll it to the back's side to make the drill more gamelike.)
7. Groups of three—halfback, inner, and wing on the same team.
   The halfback passes to the inner, who sends a through pass to
   the wing. Make the half work for the ball, as described for the
   back in No. 6.

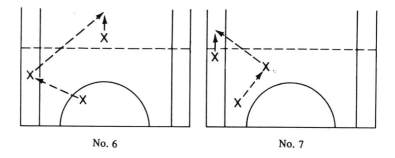

No. 6   No. 7

8. Groups of three—one defense player and her opponent and an
   attack player. The defense player must evade her opponent,
   using a dodge if necessary, so that she can pass the ball to her
   teammate. Start the ball to the side of the defense player and
   her opponent and instruct both to go for it, or have someone
   roll the ball so that the defense player can intercept and proceed with her pass.

MIDFIELD PLAY

Defense with the ball

When the opponents have the ball, the forwards should hurry back into position to receive a pass when one of their defense players obtains the ball. Long gaps between the defense and forwards make passes easy for the opposition. Figure 4:3 demonstrates how a halfback can cut off a pass to a player who is ahead of the ball. Figure 4:4 shows how the attack player can free herself for a pass.

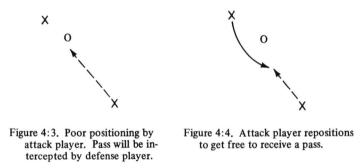

Figure 4:3. Poor positioning by attack player. Pass will be intercepted by defense player.

Figure 4:4. Attack player repositions to get free to receive a pass.

Forwards should be positioned laterally across the field. Each forward should move to the side to make a space for herself or her teammate, or to draw an opponent away from the area of play. At times, the inner should pull toward the center of the field so that the ball can be cleared to the wing. As the team approaches the attacking twenty-five yard line, the inner should pull toward the sideline so that the spaces are concentrated nearer to the goal. Figure 4:5 shows how spaces are made for the wing and inner. Figure 4:6 indicates how the inner can move to make a greater space for herself and the center.

Against strong opponents, forwards have to be careful about their positioning. Wings particularly will have to cut back and receive passes as shown in Figure 4:4. Against a weaker opponent, however, forwards can remain further upfield. This is to their advantage because it places them closer to the attacking goal.

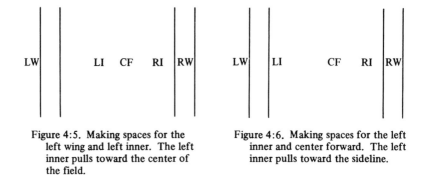

Figure 4:5. Making spaces for the left wing and left inner. The left inner pulls toward the center of the field.

Figure 4:6. Making spaces for the left inner and center forward. The left inner pulls toward the sideline.

Defense players can ascertain quickly whether their forwards are getting free. If they are not, they should be requested to come back further or to pull away from one another. If no attack player is free, a defense player can pass to another defense player, who will have a better angle for sending the ball downfield to a forward. Passing between defense players can be dangerous for beginners, and extensive passing among defense players should not be encouraged even for advanced players.

Attack with the ball

The area between the twenty-five yard lines provides liberty for individual creativity and imagination on the hockey field. No rules denote what each player should do. Rather, her actions should be prescribed by the position of her teammates, the position of the opponents, the position of the ball, and her ability in relation to that of her opponent. Considering these elements, dribbling, dodging, and passing should be used to attack the defense. Dribbling is useful when a player is free, and dodging is an evasive measure. Passing, however, is the best way to advance the ball down the field. Players, therefore, should master these techniques in order to mount a constructive attack. The technical aspects relative to the mechanical principles involved in these strokes are outlined in Chapter II. The application of these principles to the dribble, dodge, drive, push, flick, scoop, and reverse passes are discussed in Chapter III. The reader is referred to these chapters for review, if it is needed.

At this point, it is timely to consider the involvement of the forwards who do not have the ball, the player who receives a pass, and what she does with the ball after fielding it. The four *forwards who do not have the ball* are concerned with making spaces as previously described.

In the defensive half of the field, they must think of their position laterally, and also of being on line with the ball or ahead of it. If they are being marked closely or if their opponent is playing between them and the ball, a position on line with the ball will provide more spaces into which the ball may be passed. If the defense players are in a deep covering position or if they are otherwise out of position, a position in advance of the ball may prove beneficial.

In the offensive end, forwards should be concerned with staying on line with the ball so that they will not be offside. However, if a number of the defense are near the goal, the forwards should advance their position more quickly by placing themselves ahead of the ball.

If a forward's neighbor has the ball, she pulls away from her to give her ample room in which to maneuver. At the same time, each forward surveys the positioning of all the defense players so that she may establish a tentative plan of action if she receives a pass.

There may be instances when a defense player is significantly better than a forward. In this case, it may be helpful to deploy this forward for most of the game so that the efficacy of her opponent can be markedly reduced. If the forward keeps moving forward, back, and laterally, the defense player constantly will have to re-adjust her position. Also, by moving away from the desired direction of the pass, the forward can occupy her opponent so that she cannot impede the progress of the ball. When a player on either side of her has the ball, the forward should drop back slightly behind the ball to draw her opponent so that the ball can be passed ahead to another teammate. Obviously, occasional passes must be directed to the forward so that the deployment is effective.

To *receive a pass,* a player should anticipate its direction and dart to field it. Quickness off the mark should give the forward at least a step advantage on her opponent. (Forwards who are frequently victimized by an interception should analyze whether they start their cuts too late.) On centering passes, all forwards should cut as though the pass were directed to them. In this way, if a teammate misses the pass, someone is in position to field it. If a poorly directed pass does occur, some forward must try to field it. Some forwards seem content to watch opponents intercept passes. This attitude should never occur. By running at full speed and swerving toward the ball, the forward can lunge or jab and attempt to deflect the ball away from the defender.

If the forward cannot reach the ball, her appearance may at least cause the defender to take her eye off the ball and thus fail to control it.

Sometimes a pass is made erroneously to the inner position when the inner is not there. Either the wing or center should try to field the ball. If both players start for the ball, the closer player should continue while the other one pulls away. If both players are equally near, the player on the left should be given preference, since the ball is on her stick side.

Once a forward *gains the ball,* she can either retain it or pass it. If she is free, she should dribble the ball until she draws her opponent. This prevents the opponent from remaining in a covering position to intercept the subsequent pass. As soon as a free teammate in a more favorable position is spotted, the ball should be passed to her. Since a player is not always free, immediate advantage should be taken. The attack, then, is composed of successful passing accompanied by interspersed dribbling and dodging.

A variety of tactics should be used by the ball carrier. Opponents should not "know" what a player will do under any prescribed situation. A wing who invariably gives a flat pass to her inner to start a triangular pass, dribbles downfield until she reaches the twenty-five, does a right dodge followed by a centering pass at the circle does not deceive the opponents. They can devise a game plan to render this player ineffective. The forward who can do the unexpected is the player who worries the opposition. Each forward should utilize the square and the through pass in all parts of the field, attempt a dodge when it is not anticipated, use backward passes to a half or to a wing on the far side of the field, and use short and long passes. No forward should let herself become known as a rote or uninspired player. Variety is the spice of field hockey.

If the relative abilities of the opponents are not known before a game, players should use the first ten minutes of the first half to experiment and learn the strengths and weaknesses of the opponents. Each forward should evaluate her opponent in terms of: how well does she cover and mark; is she quick to recover; does she wander; how far upfield does she go; is she easy prey for a dodge; does she tend to get her weight moving in the wrong direction; is she subject to fakes; and in what direction and to whom does she prefer to clear? All forwards should evaluate the overall positioning of the defense: do they play man-to-man; do they utilize a covering back, and if so, which player do they leave free; do the fullbacks go beyond the center line; are the fullbacks speedy or slow; do they play square (parallel with one another); can they be caught square as play moves from one side of the field to the other; does one fullback linger at the edge of the circle regardless of how far upfield the ball is; do the backs field wide hits near the sidelines; does the covering half move all the way in on the inner or does she vacillate between the inner and wing? The above questions should be answered by all players soon after they dribble the ball and swing it from side to side. With this knowledge, the players have the formula for defeating the opponents. Whether they win depends on their accurate analysis of the information and their technical ability to carry out their intentions.

As Wee Willie Keeler, the baseball player, once said, the idea is to "hit it where they ain't." This over-simplification is basic to the attack in hockey. A player ascertains how the opponents position themselves and then hits around them. Fundamental to this concept is the knowledge that a defense player cannot mark a player and cover a space simultaneously, unless she is playing between the forward and the ball (see Figure 4:3). If the defender is playing goal side of the forward, she can mark her or she can cover the space; she cannot do both. If forwards would learn this lesson, their attack would be more successful.

Figure 4:7 shows the defender marking the forward. A pass to this forward should be directed into the space ahead of her. Figure 4:8 shows the defender covering the space. The forward is free for a square pass or a long pass behind the defender. A long pass is easier to give to the left because it passes the non-stick side of the defender. In midfield, the advantage of passing the ball more forward than sideward is obvious. Therefore, players should use tactics that will cause the defense to be in poor position so that the ball can be passed forward. Swinging the ball from side to side can accomplish this objective. As the defenders

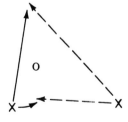

Figure 4:7. Defensive player marking the forward. The pass should be made to the space behind the defense player.

Figure 4:8. Defensive player covering the space. The pass should be made square to the forward or long behind the defense player.

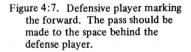

readjust their position, they may leave an opening. The effectiveness of
swinging the ball depends on how it is done. The pass across the field
may gain a lot or very little ground toward the goal. If the defenders are
playing in a covering position, the ball must be passed in front of them
for a little forward gain. If they are playing closer, the pass may be
directed behind them for a lot of forward progress. Aiming for the
corner flag is not always a good idea. If this tactic is followed regardless
of the defenders' position, the ball could be aimed not only for the corner
but also directly at an opponent!

Evading a defender is another tactic commonly used to gain a
momentary advantage. Evading can be done by dodging or by combining with a teammate to execute a triangular pass. Since the chapter
on strokes contains the technical information on how and when to dodge
and which dodge to use, that information will not be repeated here.

The triangular pass consists of a player passing the ball to a
teammate, who returns it. Both passes should gain distance, as shown
in Figure 4:9; a gain however, may not be possible if the space is
covered. In this case, the initial pass should be square. Another instance
requiring the square pass occurs when the receiver of the first pass is
behind the line of the ball, having just served as a connector between
the defense and the forward or recovering from her position in the V
formation (see Figure 4:10).

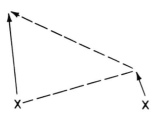

Figure 4:9. Triangular pass.
Both passes ahead.

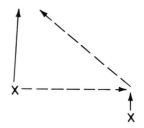

Figure 4:10. Triangular pass. First
pass square, second pass ahead.

Three players can become involved in a triangular pass. One that is
similar to Figure 4:9 could involve the halfback, inner, and wing. One
that is similar to Figure 4:10 could involve the fullback, halfback, and
inner, or the halfback, fullback, and wing. The triangular pass is an

Figure 4:11

excellent means of creating a space for a pass. It is effective to either side, but particularly to the left, where it passes the non-stick side of the defender.

Deception also is an important tactic. If a player can conceal whether she is going to pass to the left or right, she complicates the problems of her opponent. Looking to both sides (wings excepted), dribbling toward one side to pass or dodge to the other, and moving the stick deftly to imply movement in one direction with a change to another, all tend to eliminate the broadcasting effect of beginners' play.

Proper timing of the dodge or pass seems to be instinctive and improves with experience. Good judgment is a quality possessed by all good field hockey players. The pass or dodge should be made when the player has drawn her opponent and is about to be tackled. The ball also may be passed before this time if another player is in a better position to receive. Passing too soon or too late is fatal. If the pass or dodge is executed too early, the defender is likely to intercept. If made too late, the player is tackled before she can execute her play.

In passing to a teammate, a player should try to place the ball in the easiest position for the receiver to field it. This position is always on the receiver's stick side so that she can field it and continue at full speed. The receiver prefers to field a ball hit to the left near the center of her body, and the player on the right wishes to receive the ball on her right side. When hitting to the right, the passer should consider the extra distance the ball travels as it crosses the receiver's body before being fielded.

The speed with which the ball is passed is another important factor. The ball should be hit only hard enough to serve its purpose. Since speed has a bearing on distance, long passes must be hit with authority. If a receiver is free, the pass to her should be sharp but not necessarily hard. The speed of a pass depends on the opening through which it must pass and the freeness of the receiver. If the opening is small, the ball will have to be hit harder to get through before an opponent can reach it. If the defender is close to the receiver, a faster pass will reach the player before the defender can intercept. Passes hit to a nearby player should be hit slower so that they can be fielded with ease. Picture the tension that overcomes a player when she sees her teammate only a few yards away take a full backswing!

Drills

1. Groups of two or three. Forwards give forward (through) passes to one another as they progress down the field. Substitute flat passes and repeat.
2. Two inners. Pass down the field in inner positions. Cut for the ball to field it and pull away from it after passing. Emphasize proper fielding and accurate passes. Maintain spaces.
3. In two's—an inner and a wing. Left inner and right wing pass to one another, and right inner and left wing do the same.
4. In two's—center and a wing. Pass down the field. Substitute the other wing so that the center has practice in hitting to each side.
5. In two's—both wings; practice wing to wing passes.

6. Two columns. Last player in each column moves out in front to serve as a defense player. First two players start passing. If the defense get the ball, they become the attack and the other pair, defense players. Establish starting and finish lines and a time limitation, if neither pair succeeds in getting the ball over the line. Do not permit dodging; later allow it.

7. Groups of three—one defense player and an attack player opposed by a defender. The defense player passes to her forward, who dodges her opponent.

8. Groups of five—one defense player and two forwards on one team and two opponents. The defense player passes to one of the forwards, who has the option of dodging or passing.

9. Groups of five—wing, inner, and center opposed by the back and center half. The defenders are requested at various times to mark closely, mark loosely, or to play in a covering position. The wing must decide whether to pass in front of the defenders or behind them.

10. Groups of four—the two inners, center forward, and opposing center half. The inners practice inner-to-inner passes. The center forward pulls back slightly behind the line of the ball to draw her opponent so that she cannot intercept the passes. If the halfback tends to drift backward, the inner gives the center a flat pass.

11. Five forwards and three halves from one team vs. two defenders. The instructor starts with the ball and rolls it on to the field. By passing only, the forwards must advance the ball down the field. (If they fail to succeed in this drill, they never will!) If a defense player intercepts, she passes to one of the halves and play continues. Add a third, fourth, and fifth defender after the forwards see the need for accurate passing.

12. Groups of three—two forwards against one defender. Forwards may advance by passing or dodging. Stress the timing of passing and dodging to evade the lone defender. Later add a second foe.

13. Five forwards against five defense. Right wing or right inner starts with the ball. The left wing drops back slightly behind the line of the ball for a cross-field pass. Repeat from the other side.

14. Groups of three—two forwards against one defense. The forward on the left starts with the ball. She gives a forward pass, and her teammate returns it ahead to complete the triangular pass. Rotate positions and repeat from the other side.

15. Same description and directions as for No. 14, except a flat pass is given to the forward, who is recovering to the line of play.

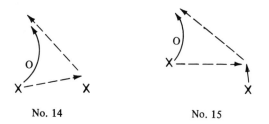

No. 14   No. 15

16. Groups of four—two forwards and their opponents. The
    defenders change their position from covering the space to
    marking, as they see fit. The forwards "read" their position
    and try to evade them with a triangular pass.
17. Groups of four—one defense player and two forwards from
    the same team and one opponent. The halfback passes to the
    inner, who relays the ball behind the defender to the wing.
18. Same directions as for No. 17, except that the back passes
    to the wing, who sends the ball on to the inner.
19. Groups of five—one defender and two forwards from one
    team and two opponents. The back gives a soft pass to the
    inner, who is forced to cut back for it. She gives a flat pass to
    the wing, who returns a through pass.

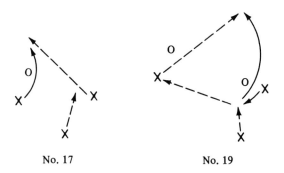

No. 17   No. 19

20. Groups of five—two defenders and one forward from one
    team and one opponent. The halfback passes to the back, who
    gives a through pass to the wing.
21. Same as No. 20, except that the pass goes from the back to
    the half to the inner.

22. Groups of five—one defense player and two forwards opposed by two defenders. The wing sees that the half cannot get a pass to her, so she cuts back to receive it and then passes to the inner or dodges the halfback.

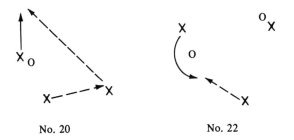

No. 20   No. 22

PLAY NEAR AND IN THE ATTACKING STRIKING CIRCLE

The merit of a forward is her ability to score. Many forwards look brilliant between the twenty-five yard lines, but when they reach the striking circle, their ability vanishes. The crowded conditions in the circle demand superior stickwork. Many forwards are deficient in this category. A good forward should be able to control the ball so well that it can be manipulated in any direction at an instant's notice. Proficiency in scoring can be attributed to stickwork, positioning, re-action time, anticipation, alertness, aggressiveness and the "desire" to score. Without the qualities of stickwork and positioning, scoring is more difficult.

Approaching the striking circle

All players should size up the defense and ascertain where the openings are as the circle is neared. At this time, each player should check her position relative to the goal so that she knows the angle she has for shooting.

If the wing has the ball, she should center it to improve the angle of shooting for the rest of the players. The wing rarely carries the ball to the edge of the circle, unless she has interchanged with the inner and approaches the circle from that angle. Any other player with the ball continues toward the circle, hoping that she can shoot before being tackled. If the defense inhibits her progress, she passes to a teammate. Meanwhile, her forwards have moved away from her and are ready for a pass.

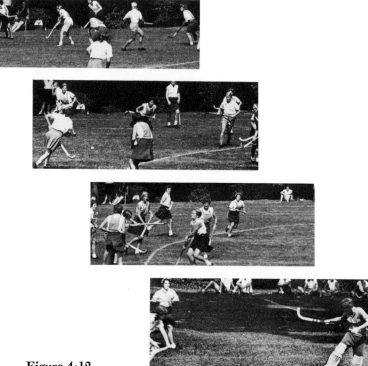

Figure 4:12

In the circle

Forwards should observe immediately whether the opponents use a covering fullback in the circle and if so, how close to the goal the covering fullback is continued. They also should know that forwards near the ball will be marked closely. Being marked closely in hockey is analogous to the pressing man-to-man defense used in basketball. To outwit an opponent, the forward must outthink her by feinting in one direction and moving in another and by being on the move constantly. The player moves forward and back (to remain on side) as the ball moves in each direction. Simultaneously, she moves laterally from left to right to make spaces as the ball shifts direction. Constant re-spacing will help prevent congestion, will force the defense to remain alert, and will force them to re-position constantly in order to keep marking. Maneuvering in the circle by the forwards is much like rocking a car on ice. You put it in forward and reverse and occasionally you slide a little to the side, but the engine always faces the same direction. Thus, the forwards move forward, back, and laterally, always facing the goal. A forward's left shoulder should be forward so that her body is rotated to the right. In this position, she is ready to shoot immediately.

The forwards will pull away from the player with the ball to make spaces into which the ball can be passed. With the ball to the right, players can cut to the non-stick side of their opponent to receive a through pass. As the ball is passed, a player must cut to meet it; she can never wait for it in the circle. When the circle is congested, a player must shoot the instant she is free.

Through passes are usually the most successful way to advance the ball in the circle. The ball can be passed into a space for a forward to cut to it and sweep it into the goal. Often, goals result after the goalie makes an initial save; so even if the goalie reaches the ball first, the forwards should not give up. If the through passes are being intercepted by a covering back, dodges may prove more successful in scoring. If a forward can evade her opponent, she should be free for a shot, unless the covering back tackles her. In that case, a teammate will be left free on the other side of the circle, and that area should be relatively clear of defenders.

The *halfbacks back up* at the edge of the circle or just outside it and try to seal off all possible angles for clears. This backing up forces them to re-position constantly as the ball moves from one side of the field to the other. For example, if the ball is near the end line to the right and fifteen to twenty yards from the goal, the right half will move toward the sideline to block off the angle to her wing. Similarly, the center half moves to her right, and the left halfback finds herself almost in the center of the field as she protects that angle. Thus, the halfbacks adjust laterally and also back from the circle as the ball moves to the other side of the field. Their position represents a notable attacking effort.

Every opportunity to keep the ball in the circle should be seized. Risks are worthwhile. A halfback may even tackle an opposing defense player if she is relatively sure of getting the ball. Smart halfbacks will drop back as though to defend against a pass. Then, when the opponent feels secure and permits the ball to go out of control, the halfback can change direction quickly and recover the ball. (Beginners should not be encouraged to attempt this tactic until they acquire considerable game sense.)

Once the ball is obtained, the halfback should try to score. There-

fore, she dribbles only as far as the edge of the circle and shoots. If an
opposing defense player moves out to tackle her, a simple pass to the
free player is executed. If an opposing attack player comes back to
tackle, she must maneuver for the shot or give a through pass to one of
her forwards. Occasionally a pass to an open halfback is good strategy.

Near the circle, it is evident that a team is only as strong as its
halfback line. The pressure on the opposing defense increases when
the ball remains in or near the circle for a long time. Given repeated
opportunities, some forward usually will score.

In advanced play, the initial hit for goal from near the edge of the
circle is usually done with a hands-apart drive. The end of the stick
can be moved more quickly and with almost as much speed as a hands-
together drive. On a subsequent shot or for any shot taken from midway
in a congested circle, either the sweep shot, scoop, or flick is used. The
sweep shot is very effective when the ball moves toward a player from
either side.

The sweep shot is executed with a sweeping motion of the stick
along the ground; the timing of the sweep is critical. The hands are
apart on the stick to give added control (Figures 4:13 and 4:14). The
forwards have their left shoulder facing the goal and their bodies facing
to the right so that as they take the sweep, the angle of the stick will
cause the ball to deflect into the goal rather than over the end line to
the left of the goal, as often happens with beginners. If the ball is

Figure 4:13

Figure 4:14

passed from behind into a space in front of the goal, or if the ball is deflected toward a player off the stick of a defender or the goalie, a flick or scoop can raise the ball, causing the goalkeeper to misjudge the timing of the shot. Players should aim for the spaces in the goal and not for the goalie's pads; they should aim for the dark area, not the white.

As a shot is taken, designated forwards should rush the goal. The two inners and the center are the main rushers. The wings wait out near the edge of the circle for defensive clears. If a wing has interchanged with an inner and shot for the goal, she has exchanged responsibilities temporarily. Therefore, the wing rushes the goal as the inner moves toward the edge of the circle.

The inside forwards start rushing as soon as the shooter takes her backswing. If an inside forward is shooting, she rushes as soon as she has hit the ball. Although a player usually is forced to shoot toward the opposite corner of the goal (if the goalkeeper is well positioned), each inner will rush the goal post on her side of the field. The center either rushes the middle of the goal or goes part way and waits for the resultant play. More pressure is placed on the goalkeeper if three players charge at her instead of two.

All players should try to keep the ball in the circle so that a goal can be scored. Forwards should learn to work harder in the circle and keep the pressure on the defense. They can rest after they score. If they would persist in a "don't give up" attitude instead of a "may I" attitude, they could save a lot of energy and have more fun. Why run all the way to the other end of the field and back before gaining another scoring opportunity?

The following tactics can help a team vary its play and produce an unhindered shot for goal. When the wing has the ball, the inner on her side can pull back slightly, drawing her opponent so that the ball can be passed behind the fullback for a sweep shot by the center. If the fullback is not lured, the inner is free for a quick sweep shot. If the wing has the ball near the goal line, a quick pass back to the center half or the side half is useful. Often these players are free. Occasionally, the center forward may pull back from the line of the ball and be free for a quick, easy backward pass, if her opponent is not guarding closely. If the opponents are playing with a covering back, a pass from either side half across to the wing on the other side may prove successful. For example, the left half can pass to the right wing. Actually, a pass from the right half to the left wing should bring better results because the left wing has the goal on her stick side.

Obviously, weather and ground conditions in front of the goal should be considered by the attack. If the ground is soft and soggy, greater emphasis should be placed on the lifting strokes so that the ground condition does not affect the hit. On frozen or hard, bumpy ground, unexpected bounces may occur with hard hits along the ground.

Shooting

If the attackers keep the distance from the goal line constant, then there is a greater space through which the ball can pass and a greater area for the goalie to defend the more nearly a player is directly in front of the goal. The further a player moves away (laterally) from in front of the goal, the more the space diminishes (Figure 4:15).[1]

As shown in Table 3, at least half of the goal is open as a player shoots from less than a foot to 6 feet to the side of the goal, regardless of the distance from the goal line. In order to have at least half of the goal open: at 11 feet to the side of the goal, a player must be at least 10 feet (approximately) in front of the goal; at 16 feet to the side, she must be about 13 feet in front of the goal; and at 26 feet to 31 feet to the side, she must shoot from about 21 feet in front of the goal. It becomes apparent that the closer a player is to the front of the goal, the more area is exposed. Obviously, a goalkeeper has more difficulty defending against a larger area; hence, the greater chance the forwards have for scoring.

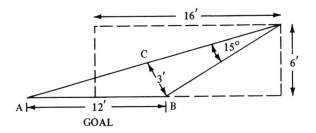

Figure 4:15. A player shoots from 6 feet in front of the goal
and 16 feet to the side of it. The ball must pass through
BC in order to enter the goal at AB[1].

Table 3 shows that from any point directly in front of the goal, the entire width of the goal is exposed. As seen in Table 4, however, the possible angle of deviation (the margin for error) is smallest at the edge of the circle and increases as the goal is approached. Thus, the center forward should shoot from a position as close to the goal as possible, provided that she is free to do so. The old adage, "shoot as soon as you reach the circle," is erroneous for a center forward (or anyone else approaching from that position), unless the forward is pressed by a defensive player.

As the shot taken is progressively closer to the sideline (with the distance into the field from the goal line held constant), the angle of the shot diminishes. In Table 4, compare the angles possible at 41 feet to the side of the goal, for example. For this reason, wings usually center the ball rather than shoot. The angle often is too acute to produce good results. As any free player approaches the striking circle, she should dribble toward the center forward's position, where the angle for her shot improves.

It is interesting to look at the deviation possible when the distance to the side of the goal is held constant but the distance from the goal line is varied. When a player is 30 feet or more to the side of the goal, the further out she shoots, the better the angle. From 26 feet to the side of the goal, it makes little difference whether a player shoots from 16 feet or 41 feet from the goal line. From about 16 feet to 21 feet to the side of the goal, the angle increases as a player moves in to the circle, and then diminishes as the goal is approached. Thus, as a player is 16 feet to 21 feet to the side of the goal, her best angle for shooting

Table 3. Distance (in Feet) That Must Be Defended by the Goalie[2]

Distances (in feet) From the Goal Line Into the Striking Circle	Distances (in feet) from the Center of the Goal Toward the Sideline									
	0	3	6	11	16	21	26	31	36	41
41	12	11.8	11.6	11.0	10.6	10.0	10.0	—	—	—
31	12	11.6	11.2	10.6	9.8	9.0	8.7	7.7	7.0	7.0
21	12	11.4	10.4	9.4	8.3	7.4	6.6	5.8	5.2	4.8
16	12	11.0	10.1	9.2	7.2	6.0	5.2	4.6	4.2	3.8
11	12	10.4	8.8	6.7	5.4	4.4	3.8	3.4	2.9	2.6
6	12	9.0	6.3	4.0	3.0	2.5	2.2	1.6	1.6	1.4

Table 4. Angle of Deviation Possible for Shots[3]

Distance (in feet) From the Goal Line Into the Striking Circle	Distance (in feet) from the Center of the Goal Toward the Sideline									
	0	3	6	11	16	21	26	31	36	41
41	16	16	16	15	14	13	13	11	—	—
31	22	21	21	19	17	15	13	11	9	9
21	32	31	29	25	21	17	13	10	8	7
16	41	40	37	29	22	16	12	9	7	5
11	57	54	47	32	21	14	10	7	5	4
6	90	83	63	30	15	9	6	3	3	2

Figure 4:16

is about midway in the circle or slightly closer to the goal. Directly in front of the goal, the angle increases as a player nears the goal line.

When a player shoots from 41 feet from the goal line, there is little difference in the angle from any place in the circle. The angle ranges from 16 degrees directly in front of the goal to 13 degrees at 26 feet at the side of the goal, a difference of only three degrees. As a player gets midway into the circle, the angle is 32 degrees in front of the goal and 8 degrees 36 feet to the side of the goal, a considerable difference. Six feet in front of the goal line, the range in angles is even greater— from 90 degrees directly in front to two degrees at 41 feet to the side of the goal. Thus, when a player is forced toward the sideline, she should shoot as soon as possible and aim for the opposite corner of the goal. If she is in approximately the inner position, she should shoot midway in the circle. The center should attempt to get as close to the goal as possible before shooting.

Drills

Most of the following drills can be done either with or without a goalkeeper. If a goalkeeper is used, be sure that she is ready before a subsequent shot.

1. Individually. Each forward starts from her normal position at the twenty-five yard line. In turn, each dribbles into the circle and shoots. The center forward dribbles in close to the goal, the inners midway, and the wings midway and in the inner's position before shooting.
2. Groups of three—two attack against one defense. The two attack players start with the ball at the twenty-five, and the opponent defends against the forward, who starts with the ball. The attack player dribbles forward, dodges her opponent, or passes to her free teammate. In the circle, the ball is shot at the appropriate time, and both forwards rush the goal (even if a goalkeeper is not used to develop the concept of always rushing).
3. Columns—three, at the center and inner positions on the twenty-five yard line. One defense player stands facing each column midway between the twenty-five yard line and the circle. The first forward in each line dribbles, dodges the defense, and shoots at the appropriate time. Let the defense players act as posts at the start; later, let them attempt to prevent the dodge. (Do not use a goalkeeper unless only one forward advances at a time.)

4. Partners—wing and inner (or center). Both players start midway in the circle. The wing takes one dribble and then centers the ball. The inner attempts a sweep shot for a score. Try from both sides.

5. Individually. Each player places a ball in the circle (no more than three at any one time) and moves back five yards from it. On signal, one after another runs in and flicks, pushes, or scoops the ball into the goal. (Do not use the scoop unless the ball is close to the goal.)

6. Groups of three—two attack and one defense. The two attack players start at the twenty-five yard line with the defense player waiting midway in the circle. The instructor (or an extra player) stands with a bag of balls near the goal. When the goalie is ready, one forward dribbles toward the circle. The defense player is asked to delay her tackle and just exert some pressure on the dribbler so that she is forced to shoot from the edge of the circle. After the shot, both forwards rush the goal and attempt to push, flick, scoop, or sweep the goalie's clear into the goal. If a goal is scored, the instructor rolls out an extra ball for the follow-up shot.

7. Groups of three—two forwards and a halfback backing up. The half has the ball about ten yards behind the twenty-five yard line. She passes to one of the forwards, who passes to the other forward, who shoots when she reaches the circle. Forwards rush and the half waits at the edge of the circle.

8. A forward line against a marking defense in the circle; no ball. On signal, the forwards rush toward the goal and the defense continue to mark; on signal, the forwards pull back and the defense re-position accordingly. Emphasize that players run forward and backward so that the forwards constantly are facing the goal and the defense keep their backs to the goal.

9. Forwards and their halves against the opposing defense. The forwards move midway into the circle with the defense marking. From back of the end line, the instructor sends the ball behind the forwards to a halfback at the edge of the circle. The forwards make spaces for the halfback's shot, and the inside forwards rush the goal on the backswing for the shot.

10. Forwards and their halves against the opposing defense and one of their forwards. Same directions as for No. 9, except that the halfback is forced to pass the ball to one of her forwards as an opposing forward tackles back on her to prevent the half from shooting. The half gives a through pass to a forward for a shot; the inside forwards rush.

11. Forwards and halves against the opposing defense. A side half has the ball, and the wing on the opposite side pulls back on

line with the ball. The half passes to the wing for a shot; inside forwards rush.

12. Forwards and halves against the opposing defense. One half-back starts with the ball just outside the circle. She dribbles to the edge of the circle as the forwards pull away to create spaces. She shoots from the edge of the circle, and the inside forwards rush. Alternate halves.

13. A forward line—no defense used. The wing starts with the ball outside the circle about 10 feet from the end line. She centers the ball, and players attempt to sweep it into the goal. Alternate sides.

14. Forwards and halves against the opposing defense. The wing has the ball outside the circle about eight yards from the end line. She centers it behind the fullback and the inside forwards rush for a sweep shot. Alternate sides of the field.

15. Same formation as for No. 14 except that the inner on the side with the ball drops back from the line of the ball. Her fullback fails to mark her, and the wing pushes a pass to her for a shot. Later, let the inner drop back and give the fullback the option of whether she marks or "dozes." The wing must consider the position of the back and execute the pass to the free space.

16. Forwards and halves against opposing defense. A halfback starts with the ball at the twenty-five yard line. She passes to the nearest wing, who returns the pass to the half at the edge of the circle. The halfback shoots, and the inside forwards rush.

17. Forwards and halves against the opposing defense. A halfback has the ball at the edge of the circle, and the forwards are midway in the circle. The halfback passes to one of the forwards, who executes a back pass to the half for a shot. Inside forwards rush. Alternate halves.

18. One forward against a goalkeeper. The forward starts near the twenty-five yard line and dribbles into the circle directly in front of goal. (The forwards start in their normal position, then angle to the center as they approach the circle.) The forward shoots just beyond the reach of the goalie, if the goalie does not move out toward her. If the goalie approaches the forward, the forward shoots when the angle is optimum or dodges the goalie for a closer shot.

ATTACK PLAY ANALYZED

The author would like to raise the question of whether hockey attack has become too stereotyped. Observing play, it seems as though one can almost predict where the next pass will be made. Has the game become too machine-like? too pre-determined? Certainly, the general concepts of strategy must be identified and learned by beginners, but it seems that punch card standardization is unnecessary at higher levels of play. During regular class play, the ordered tactics of passing to the wings in the defensive end and of the wings centering the ball at the center line or slightly later are used. The inners and center forward are encouraged to swing the ball. All too often, these unimaginative tactics are followed by varsity and club teams. Perhaps dogmatic coaching suggestions have deprived players of individualistic efforts for taking advantage of opportunities.

In advanced play, the halfbacks should be used to a greater extent on offense. They could be used more extensively near the striking circle, as well as anywhere in the offensive end of the field. When the opposing defense seem to have the desirable angles blocked, a backward pass to one of the halves can give the attack time to re-position. Meanwhile, the half can dribble the ball down the field until an opening occurs. It is questionable whether she would have to dribble very far, but if she succeeds in drawing an opposing defense player, the opening for the pass presents itself.

The halves also can pass the ball among themselves and wait for a defensive lapse before passing the ball forward. Since the halves and the wing on the far side of the field are free, a pass from one side half to the other will force the defense to re-position, and the opening may occur for the through pass to the forwards. This plan seems more sensible than having the forwards pass into a well-positioned defense.

It is true that the halves must work harder under this tactic, but it should be more rewarding to them to recognize that while backing up their forwards their function is not only defensive (intercepting opponent's passes) but also offensive, in that they can take part in the battle of wits involved in scoring. This tactic also can force the opposing forwards to alter their game plan. Being forced to tackle back to a greater extent may cause them to be ill-positioned on offense. Because the opposing forwards must work harder, their stamina may diminish in the later stages of the game, thus decreasing their effectiveness. Psychologically, a team is affected when players are forced to change their position to help out more defensively.

Coaches in other team sports seem to spend more time establishing a game plan, either before the game begins (if the quality of the opponents is known), or during the game as their strengths and weaknesses are assessed. Let me provide some situations. How many times does a team attempt to hit the ball to their right wing (for example) when she is opposed by the strongest defender on the other team? Time after time they see the ball intercepted, and yet passes are continually sent to her. Reaching her once or twice in ten attempts is a poor percentage. How long in a game of basketball would a forward play, with that shooting percentage?

If the forwards on one side of the field are having more success advancing the ball down the field, why not play it to that side more often? The maxim of "distributing" play is not satisfactory when one side of the forward line continually loses the ball. Give the ball to the players who are successful during a particular game. During one game, the right side of the forward line may be successful and the left side in the next. If one side of the forward line receives the ball infrequently, the opposing defenders may edge closer to the middle of the field to clutter the spaces. At this time, the attack can take advantage of the defenders' poor positioning by swinging the ball to the players who have not received it and they may get a breakaway.

Occasionally, a very strong forward is opposed by an exceptionally skilled defense player so that the individual duel between the two becomes a stalemate. This situation can be corrected by moving the forward to another position against a weaker opponent. An inner might move to center or to wing, for example, or a center might move out to either an inner or wing position. It is difficult for a wing to move in to the center of the field where more refined moves and stickwork are necessary. If the opponents counteract this measure by moving their strong defender, the tactics have reached another stalemate. However, it may be more difficult for a fullback, for example, to move to a halfback position than it is for the forward to change positions.

These are a few adjustments that can be made offensively during a game. Students of the game can think of many others and will find that creativity in field hockey offense leads to victory.

FOOTNOTES

1. MacLean, Dorothy and Broer, Marion R. *Angles in Hockey Goal Shooting*. Unpublished study, University of Washington, 1949.

2. *Ibid.*

3. *Ibid.*

V

POSITION PLAY BY FORWARDS

THE WINGS

by Alison Hersey[1]

The position of wing is a combination of many emotions. It is the exhilaration of chasing a free ball, the challenge of getting to it before it goes out of bounds or onto the stick of an opponent. It is the patience of waiting to be remembered and used by the rest of the team. It is the relief of fielding a ball on the sideline and keeping it in play. It is the satisfaction of a good, hard, well-directed hit.

QUALITIES

To be successful, a wing must have endurance, the desire to run, and the ability to sprint. Her stickwork must be strong and in pace with her feet. To reach a level of stickwork equal to her natural ability to run, a wing must practice all the skills required of the other forwards. In addition, there are specific skills that are important for a wing to learn.

Wings must be reliable fielders. Because they are the outside players, it is their responsibility to keep the ball in play. A team can easily become discouraged from passing out to the wing who continuously loses the ball over the sideline. A wing hopes to receive the ball while moving at top speed towards the goal, taking full advantage of her speed. She hopes to receive the ball on the sideline and deflect it forward into position to make the next play. The difference between the right and left wing in receiving the ball is in relation to the player's feet. A left wing accelerates to get ahead of the ball and field it slightly behind her feet. A right wing chases the ball and fields it by reaching ahead. Each wing controls the ball's direction by guiding it rather than hitting it. By keeping the ball close to her stick, the wing is ready to play it immediately.

An emergency stroke, especially for the left wing, is fielding the ball with a reverse stick. This stroke, which requires strength and a good eye, should be used only when the player cannot catch her feet up to the ball.

A wing cannot always ask for the ball while she is sprinting towards goal. Often, she must cut back to help a harried defense player. She must be able to collect the ball dead on her stick and quickly get her feet and ball headed towards goal.

A wing, more than any other player, must have a strong drive. However, a random centering pass is not enough. A good wing also must be aware of the positioning of the opposing defense and get her centering pass through by design and not by accident. A right wing keeps the ball ahead and in front of her left foot to achieve the maximum effect of the swing. The left wing must get ahead of the ball and either by a pivot or body twist, get herself around to get a full swing. It is important for each wing to get her feet to the ball rather than the ball to her feet. She must take small, quick steps to get her feet into position, in order to get an effective center.

A left wing also has the option of a reverse stick hit when she is being pressed by an opponent or when she needs a quick, less powerful, center. Both wings vary the speed of the centering passes according to the situation. Many times, they may use a push or scoop pass to put the ball exactly where it should go.

A wing often needs to use a dodge. She should be able to use all types of dodges. A left wing should be adept at the pull to the left and the scoop. A right wing usually uses the dodge to the non-stick side and the scoop. These dodges help keep the play spread by using the un-marked space.

Defensively, a wing should tackle back on her opponent to force a pass and allow her halfback opportunity to cover the space. A forward often can force the play enough to give her defense the chance to intercept. This extra effort often will save a long exhausting run in the wrong direction. A wing should keep up with the play in both directions. She cannot afford the luxury of waiting and watching on the fifty-yard line. She must go back with the play and be available when her defense gains possession of the ball.

PLAY IN THE DEFENSIVE END

Defensively, the wing's position at the twenty-five yard line varies with the ball's position. When the ball is on the far side of the field, a wing can afford to play up from the twenty-five yard line in anticipation of the center. When the ball is on her side, however, a wing should be back and available to her defense. A wing is not useful if she expects a pressed defense to clear the ball up to her in midfield. Even if she is tired, a wing should return to the twenty-five yard line and rest there. From this position, she is ready to cut back and pick up a hurried clear, or even to go back to collect her goalkeeper's clear out to the sideline. A pressed defense appreciates the extra effort by their forwards to get free.

A wing often has to cut back to receive a pass. She must time her movements so that she arrives in the space at the same time as the ball. Having received the ball behind her own line, she has two options. She can clear quickly across the field. Her other choice, which is more unexpected, is to pass the ball up her own alley. The inner cuts and centers, leaving the halfback and fullback hopelessly behind.

The earlier a wing is used in a game, the more effective is her center. If the wing receives the ball deep in the defending half of the field, she can center the ball before reaching the fifty-yard line. This action allows her a deep angle and maximum space to put the ball across field. The farther downfield a wing goes, the more difficulty she has finding the space. She must be used early and not hold on to the ball. If she has a well-established defense against her and carries the ball in extended dribbling, she succeeds only in reducing the angle of her center. The farther downfield she goes, the flatter the center must be.

Carrying the ball downfield is not the wing's main function. Her center is not useful if the fullback can mark the only available space and make an easy interception. Extended dribbling also gives a passed defense time to recover and get back into position. The only times a wing is justified in dribbling is either when she is ahead of all the other forwards or if she has beaten one fullback and dribbles to draw the covering back.

To receive a pass from her defense, a wing should be up ahead and out to the sideline. A left wing should always receive the ball from the right side, and the right wing from the left side. A wing also must be ready to cut back if she is closely marked, and to make herself free for her defense. Many times a harried defense player is relieved to see a wing emerge and offer a stick for a pass.

MIDFIELD PLAY

A wing is at her maximum effectiveness in midfield play. She has two jobs to do. One is to stay out to keep the play open and the players spread. The other is to split the defense, get them wrong-footed, and set up a goal-making situation by using intelligent passing. When a wing stays out near the sideline, her team can use maximum space and make it as difficult as possible for the opposing defense. A team that does not use its wings destroys the effectiveness of their positioning. A player not used will not be a threat to the defense.

Besides keeping wide, a wing must effectively position herself to receive a pass. If one of her forwards has the ball, the wing must stay on line with the ball, anticipating either the flat or through pass. If she gets even a few steps ahead of the ball, she allows the half to mark both her and the space and she risks being offside, an occupational hazard for the wing, especially the left wing.

PLAY IN THE ATTACKING END

When the wing is at the attacking twenty-five yard line without the ball, she should still present herself as a potential threat. She should stay out to keep the spaces open, and she must stay onside. At the edge of the circle, the wing should anticipate a through pass from the inside forwards, halfbacks, or even a hard pass from her opposite half; for example, from the left half to the right wing. When the ball is on the opposite side of the field, the wing is the freest player for the shot. Unfortunately, she often is the most neglected player. A quick hit to her across the circle behind the other line players often can result in a goal.

When she has possession of the ball at the twenty-five yard line or in the circle, the wing should consider herself a scoring threat. Many options are open to her. The more varied her play, the more effective she becomes. Her most obvious choice is cutting in and shooting at the edge of the circle. She can cut in to draw the fullback and then push pass through into the space behind the fullback for the inside forwards to score. Another effective play is for her to dribble almost to the edge of the circle and then pass flat across behind the inner and even the center, who have pulled ahead a few steps, to an inner or wing waiting at the edge of the circle on the opposite side.

Sometimes play is forced to the endline. Here, the wing has the option of either a hard, flat hit across the mouth of the goal or a hit back to the edge of the circle. This option depends on the position of the defense. The wing must use the space available to her and not depend on luck or brute force to get the ball through to a teammate's stick.

A wing also should anticipate the clear from the goalkeeper and be in position to get the rebound shot from the clear. If the clear goes out to her own halfback, the wing must be ready to do two things. She must get onside and in position to receive a pass by pulling back and out. If the half wishes to sustain her own attack, the wing must interchange and assume the halfback's position until the halfback can recover.

Both wings have a responsibility in executing a strong, well-directed corner hit. This skill is neglected too often. The failure of the corner is laid to the inside forwards. A wing must have a reliable, flat, hard, direct hit. It must be precise so that the inside forward has maximum time and chance to make her stop and shot. A wing should gain satisfaction in any goal scored from a corner because half of it was her doing.

SUMMARY

Specifically, a wing needs to practice passing and receiving at top speed. She should be nearly perfect in both these skills. She should continually practice receiving the ball from all angles and passing it quickly, striving for accuracy and distance. The left wing should concentrate on her right drive and the right wing on her left drive.

Dribbling and dodging can be practiced together to develop ball control, good footwork, and wrist strength. Dribbling from an extended position, reaching out as far as possible, and one hand dribbling all develop strength. Dribbling with a series of pulls and taps and dribbling with reverse stick pulls and taps develop footwork and ball control. These qualities are essential for effective field play.

A wing easily can become typed as a player who always does the same thing. It is up to each individual wing to be elusive, deceptive, opportunistic, and unorthodox. She must be quick to the ball and accelerate to receive the pass. A change of pace puts off the defense's timing and makes her misjudge her tackle or interception.

A wing should never stand still; she should keep moving up and back, forcing the half to concentrate on her instead of on the ball in play. Moving is especially important in the circle. The quicker the wing passes the ball, the more difficult she is to play against. A wing who carries the ball can be caught and tackled, but one who passes and accelerates for the pass back is out of range of the passed defense. A wing always should be a scoring threat. One who only fetches and carries will soon be ignored in the circle, causing a concentration of defense on the inside forwards.

At all times, a wing should concentrate, anticipate, and react quickly to each new situation. She should never let her play become routine and common. She must create her own options and prove to her teammates that she is a valuable, essential part of the team.

THE INNERS

by Mary Ann Harris[2]

QUALITIES

A good inner should be aggressive, speedy and well-coordinated. Also, she should be quick off the mark, scheming and clever, and have quick reflexes, a good eye, and good footwork.

An inner's feet are always oriented toward her goal. She attacks and also is willing to defend and tackle back. She demonstrates good ball control. She shows strength in the circle; and of course, she scores. She can capitalize on defensive errors, particularly in the attacking area.

STICKWORK

A good inner must be able to control the ball. Vera Chapman (former All-England right and left inner), is a good example of a player with excellent ball control. She once dribbled past four defenders and scored, beating the goalkeeper with a hard shot to the right hand corner. Stickwork can improve only with practice.

Both inners should have various dodges. Each inner should concentrate on the dodges that work best for her in given situations. The left dodge is the best dodge on the left. The right dodge to the non-stick side of the defense is the most effective dodge on the right.

Good stickwork also includes ball control in dribbling and receiving passes, and the ability to stop with a reverse stick, to stop opponents' hits, and to stop corner hits. An inner might have to interchange with the wing, and therefore should feel secure that she can center the ball.

An inner must have a variety of shots, including hard drive, flick, push, scoop, and reverse stick shot. She should practice directing a moving ball into the cage. She should pass accurately and know the kinds of passes needed in different situations. Passing skills should include a right drive, push pass, and reverse stick pass.

The essential difference between the right and left inner is the position of each in relation to the goal and to the other players. It therefore takes practice for a left inner to switch to the right and accurately get a through pass to the right wing.

The left inner should move a lot in order to get around and ahead of the ball and into position for playing the ball to the right. The left inner should be able to drive right, driving off her forward right heel and twisting her body in order to swing the stick. She also should be able to drive to the right by running quickly ahead of the ball, turning, and driving with her right shoulder toward the sideline.

Drill

1. Groups of six—an inner, a goalie, and four defense players between the far twenty-five yard line and the circle. The inner tries to dodge the defense players, who try to stop her. They cannot chase her if she passes them. The inner then tries to score.

PLAY IN THE DEFENSIVE END

Preventing goals is not an inner's objective. Even though defensive playing is less important than offensive playing, it is necessary.

When playing defensively, the inner on the ball side of the field should drop back to a slightly deeper position, where she will avoid crowding her own defense and where she may be able to help. She may be able to take the opposing halfback who is going for a shot. The inner should always be in a position to receive a pass from her defense when they get the ball again. She should be ready to attack.

On a defense hit, she may try to create spaces to get the ball through to other players, or she may move close to receive the ball on her stick or in the space to which she is moving.

An inner can be a popular player with her own defense if they can always find and use her.

MIDFIELD PLAY

Midfield play is the intermediate step in attacking and scoring. But too much of a game should not be spent here. If the offense takes too long in midfield to set up an attack, their intentions are revealed.

When playing in midfield, an inner should have several thoughts. In concentrating on the situation at hand, she should be aware of what could happen. She should know her opponent's position and anticipate her own team's strategy. She should position herself so that she is prepared to receive the ball from her defense. Her feet should be oriented toward the goal, and she should look for an open field, where she will have room to maneuver.

An inner's purpose is to score goals. Her methods should be to catch the defense, confuse them, run them, lose them, and then beat them.

During a game an inner often is confronted with her own special problems. An inner is concerned about how far back down the field she should come. When the ball is on her side, she should return across her defending twenty-five yard line to a position where she can be free. She should watch carefully the positioning of her opposing halfbacks.

If she receives the ball when no back is immediately upfield to take her, but is coming, she can pass to the center if she can avoid the opposing center half. Or, if she finds her wing free, she can give her a flat or through pass. Or she can speed toward the back and pass when she reaches her to remove her from play. Then, if the inner accelerates around the back, the inner is free on the path to the goal.

If a halfback tackles the inner, the inner should pass to the free wing.

If an inner sees that her wing is marked closely, the inner should pass on an angle behind the halfback to the space. In some cases, the inner should pass straight ahead to her own position for the wing to run onto. If the wing is not marked closely, the inner should give the wing a flat pass to draw the half. The wing passes back to the inner, and then the inner sends her a pass to the space angled behind the halfback.

If the inner wants to use the wing to take out a fullback, she should make a flat pass to the wing, who should pass diagonally ahead to the inner behind the fullback.

If the inner finds the fullbacks square, she should use a through pass for herself or for any other forward to run onto.

An inner should use her center forward, who enjoys running on well-placed through passes behind her center halfback. The right inner, who is on the non-stick side of the center half, can make this pass work quite well.

If the ball is on one side of the field, the inner should pass to the opposite inner and wing.

On free hits in midfield, the inner should maneuver so that she can take advantage of the hit to force the attack from a stopped position.

An inner should work out roll-in situations with her wing and halfback. By having the wing drop back to draw the opposing defense player, the half can roll unexpectedly hard along the sideline. By anticipating the roll and quickly cutting into the alley to pick it up, the inner actually becomes the wing. It will not help just knowing the various possibilities; practicing for accuracy is necessary in such a situation.

The inners should pass to each other often. For example, when the right inner receives the ball from the defense, she can immediately pass behind the unrecovered center half to the left inner. The left inner carries quickly to draw the right back and then passes back to the right inner, who immediately passes back to the left inner. The left inner passes ahead on an angle, toward the covering back, to the right inner, who receives in front of the back, takes the ball around her to the left, and shoots to the right corner of the goal.

A good pass to the left inner is one made by the right inner as she approaches the fifty-yard line. The ball is angled toward the covering back, looking almost like a pass to the center forward. This pass enables the left inner to run onto the ball, take it around the back, and shoot from the right side.

PLAY IN THE ATTACKING END

When the play is in this area of the field, the inner again has her own special duties and problems.

An inner should continue on pace. If she finds that the defense is marking and that none of the attack is moving, she should use her halfback in an attempt to open play. On free hits, the inner should pull away. If the defense is marking, she should expect the ball to go to a space. If she is unguarded, she should either stay or move, and expect the ball to be on her stick. It is the inner's job to defend on a defense hit. She should either ring the hit with her other forwards, or play man-to-man on her opposite player. An inner who wants her backs to back her up must be prepared to begin the attack again.

Scoring

Here are some specific tactics an inner can use when trying to score. If the backs wait or back up, dodge or pass, or if there is room, the inner should get the ball just inside the striking circle and shoot. If the circle is crowded, the inner should pass out to the wing, pass back to her halfbacks, or look for an opening for a through pass.

An inner should give her center forward the room she needs to maneuver and should follow up on all shots.

An inner should be sure that the wings don't crowd her. When the inner is crowded, the defense's job is easier.

When the forwards interchange in the circle, the inner should be ready to adjust until the play is finished.

If the wing shoots, the wing may follow up her shot. If this is the case, the inner goes to the wing's position. If an inner's halfback shoots, the inner should follow the shot.

An inner should have the proper shot for each situation. She can push or flick if there is not enough time for a backswing or if she fields a rebound from the goalkeeper. She can use a hard, accurate drive on a corner hit or on any shot at the edge of the circle. If the circle is crowded, the inner can use a scoop to the top corner of the cage if she can find room to use it safely. She can sweep or direct a centering pass. A left inner will find a reverse stick shot very helpful.

The inners should rush at the goalkeeper's pads. Sometimes an inner finds it better to field the ball as it rebounds. Regardless of where she fields the ball, both of her hands should hold firmly on to the stick, which is on the ground in front of her, away from her feet.

WHAT TO PRACTICE

Stickwork practice sessions should include individual work on skills, skill-drill formations, and actual game situations.

Players should think about what strategy to use in all situations. They can make some discoveries about their team's positioning by using this technique. Each player should practice concentrating on her own opponent, her positioning, and her strong and weak points.

A well-practiced and well-coached team enjoys playing field hockey. Practice sessions, therefore, should follow a plan to some measure of satisfaction.

HOW TO MAKE PLAY DIFFICULT FOR THE OPPONENT

Being physically fit, playing a determined game, and trying to outwit the opponent are three general ways an inner, or any other player, can make a game more difficult for the opposition. Here are some specific suggestions on how an inner can accomplish this task.

An inner can confuse her opponent by changing her pace often, by concealing her plans, and by varying her play. By studying the position of her opponent, an inner can learn what is difficult for her. A right inner can be successful with a dodge to the non-stick side of the left back. The right inner can make passes behind the center half, and she will have her running in circles. An inner can pass to spaces if her opponents are marking closely, and to the player's stick if she is free.

An inner should do the unexpected. She should go into another position to shoot, for example. She rushes the goalkeeper on shots for goal. An inner tackles back on her opponent when she has the ball. An inner should try to fake with her stick, eyes, and body movement. If the left inner can fake the pass right and then pass out to her wing instead, she moves the opposing fullback off balance. On a corner, an inner can fake the drive, dodge, and get a clear shot.

THE CENTER FORWARD

by Diane Crowley Treese[3]

QUALITIES

As in any forward position, a center forward should be speedy, be able to accelerate quickly, and have body balance and control with neat footwork. She should be aggressive and desire to score goals. She should be able to take the initiative and, if necessary, be willing to attempt to score alone and unaided. Yet she should be able to combine with her teammates to produce total team aggression. She must not, however, become interested only in scoring. She should always be ready to turn around and help her defense by tackling back. A center forward should be able to pass accurately or score goals under the pressure of a large audience or an important game. The few perfect scoring opportunities in a game should be fully exploited and utilized.

The center forward position requires the same qualities of temperament, footwork, and stickwork needed in other forward positions. Certain aspects of this position are specialized; they require knowledge and practice of skills particularly appropriate to center forward play. Therefore, teaching forward play is a difficult assignment in hockey.

A stereotyped attack will usually be nullified by a stereotyped defense system. So it is the surprise element, the individual spark, and
the quick and unusual reaction of a forward player that will break
through the defense. Thus it is important for a center forward, as for
all forwards, to have initiative and a sense of adventure. These qualities,
however, must be combined with perfect footwork and stickwork to
control the ball closely in any given situation, if the launching of unusual attacks is to be successful.

FOOTWORK AND STICKWORK

National and modern dancing, matwork, tumbling, and gymnastics
are several ways of acquiring good footwork. At the high school and
college level, time in hockey practices should be given to running activities to build up stamina, to quick sprints, and frequently and suddenly
changing direction to the whistle with good body control. The importance of quick, light footwork combined with good body control cannot
be overemphasized.

Since a center forward is positioned in the center of the field most
of the time, she must learn to receive and control a ball passed to her
from any direction. In midfield, she is likely to receive a pass from her
own defense angled from behind, or a forward pass from an inner.
Nearing the attacking circle, she may receive flatter passes from her
wings. In the striking circle, a center must be prepared to use flat or
even backward passes from either the right or left wing or inners.

When she has received and controlled the ball, the center must
then use one of a variety of strokes to further the play. In midfield, she
distributes the ball to her wings, either strongly with a hard drive or
firmly and with control with a strong push. In order to avoid a defense
player as she passes the ball, she may wish to flick or scoop the ball
to a teammate.

In the striking circle, she may use the drive, long push, or flick as
potential scoring strokes. However, a center often has to receive a flat
pass just in front of the goalkeeper as she is moving in at speed. Thus,
she must develop a quick, wristy flick, a sweeping push for a pass from
the right, and a deflecting stroke for a flat pass from the left. Often,
when a center forward has control of the ball in front of the goalie, a
quick pull to the left·followed by a reverse stick drive is highly effective.
A center forward, therefore, needs to be skilled in every stroke in the
game of hockey.

Because a center forward lacks room to move in the striking circle, she may develop her own characteristics when performing conventional strokes. These time-saving devices enable her to perform effectively and more quickly in her confined space. Such a characteristic may be a small backswing when driving the ball, compensated by the hands being slightly apart. Sometimes, if a player has developed strong wrists, she can flick with a smaller action. A pushing jab with the stick at right angles to the goal can be performed quickly and effectively to deflect a flat pass from the left into the goal.

A center forward is marked man-to-man by an opponent more than any other player on the field. She also has less space to move in, being backed by her own center half and edged by her inners. She therefore must learn to perform all dodges effectively and skillfully in a confined space, particularly in the striking circle.

In all, a center forward needs quick, controlled footwork and movement, combined with delicate stickwork and a complete repertoire of strokes for all occasions. Playing this position well requires constant practice.

PLAY IN THE DEFENSIVE END

When the opposing team attacks, the defensive forward line usually has a system of formations enabling them to be ready to help their defense. Some of these formations, including the M shaped one, the W, the V, and the inverted V, have been described in Chapter IV. A formation will be selected according to the strategy of a team and its coach. This is almost the only time in the game when the center forward is unmarked by her opposing center half, who should be supporting and backing up the attacking forward line. Thus, in the M and V formations, the center forward should be ready to pounce on any short pass from her defense player. She then will be free with the ball momentarily and should quickly pass to her inners or wings to clear the ball from the danger area. In the M and V formations, she also should be prepared to move quickly to tackle the opposing center half, if she should take the ball into the circle to shoot.

In formation W, an inner receiving the ball near her defensive circle often will put a "through" pass to the waiting center forward, who is free of defensive opposition. The center forward previously should have assessed the position of the opposing fullbacks. If the left fullback is covering, then the center forward's right wing will be comparatively free, and a long, strong pass to her will be effective. If the right fullback is covering, then the converse will be true (Figure 5:1).

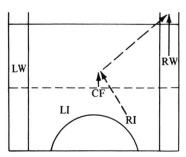

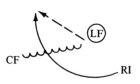

Figure 5:1. W formation. Inner to center to wing pass for a break-away.

Figure 5:2. Interchange of an inner and center forward for a breakaway.

The center forward may wish to vary this strategy and dribble the ball herself, as in the inverted V formation. While she is unmarked, she should move at top speed and dribble loosely; as she nears an opponent, she should change to closer, controlled dribbling.

MIDFIELD PLAY

As a center forward dribbles away from the defensive quarter of the field to the midfield area between the twenty-five yard lines, she must have a plan. Remembering that her opposing center half may be able to move faster without the ball than she is able to, she must constantly be listening for footsteps and breathing behind her. At the same time, she must watch her opposing fullbacks and halfbacks so that she times her pass to a wing or an inner before the full defense system has time to re-position itself.

As she dribbles from the defensive end of the field, she may go in a straight line, hoping that the nearest fullback will tackle her, thus freeing the inner on that side for a pass at the most opportune moment. Or, she may dribble straight at the nearest fullback, knowing that the inner on that side will drop into the center and be free for a pass (Figure 5:2). Or, she may dribble diagonally toward the covering full-back, causing the fullbacks to switch their covering defense. When the fullbacks are crossing and level with each other, the center forward may then put a through pass between them for an inner to run onto (Figure 5:3).

These are a few ideas for the center forward from an M or in-verted V formation, dribbling away from her defensive end of the field and starting an intelligent attacking movement. These ideas will not

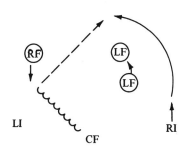

Figure 5:3. Fullbacks duped into a square
position followed by a through pass
between them.

work if the center forward has not assessed and planned before receiving
the ball and if she does not move at top speed away from her opposing
center half, who has been backing up her own forward line near the
edge of the circle.

During midfield play, the center forward usually is marked closely
by the opposing center half, who will try to position herself on the ball
side of the center forward and in line with a possible pass to her. Thus,
the center forward must work as hard when she does *not* have the ball
as when she is in possession of the ball. She must try to distract her
opposing center half by continually moving forward, backward, and
sideward onto the ball side of the center half. Thus, the opposing center
half has to watch continually and move with the center forward, making
her defensive job more difficult.

The center forward can help an inner who may want to use a
flat pass to the other inner. The center moves quickly ahead taking her
center half with her, thereby opening a clear space for an inner-to-inner
pass. As a cross pass from an inner or wing heads for the center forward,
it is a temptation for the center forward to stop it. She must learn that in
midfield, if the ball is allowed to pass by untouched to the inner or wing
on the other side of her, the opposing defense system is forced to change,
possibly opening up holes in its system, which may be penetrated by
the attack.

Thus, the center forward's job in midfield is twofold. First, she
may distribute the ball to others on the line; and, second, by constantly
moving and repositioning, she may draw her opponent with her, thereby
opening up clear spaces for inner-to-inner passes.

In both the midfield area and the attacking quarter of the field, a
center forward should avoid the temptation to drift towards an inner
who has possession of the ball. The center forward should move away

from the inner. This movement will draw the opposing center half further away from the ball and will give the inner a larger area in which to maneuver. It also will open up a clear space into which the inner may pass the ball to the center forward to run onto (Figure 5:4).

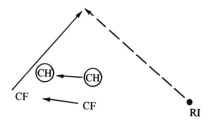

Figure 5:4. Center forward pulling away from the player with the ball to make a space for a pass.

PLAY IN THE ATTACKING END

In the attacking twenty-five yards, the center forward, as part of the forward line, should try to combine to produce a strong attack, hopefully resulting in a goal. It is impossible to designate specific movements for an attacking line of forwards. The game situation is continually changing as the ball passes from player to player. Because of the limited space in the striking circle, passing must be quick and accurate, and opportunities for shooting at goal must be quickly exploited. Forwards should try to shoot quickly or pass quickly. In the circle, a forward rarely dodges twice successfully. Therefore, if a center forward receives the ball on the edge of the circle and has time, she should drive it hard for goal. If she is about to be tackled, she should pass, or dodge and shoot immediately.

If another forward shoots for goal, the center forward immediately should rush towards the goalkeeper's pads with her stick down, ready to push or flick a rebound straight into the goal. This cleaning up action is one of the center forward's most important roles, both in general circle play and in a corner situation when an inner has received the ball and has shot at the goal. The center forward must be poised and ready to run, for she must surprise the goalie by arriving almost simultaneously with the ball. She also must be aware of the danger of being offside and should be ready to run off the field or retreat backwards if the goalkeeper clears the ball behind her as she rushes.

When the attacking center half receives the ball, either in general play or at a corner, and is dribbling in to shoot, the center forward immediately should pull to one side to allow the center half a clear shot. At the same time, when she sees the downward swing of the center half's stick or hears the stick hit the ball, the center forward should run straight for the goal, ready to rush a possible rebound off the goalie's pads.

Even though it is impossible to explain exactly how a forward line should penetrate the defense system, due to the ever-changing game situation, there are some situations in which certain types of passes are most suitable. If one player wants to pass to a player who is marked man-to-man, she should not pass to her stick but to a space behind the defensive player. Conversely, if a defensive player is marking the space and is not close to the player, the passer should pass the ball to the player's stick.

Often when a forward line arrives on the edge of the attacking circle, it finds the whole defense system is in position and marking and covering closely. This means that the only free forward is the wing farthest from the ball. A surprise move is a direct flat pass to the free wing, who may either quickly take a shot at the goal or cause a shifting of the defense, which opens up further possibilities of attack. Forwards should remember that the defense is most vulnerable when shifting; hence, they must shoot quickly. The center forward, specifically, always must be ready to cut to the ball side of her center half and pounce on a loose ball.

BULLYING

With the elimination of the rule for the twenty-five yard line bully, the center forward becomes the person primarily responsible for bullying. She should have a repertoire of methods that she will vary according to the tactics of her opponent. Basically, she may push or pull the ball away from the center, or relax her stick and induce the opposing forward to hit to the attacking center half; sometimes a scoop over the opponent's stick is possible, or a reverse pull followed by a quick drive to the non-stick side of the center forward. When bullying, the center forward should make small movements, especially on the third tap. Speed, quickness, and variation in timing are essential qualities that can be developed by constant practice. A center forward should remember that the opponent also is trying to outwit her and that she is not likely to be successful all the time. One would hope, however, that during a penalty bully, the center forward would win, for the goalie is encumbered and lacks practice in bullying. For this situation, the center forward should use her most reliably controlled method, being ready to adapt to the goalie's slower pace, and moving quickly after the third tap.

A SUMMARY OF SKILLS TO PRACTICE

Wherever possible, all practices should be in gamelike situations when specific skills are sufficiently competent.

1. *Footwork*—devise practices for quick, light, neat steps, moving in all directions.
2. *Body control*—closely connected with footwork; emphasis should be on control and balance.
3. *Stickwork*—devise practices to develop skills described under the section on stickwork.

FOOTNOTES

1. Named to the United States or Reserve Team as left wing for the past ten years, Alison knows the wing position well. She has represented the United States on five touring teams—to South Africa (1958), Europe (1959), Great Britain and Denmark (1962), the IFWHA Conference at Baltimore (1963), and Europe (1967). She is a Sectional B umpire. Alison received her Bachelor's degree from Mt. Holyoke College and her Master's degree from Tufts University. She coaches hockey at Germantown Friends School (Pa.) and Merestead Hockey and Lacrosse Camp (Maine).

2. Mary Ann Harris is a graduate of Temple University and is currently teaching at the Sidwell Friends School, Washington, D.C. She played for the Philadelphia and Southeast Sections and made the United States Reserve Team in 1958 and the United States Team from 1959–1967. She has been on touring teams to Europe (1959), Great Britain and Denmark (1962), IFWHA Conference in Baltimore (1963), Penn Valley team to Jamaica (1964) and to Europe (1967). She has had coaching experience at the high school level, at day camps and Merestead Hockey and Lacrosse Camp. She is a Sectional B umpire.

3. An All-England hockey player, Diane Crowley Treese came to the United States in 1962. She graduated from Bedford College in England and is presently teaching at the Baldwin School, Bryn Mawr, Pennsylvania. She played for Surrey County, South of England, All-England, and since coming to this country has played for the Philadelphia team, being named captain of that team for two years. She has coached at the Pocono Hockey Camp for seven years and at a camp at Westown, Pennsylvania for Sectional and United States players for three years.

VI

THE DEFENSE

The role of a defense player coördinating with her teammates is a matter of being in the right place at the right time. Where that place is depends on the location of the ball and the position of the other players on the field.

Because of the nature of the game, the defense has the advantage over the attack. Therefore, the final score in field hockey is low. This is because the ball is propelled along the ground at one level rather than through the air at several levels. By proper positioning, the defense can prevent a team from scoring. A score results when the defensive team makes a tactical error.

GENERAL CONCEPTS OF DEFENSE

Defense players must be good fielders. They should be able to field balls that approach from any direction, whether they are rolling or bouncing over bumpy turf. They should be able to stop the ball and to start an attack. Little is gained if the ball is intercepted and then passed back to the opponents, as often happens in beginning play. Particularly when a ball approaches from the left, a beginning defense player incorrectly sets herself in a stationary position and places her stick so that the ball is deflected back toward its starting point.

At times, a defense player wants to stop the ball; at other times, she wants to deflect the ball. If the opposing forwards are close, the defense player should deflect the ball forward past the onrushing forwards. This tactic gives the defense player time to look for a free teammate and removes her from the congestion. She cannot wait too long, however, because the opposing forwards will tackle back. Using this tactic, the player is running forward as she intercepts. She does not stop the ball completely, but angles her stick so that the ball is deflected forward. This action permits her to continue running into a free space. If an onrushing forward might intercept the deflection, the defense

119

player should stop the ball and do a quick, neat dodge around her to gain time to look for a receiver. If a long, through pass is received, the defense player desires to control it, look for a free player, and then pass accurately to her. Under no circumstances should the ball just be hit; it should be passed to a teammate.

Players and coaches should be aware of the danger of hitting an oncoming ball without previously controlling it. Controlling means that the ball is deflected or stopped, but not necessarily motionless. Hitting the ball without controlling it often causes the ball to be raised into a dangerous hit. Uncontrolled hits are dangerous and should be penalized. Beginning players often forget to control the ball before hitting it. Immediate steps should be taken to insure that this practice is not habit forming. Penalties should be assessed immediately at any level of play when an uncontrolled hit is executed.

Players should not be permitted to drive the ball into the legs of an opponent who is close by. This, too, is a dangerous hit. It often occurs when a defense player hits the ball hurriedly and impulsively directly into an opponent's legs. A dodge would avoid this dangerous hit. The same situation occurs when a defender approaches to make a tackle and has the ball driven into her shins.

In addition to being dangerous, uncontrolled hitting often discourages players from participating in recreational hockey. For students in physical education classes and for all hockey enthusiasts, the game should be both safe and enjoyable.

Fielding the ball requires certain skills. The most important skill is the position of the player relative to the ball. The player should have her feet and body facing the direction she is attacking. This means that she faces the ball only when it comes from directly in front of her. The defense player may cut toward the ball to intercept it; but as she fields it, her body and feet turn so that she can proceed toward the goal she is attacking rather than toward the sideline. A defense player becoming proficient in this tactic would not hit the ball sideward and directly back to an opponent. This dangerous habit could be eliminated if the defense player would thrust her left foot, hip, and shoulder forward while intercepting and continue to run forward (Figure 6:1).

As a player learns to face properly, she also must learn to stay on the ball side of her opponent (Figure 6:2). If players would become more interception-minded, they would see the necessity of being closer to the ball than is their opponent. Once players recognize how much more difficult it is to get the ball after their opponent has it, they should understand the value of intercepting it first.

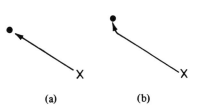
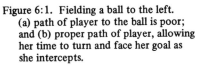
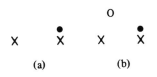
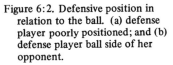

(a)   (b)   (a)   (b)

Figure 6:1. Fielding a ball to the left. (a) path of player to the ball is poor; and (b) proper path of player, allowing her time to turn and face her goal as she intercepts.

Figure 6:2. Defensive position in relation to the ball. (a) defense player poorly positioned; and (b) defense player ball side of her opponent.

Intercepting the ball is a matter of anticipation and concentration. Anticipation can be developed by an understanding of the theory of attack play. Knowing the game develops game sense. By recognizing where an opposing defense player is likely to pass under varying circumstances and by knowing where attack players are likely to pass in different portions of the field, a player knows where to intercept the ball. Concentration is the key to being prepared. Being prepared, anticipating, and then being able to make a quick, confident decision enables a player to make the interceptions that can demoralize and frustrate the opposing forwards.

While the ball is in play, the defense players usually are moving. As the ball changes position, whether it is dribbled or passed, every defense player must react to the new positions of both the ball and the other players on the field, both teammates and opponents. The defense changes position forward and back as the ball moves up and down the field. They also change position laterally as the ball moves across the field. As the ball is passed from one forward to another behind a defense player, each inside defender (fullbacks and center half) must move laterally to the other side of her opponent so that she remains on the ball side of her. Figure 6:3 demonstrates this tactic. The diagram also indicates that when lateral movement is involved, the player has further to move to regain the same relative position. The defense player therefore must react quickly and move more swiftly than her opponent to stay in a good defensive position. Attaining a good defensive position is easier when the ball is passed from her left to her right because the ball is on her stick side and her opponent's non-stick side. As the ball

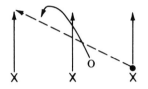

Figure 6:3. Defense player regaining
ball side defensive position as the
ball is passed.

is passed from her right to her left, her problems are greater because
the ball is then on her non-stick side.

The good defense player must develop endurance. Practice sessions
should be planned so that she can gain more stamina than she would
need during any contest. If players do not have the energy to move
into proper position, their defense weakens because it has gaps; a defense is only as strong as its weakest player.

FORWARDS' DUTIES ON DEFENSE

As soon as a forward loses the ball to her opponent, she should
tackle back immediately and try to regain the ball. Even if she fails to
regain the ball, she at least has hurried the opponent into passing sooner
than she might like. The reaction to tackle back must be immediate.

Sometimes it is obvious that a pass will be intercepted. Instead of
blaming a teammate for a poor pass, the closest attack player should
hurry to tackle the opponent as she fields the ball. The attack player
may succeed in getting the ball or may cause the opponent to pass
poorly. Attack players must assume more responsibility in tackling back
on the opposing defense. It is disheartening for the forwards' own defense players to see opponents progressing down the field unimpeded
and able to look for a free player and give her an accurate pass.

Nevertheless, attack players must not tackle back on opposing
attack players. This is the job for their defense (Figure 6:4). When
attack players are permitted to tackle an opposing forward, the play
becomes confused and congested, because at least three or four players
are trying to get the ball, including an inner tackling back on the opposing inner and the fullbacks trying to tackle their own inner. Further-

more, if the defense player succeeds in getting the ball, she has no forward ahead to whom she may pass. When members of one forward line are playing the ball, the opposing forwards should stay about ten yards behind the ball toward the goal they are attacking and let their own defense players get the ball (Figure 6:5). Advanced players may alter this position somewhat, especially in the defensive end of the field when they may find it advantageous to vary the straight line pattern of the forwards to a W or diagonal in order to have a better chance of springing a player free.

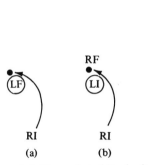

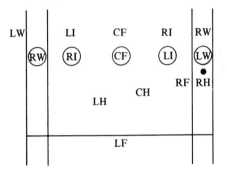

Figure 6:4. Forwards tackling back. (a) an inner tackles back on her opposing fullback; and (b) poor play by the inner who tackles back on an opposing attack player and muddles the defense.

Figure 6:5. Position of forwards on the team that does not have the ball. Forwards allow their defense players to get the ball and position to receive a pass. Note: The defense players opposing them have been omitted intentionally to make the diagram more clear.

Another defensive duty of the forwards is to prevent the opposing halves from shooting unimpeded. The various formations that can be used to prevent this were discussed in Chapter IV. The use of the W, M, diagonal, V, or inverted V depends upon the strengths of the forwards and the abilities of the opposing halves. Whether the inners, center, or wings are deployed for this purpose makes little difference as long as someone prevents the opponents from increasing their attack to an eight-on-five situation. Of course, if the halves do not shoot when the opportunity arises, there is no reason to deploy an attack player to defend. The attack player can be used to better advantage up the field to wait for a pass.

DEFENSE TECHNIQUES

Marking

Defense players mark an opponent, but attack players *are* marked. The only exception to this rule occurs when attack players mark opposing forwards on free hits and rolls-in to permit their defensive teammates to cover the spaces. Otherwise, forwards never mark opposing forwards.

Marking implies that a player is on the ball side of her opponent, on the goal side of her opponent, and within a stick's length of her opponent. Being positioned this close to the opponent discourages a pass directly to the marked player. The defender therefore forces the opposition to give a through pass to the attacker. For this reason, defense players are most likely to mark in or near the circle, where the space ahead is more limited. Because the attack needs little forward progress in the circle, their passes become more square. By marking, the defense is in a good position to intercept the pass. In the circle, a defender should not permit her opponent to take a shot at goal at any time. For these reasons, marking is a necessity in the circle. In midfield, marking is less desirable because the forwards prefer to pass ahead, and marking enables them to do so.

Covering

Defense players cover a space; that is, they position themselves so that a through pass hit to their opponent will have to cross the area in which they are positioned. A defender cannot mark and cover at the same time, except when a defense player has the ball and an opponent stands between her and the player she is marking. If the defense player marks, she encourages the through passes (Figure 6:6); if she covers, she encourages the flat passes (Figure 6:7). Because the defense wishes to delay the forward progress of the attack, they cover in the midfield area. This concept is difficult to get across to beginning defense players, as they tend to think they are not doing their job unless they are quite close to their opponent. Figure 6:8 shows typical positioning of defense players. Figure 6:9 shows how much better the spaces are defended by a slight altering in the defensive positioning. Once the concept of

Figure 6:6. A defense player
marking

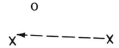
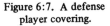

Figure 6:7. A defense
player covering.

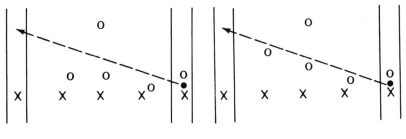

Figure 6:8. Poor covering positions
by defense players.

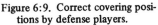

Figure 6:9. Correct covering positions by defense players.

positioning oneself in the path that the ball will have to take in order to
reach the receiver is acquired, covering becomes more understandable.

Covering also is the term applied to the fullback, who plays deeper
on defense. The covering fullback may move to intercept long, through
passes or to tackle a free player as she approaches the striking circle.

Tackling

A tackle is a means of taking the ball away from an opponent. The
tackle used most often is the straight tackle. The defense player must
be deceptive to be successful. It is fatal to run toward the attack player
and attempt the tackle. The dribbler will time the defender's speed and
easily dodge her as the defender's momentum carries her beyond the
dribbler. An intelligent defense player will approach the dribbler with

care. Her speed is reduced and her weight is evenly distributed so that she may move in any direction—forward or backward or sideward. She may feign a tackle and pull away; she may hover; or she may feign inattention or lethargy in an attempt to disrupt the timing of the forward. The defender may then tackle the ball at the critical instant.

Before the tackle, the rest of the defenders are preparing for a dodge or a pass by the dribbler. If the tackler forces a pass, the rest of the defense should be in position to intercept it. If the dribbler succeeds in dodging, the defender must recover immediately and tackle back. Meanwhile, the rest of the defense gives their teammate time to recover, even though it is tempting for another defender to rush out to the free player as she dribbles down the field unimpeded. However, the defense must discipline themselves to remain in position against their own opponent. Unless the circle is near, their teammate should have time to recover and tackle her own opponent. If she does not and a free player approaches the striking circle, then the covering back tackles her. But she must not be tempted to go too soon. If she is drawn from her covering position before the circle is reached, then the defense is in a poor position if she is ever passed (five attack against three defense). Therefore, backs must discipline themselves to wait until the free player moves near the circle. Fullbacks should remember that the opponents cannot score until they reach the circle; therefore, even if the player is free and proceeding unimpeded, she is not dangerous until she reaches the circle. When the fullback is forced to tackle the free player, the recovering defender continues to hustle back in to the circle to a position where she will be of the greatest help.

As a defender tackles back, she runs back on the goal side of her opponent and tackles at the appropriate time. The left halfback and left fullback must make a circular tackle, and the right halfback and right fullback, a left hand lunge. The center half has her choice of either tackle. In a desperate situation, the jab or cut may be used strictly as a defensive measure.

Interchanging

An interchange occurs when two players exchange positions temporarily. An interchange can occur when a long, through pass is directed down the field to the wing. The covering fullback, knowing that she can reach the ball before the wing does, moves over to intercept it. At this time, the halfback should move in and be responsible for the inner. If the fullback intercepts the ball and passes to one of her forwards, both the halfback and fullback can return to their normal positions. However, if the fullback misses the ball or if the wing reaches the ball sooner than anticipated, the fullback stays with the wing and the halfback stays on the inner. They retain these positions until the ball is cleared.

The same type of situation occurs when a free attack player nears the circle and the fullback goes to tackle her. The fullback stays with the attack player until the crisis is passed and a teammate marks her opponent for her. On an interchange of this type, the players nearest the ball should be marked. As the defender recovers, she moves to mark a player further from the ball.

Although usually thought of as a defensive tactic, an interchange also is used by attack players. On a long roll down the alley, the inner may be in a better position than the wing to field it. On a pass to the inner's position, the center may be in a better position because the inner has been left behind. The halfback may field a ball near the sideline and opposite the offensive striking circle. In this case, the wing may wish to replace her as the halfback. In situations such as these, the players temporarily exchange positions so that crowding does not occur. The players remain in their new positions until the ball moves to the other side of the field.

An interchange must be decisive. Interchanging is consistent with intelligent play if used wisely, but excessive interchange is unwarranted. If used too frequently, it loses its purpose and tends to confuse one's own team as well as the opposition.

DEFENSIVE POSITIONING

The defense is concerned with three areas of the playing field— midfield, in the defensive striking circle, and in the attacking striking circle. The positioning of the players varies considerably according to the area of the field in which the ball is being played.

Players often are confused about the positioning for play in each area because they fail to consider them separately. It is impossible, of course, to indicate exactly where each player should position herself in the three areas of the field; the exact position depends on the location of the ball and of the other players. The number of passes possible at any given moment increases the complexity of the defense. Nevertheless, a knowledge of the theory of defense and attack play will enable each defender to anticipate and thwart the opponent's efforts.

Midfield Play

When in the expanse between the two striking circles, the opposing attack wants to get the ball down to the attacking striking circle as quickly as possible. The defense players therefore position themselves to prevent a rapid breakthrough by covering the spaces into which through passes to their opponents would be made. Here, defense players do not mark. By covering, they try to force the attackers to make passes that are more square, and thus slow down their forward progress. A square pass usually cannot be intercepted. A good defense does not attempt an interception because this is what the attack hopes for—a defense player out of position. Instead, the defense waits, and an impatient attack soon will try a through pass, which is just what the defense is waiting for.

A basketball player or coach can see an analogy between a zone defense in basketball and the covering tactics of the defense in hockey. The purposes of the two defenses are quite similar. In both, some freedom for passing is given when players are distant from the goal. In basketball, players are permitted to pass beyond the key relatively unhindered, and in hockey the square pass is the most "open" pass.

One objective of the zone in basketball is to protect against passes going to players in front of the goal. The players on the periphery are paid least attention and often remain free. They may be able to shoot from a distance from the goal, or the defense may have time to recover and at least pose a threat to the shooter. In hockey, the inners and center are well-guarded at all times, and the wing on the side away from the ball has the greatest amount of freedom.

Another objective of the zone is to position so that the angle of a pass to a forward is covered, thus allowing for a number of interceptions. The same principle is followed in hockey. Any player out of position in the zone defense in basketball or the covering defense in hockey makes the defense vulnerable. A coördinated effort of all players is necessary for a stalwart defense.

In the covering position in hockey, the fullbacks play on an oblique angle; the fullback on the side with the ball plays up, and the fullback on the other side plays back and in toward the center of the field. The center halfback is responsible for the center forward only. Her defense is man-to-man; she should not wander from the center to defend against any other attack player. The side halves coordinate with the fullbacks. The half on whose side the ball is covers her wing, and the halfback on the other side of the field moves in and covers the inner, allowing her own wing to go uncovered. The right half and right back will play deeper and more in toward the center of the field than do the left half and left fullback, because the ball is to their non-stick side. They need more time to cross over to be stick-side when the right back becomes the covering back and the right half moves in on the inner. This means that when the ball is on the far side of the field, the right half may be in almost to the center of the field to cover the space to the opposing left inner.

As the ball is moved from one side of the field to the other, the defense players readjust their positions. The center half moves to the other side of her center forward, the fullbacks change up and back positions, and the halves move to their new position. These changes in position are done simultaneously. The side halfbacks should not hesitate, especially when the fullbacks are changing their position. If the side halfbacks do hesitate, a dangerous inner is left free.

The fullbacks should be careful during their adjustment that they do not become "square," that is, parallel with one another. As the halfbacks move in on the inner, they must be careful not to hover between the wing and the inner; they should get on the ball side of the inner. They also should recognize that they are not covering spaces if they only are on-line with the inner. In order to cover spaces with the ball on the far side of the field, they should move back toward the defensive goal and in toward the center of the field.

The most vulnerable time for the defense is during this readjustment period. Therefore, the selection of a team's defense players should be made at the earliest possible time, to give them time to refine their moves. Coördination with each other comes only through experience in playing together.

If a pass is made across the field to an inner, a well-positioned halfback will try to intercept. If she misses, she allows the fullback to move up to take the inner with the ball. The halfback then returns to her own wing, snce the ball is now on her side of the field. Similarly, if the halfback is in on the inner, and the opposition hits a ball to the free wing, the halfback leaves the inner to go to the wing as the back on her side moves up to cover her own inner. This adjustment should become second-nature to the players.

It should be emphasized that the center halfback has only one responsibility—her opposing center. The side halfbacks and fullbacks each have two responsibilities. Each side halfback is responsible for her own wing when the ball is on the halfback's side of the field and is responsible for the inner on her side when the ball is on the other side of the field. Thus, the halves are continually moving from one position to the other, depending upon the location of the ball. Each fullback is responsible for her own inner when the ball is on her side of the field and is responsible for through passes that escape all of the other defense players and for *any* free player who approaches the striking circle. A free player is permitted to proceed unhindered anywhere up the field away from the circle to allow her own defender a chance to recover.

Further comments. Occasionally, forwards will pull back slightly behind the line of the ball to coax the defender to follow. This move creates a space behind the defender through which a pass can be made. All defense players should be aware of this offensive tactic, especially the center half because the center forward frequently assists an inner-to-inner pass.

Each defense player should reach as far to her right as possible to protect the non-stick side of the defender on her right. But this is not true of players reaching to their left. The use of the reverse stick stop while the defenders are marking in the circle is undesirable. Each player (except the left halfback) has a defender to her left who can more easily field the ball on her stick side. An attempt at a reverse stick stop may deflect the ball out of the reach of a teammate. If the ball goes to the stick of an attack player, a goal can result.

The situation upfield is different. In many cases, a defender can make a spectacular stop of a ball hit into a space behind her. Players who are adept at this method of fielding can cover more area and therefore are valuable to their team.

Drills.

1. Pairs. One player dribbles and the defense player attempts a straight tackle. Emphasize a cautious approach for the tackle.
2. Groups of threes—two attack players against one defense player. One attack player dribbles toward the defense player and has the option of passing or dodging. The defense player should practice feinting movements to harass the timing of the dribbler. The defense player tries to tackle or intercept the pass.
3. Groups of threes—two attack players against one defense player. The forward on the right without an opponent starts with the ball and passes to her marked teammate. The defense player runs forward to intercept. Later, pass from the left. Add a fourth player so that the defense player can clear to a teammate.
4. Same formation and description as No. 3, except the defense player starts further from her opponent to allow the first pass to be successful. She is then forced to run backwards as the forwards pass and to time her dart forward for the interception.

5. Three attack players against three defense players in midfield. No ball is used initially. To practice positioning, the instructor identifies the attack player with the ball and the defense players move to the ball side of their opponent. With practice, the instructor increases the speed in identifying the position of the ball.

6. Five attack players against five defense players in midfield. Same description as No. 5. Emphasize the halfback and fullback covering positions, particularly in terms of lateral position and depth on the field.

7. Same formation and description as No. 6, except that a ball is used. Initially, forwards are told not to pass until instructed to do so. This permits the instructor to be certain that the defensive players have adjusted to each pass correctly. Later, let the forwards pass at their own speed. When the defense obtain the ball, they pass to the instructor or to spare players.

Play in the Defensive Striking Circle

The area that must be defended is reduced when an opposing team reaches the striking circle. The forwards are drawn closer together as they move toward the edge of the circle, and they have little distance to travel before the goal line is reached.

Using a covering back when the ball is out near the edge of the circle is advisable. The covering back plays only about midway in the circle and is able to intercept many short, through passes. If a pass goes to the free wing while the back is covering, the halfback should remain marking the inner and the fullback takes the wing. This tactic is different from those suggested for use when the ball is between the striking circles because of the danger in leaving a player free in the striking circle. If the back goes to the wing, there is a change in positioning by only one player rather than two, and the inner remains marked constantly. Also, in the circle, the back has to go only a few steps to reach the wing. As the ball is advanced midway into the circle, the covering back moves to a marking position and the half moves out to her wing. In this way, the covering fullback never moves back so far as to obstruct the goalkeeper's view of the ball. In this portion of the circle, each defense player marks her opponent so closely that she always knows her exact position.

The left half and left back mark directly in front of their opponents. This permits them to be on the goal side of them and also in position to tackle an opponent on their right if she becomes free. The right back and right half mark on the stick side of their opponents so that they remain on the goal side of them.

As stated earlier, the covering back does not immediately tackle a free player beyond the striking circle. Rather, she gives the defender a chance to recover. Once the free player reaches the striking circle, the back should move to tackle. At the same time, the defender, who is still in pursuit, drops back into the striking circle in a covering position. Under other circumstances, when a player becomes free in the circle and starts to shoot, the defender on the stick side tackles or jabs to hinder the shot. When necessary, the left half tackles the right inner, right half, or right back; the left back tackles the center forward, center half, or right back; the center half tackles the left inner, center halfback, or left back; the right back tackles the left wing, left back, or left half; and the right halfback tackles the left back or left halfback. However, under no circumstances should a defender try to stop a shot as it moves toward the goal. This is the goalkeeper's job. Too many shots are deflected by defense players into the goal past the goalkeeper. The goalkeeper's goalie pads provide a wide surface to stop the ball. Other defenders should demonstrate their confidence in the goalie's ability by letting her perform her own duties.

Further comments. When a defense player gets the ball, she should clear it immediately. She has no space for dodges and only a little time before an opponent will tackle. Halfbacks should be prepared to recover goalie clears along the endline and pass them up to the wings or any other free player. Free hits and defense hits should be taken quickly so that the opponents do not have time to block the angles.

Drills.

1. Five attack players against five defense players in the circle. No ball is used initially. Instruct the attack players to rush the goal and then pull back, rush, and pull back on signal. The defense players move so that they remain marking their opponent. Later, let the forwards use their own initiative to rush the goal or re-position.
2. Same formation and description as No. 1, except that the instructor identifies who has the imaginary ball. This forces the defense players to move forward and back with their opponent, and to move laterally to stay on the ball side of their opponent.
3. Same formation and description as for No. 1, except that a ball is used. If the ball goes out of the circle, stop play and return the ball to the forwards. Add halfbacks to back up the forwards to keep the ball in play.
4. Five attack players against five defense players with the for-

wards behind the attacking twenty-five yard line. One forward starts with the ball, with her opponent ten yards behind her, as though evaded. On signal, the forward starts dribbling, and all forwards advance toward goal. The defense player attempts to recover. An interchange is effected only at the edge of the circle, if necessary. Alternate forwards who start with the ball.

5. Five attack players and their halfbacks against five defense players. The attacking center half starts with the ball just outside the striking circle. She passes to the free wing, and the covering back goes out to tackle. Let play continue. Practice to both wings.

Play in the Attacking Striking Circle

When a team has the ball in the attacking striking circle, the halfbacks back up their forwards and think of defense only in terms of blocking the angles of clears out of the circle. The fullbacks, however, must decide how far up they will play. One fullback will stay at the center line, but the other fullback can go down to back up the forwards, if she is quick enough to recover. At the same time, the backs should be concerned with the position of the opposing forwards. If the forwards are in a straight line, there is little chance for a breakaway. If they are in an M formation, the inners are in position for the breakaway. Depending upon the speed of the backs, the back who is playing up may be forced to play more defensively to guard against a breakaway of two inners versus one back. If the opposing attack uses a W formation, the wings are the breakaway players and the backs may edge slightly toward the sideline to intercept the long pass to them. This play is possible because the wing is ahead of the inner, and if the back misses the interception, the back still has time to recover and defend against her rightful opponent. As other systems are used by the attack, the backs can make necessary adjustments, but at no time can they ignore the position of the opposing attacks.

Drills. The drills in Chapter IV for attack play in the circle are appropriate here.

DEFENSIVE IMAGINATION

A defense player whose opponent is inept and unused can concern herself with other players. She can help out a troubled defender and aid on offense. She can take risks without influencing the efficiency of the defense. By keeping the ball in the offensive end, she can have more fun and be less tired at the end of the game.

When playing against inexperienced teams, the side halves (particularly the right half) can move in toward the center of the field and block off the angles. By hurrying the inners, the halves may force them to make a pass to the wing so flat that it goes over the sideline. The resulting play is like the basketball team that cannot get the ball over the center line.

When the opposition has one strong forward who is the key player, a defense player with a weak opponent can assist her teammate. The two defense players can double team the strong opponent. By using this defensive adjustment, the defense can completely stop the opposition's offense. But if all members of the opposition's forward line are effective, the complete double team is impossible because a defense then becomes susceptible to a breakaway that could be dangerous. An intelligent defense player, however, can deploy to some degree to double team the strong player partially, and yet be ready to move out to her own opponent when necessary.

A defense in which the fullbacks play square is usually vulnerable. Under certain circumstances, however, this defense can be effective. When the opposing team has the ball or is attempting to gain the ball in their defensive end of the field, both fullbacks, by playing up, can thwart the opponents' attempts to clear the ball to their attack players. By playing further downfield than is customary, the backs can establish a barrier behind the halfback line and defensively stop the opponents before they attack. The additional player provides more coverage of the possible angle for passes; thus, the "zoning" process is more effective. Even if the opponents get the ball through, the defense players have a chance to recover before the striking circle is reached. When the opposing attack gains the ball in the midfield area, the defense should place less emphasis on the squareness of the backs and revert to the more common defense measures.

However, there is value in altering defenses during a game. It forces the attack to become more alert and to check on what the opposition is doing. A team that fails to check the opposition's tactics may be surprised by the innovation of different defensive tactics. Psychologically, occasional changes in defensive tactics are profitable. They force the opponents to think about one more thing, thus, placing greater stress on their actions.

VII

POSITION PLAY BY THE DEFENSE

THE HALFBACKS

by Marilyn O'Neill[1]
in collaboration with Vonnie Gros

A look at the halfback position by a fullback, from behind the halfback play, can offer interesting insight into what makes for good halfback play.

QUALITIES

Fundamentals in which halfbacks should become proficient are tackling, passing in any direction with any stroke at the desired speed, rolling-in, and quick hitting. Accuracy and quickness of performance, which separate the average from the superior competitor, come only from desire and long hours of practice. However, there is always the danger of becoming too involved with mechanics and details. As Alice Putnam Willets, former U.S. halfback, said, "If we become too involved in mechanics and individual faults, we may fail to enjoy the activity and team coöperation that is offered."

Halfbacks are part of a unit that is similar to a zone defense in basketball in which each member moves according to the movement of the ball. Hockey defense is played under the same principle. If all defense players move together, then when the ball reaches a particular area, a defense player will be there, not be arriving there.

ATTACK PLAY

If the halves think attack, they can confuse their opponents. Many teams expect the opposing halves to send the ball across the field when they reach the twenty-five yard line. By doing the unexpected and distributing the play to both sides of the field from any position, the halves can break the opposition's defense and allow a play to go through. The halves should send passes to any available player or space in any part of the field. Hockey is more than a game of skill; it also is a game of wits and a tactical battle.

Halves have more opportunity to play the ball than do other players. Therefore, a good halfback must have the awareness to find the opponent's weaknesses and to capitalize on them. She must watch the ball and the relative positioning of the players. A wing, pulling out or dropping back, is a constant threat. A half must learn to think as her opponent does. The side half must be aware of her own fullback and her relative position on attack. If the right fullback is up on attack, the right halfback should be out on the opposing left wing. A through pass by the opposite defense can be fielded by the right fullback, thus eliminating the half's dilemma of being caught out of position.

All halves should enjoy attacking and should shoot at goal whenever they have an opportunity. Outside the attacking striking circle, the side half must be aware of the ball position. Crowding into the center can leave her opposing wing open to start an attack. During a corner, the object is a score. The possibilities of halves assisting toward a goal from a corner are numerous. For example, whether the half in possession of the ball outside the circle passes to the near wing, the far wing, or her own fullback, or whether she takes the shot herself, depends on the half's knowledge of the situation and players and on her initiative to try an unusual maneuver.

The wing halves should know why and when to stand square with their own backs when a free hit by their team is being taken. A square pass often can start an attacking movement simply by causing an opponent to re-position. All halfbacks should understand the value of using a square pass, a through pass, an angle pass, or even a back pass. Move your opponent, then eliminate her.

DEFENSIVE PLAY

Because about half of their job is defensive, halfbacks should position themselves behind the attack so that they close the ring of the opponent's defensive pass. At the same time, they should be aware of at least three possible receivers on their own forward line. Intelligent moves by forwards make the halfback's job easier. For example, no one opposing forward should be more available to receive a pass or to decoy for a pass than any other forward.

The halves should finish their assignments and stay with the play until the situation changes. The object of the defense is to start a constructive attack for their team, regardless of the system used. If the play pulls the back away from her own inner, the fullback counts on the half to mark the opposing inner in the deep, defending half of the field. Timing and an intuitive response to this situation will bring that side half in at the right time. Unfortunately, many halves come in on the inner at the fifty-yard line. This fault begins with the wing who has been neglected and moves in, narrowing the field of play by about ten yards. A half, moving too soon or too late, allows a smart opponent to capitalize on the mistake. Halfbacks caught out of position can ruin their own defense. Concentration on the entire game can help prevent bad positioning.

HOW TO MAKE PLAY DIFFICULT FOR THE OPPONENTS

These "Do's" and "Don'ts" written for a right fullback can be helpful to halfbacks.

Do's

1. Always concentrate.
2. Play every position on both teams mentally to help anticipate play.
3. Be aware of opposing forwards who do not have the ball.
4. Keep your feet moving at all times.
5. Recover quickly after being passed.
6. Take pride in fine stickwork, footwork, and control.
7. Have confidence in your goalkeeper; she often is in a better position to field a ball than you are.
8. Be sympathetic and intelligent in your passing.
9. Give your other halfbacks confidence by covering.
10. Think "attack."

Don'ts

1. Don't be afraid of an unusual move if the situation calls for it.
2. Don't hit the ball; pass it.
3. Don't obstruct your goalkeeper's view.
4. Don't fail to mark closely in the circle.
5. Don't stereotype your game with the same passes and dodges.
6. Don't hold the ball; send it on attack as soon as possible.
7. Don't ever act out of desperation by using a flying hit or a crude obstruction.
8. Don't field a ball while getting into position; be in position.

9. Don't be satisfied with a well-executed tackle or interception unless you have followed it with a pass that has started an attacking movement.
10. Don't ever give up. Dogged determination has won many a game.

A good, intelligent halfback is the greatest asset to a winning team. By knowing the game and being able to anticipate the moves of other players, she keeps her team on the attack. Because she is a vital part of the defensive unit, a half's role is somewhat stereotyped. Therefore, a wandering halfback helps only the other team. In daring to be different, the half must also be reliable. The main concern in winning should be purposeful movement and an understanding of the game. Dare to be different; try something new. You might enjoy it and be successful.

THE FULLBACKS

by Adele Boyd[2]

What makes a player decide to play the fullback position? Before reading further about the fullback position, players should dispel the image that sometimes accompanies this position. Some people may think that the fullback and goalkeeper are ideal positions for anyone overweight, over-age, and underactive. This erroneous conclusion may be the result of "gym class hockey," where a girl who wants to chat with a friend chooses to play fullback. Experienced players may enjoy modifying this position to fit into the range of their abilities, but a player does not "retire" to the fullback position in good hockey.

QUALITIES

All hockey players should be able to run quickly and with agility and endurance—both physical and mental. Footwork also is an important part of good play and can be learned and practiced. A player whose feet are clumsy can practice running with short steps sidewards, backwards, and with a change of direction. It is a good idea to place obstacles on the ground and run around or between them with short, quick steps.

Good reaction time, good peripheral vision, and a good sense of timing are qualities that all athletes would like to possess. Players can concentrate on these items and improve their ability. A player who can react to a situation that has occurred before without having to consider and react to several ideas in the process, is a necessity on a team. A player who knows what to look for out of the corner of her eye, such as a wing in the corner or her own side halfback ready to help, is more likely to see these things. And a thorough knowledge of basic skills allows a player to time her passes, dodges, and tackles at her own rate. By the experience of playing against different opponents, she learns how to use her speed and how to modify her skills to deceive any opponent.

Physical and mental strength help a defense player to keep her team from letting down in crucial periods. Sometimes the team must hold on for just a few minutes while forwards and the team are able to coördinate another offensive attack. Sheer determination can keep a defense together, even in the last exhausting minutes of the game. Just as forwards must practice quick sprints to the goal, a fullback must be prepared to run out of a corner situation time after time. The grueling fifteen-yard sprint that occurs on a penalty corner can deaden the legs quickly if a player has not conditioned for this event.

Stability in the entire defense is the key to success. A fullback should have a complete overview of the way her defense works; she must know how and when every player fits into the overall pattern. With this pattern in her mind, she must work to create the security of a strong and stable backfield for her team. Because halfbacks are responsible for getting so far up on the attack, the job of balancing the defense is often left to the fullbacks. A team will not worry if it realizes that a dependable fullback is always ready for an emergency.

The ability to work constructively under pressure will be achieved by a poised, reliable, and disciplined player. When one or more attacking players suddenly break through and come down the field toward a lone defense player, the back should be able to cope with the situation.

The initiative that any player takes makes the difference between mediocrity and brilliance in her play. If she can quickly assess an opponent's ability and intention, she must then complete her own reaction with a sound and creative move. A fullback must try to anticipate the opponent and outthink or outwit her. If a forward can outrun a fullback, the back should play her so as not to be left far behind, chasing her as she goes toward goal.

If a fullback is to be successful in hockey, she must have a sound understanding of the strategy and rules of the game and of her responsibility. As part of the team of eleven, she must work to understand what part she plays.

A defense player must have the ability to adjust and readjust to backfield situations. She should learn to recover quickly if passed, to control a situation when another player is recovering, and to assist all teammates (including the goalie) in doing a better job.

Coördinating the attack and defense of a team is easier when players are sensitive to each other's needs. A fullback should be able to pass to a forward and should not rely on a desperation hit or aggressive drive in the direction of the goal.

Any defense player knows how necessary it is for all eleven players to work during the entire playing period. A fullback needs the help of an inner who will tackle back, and of a halfback who does a little extra work now and then to spoil the plays of the other team. Appreciation of this help is important. An unselfish player will never hesitate to acknowledge her appreciation; this is how team effort is achieved.

STICKWORK

The basic strokes and skills in hockey are the most useful. The game can be played in any position if the players can control the ball and then hit it. Therefore, constant practice and complete mastery of getting the ball and then accurately sending it are invaluable.

In the fullback position, a quick, strong drive is a necessity. Both the left and right fullbacks should be able to drive on any angle accurately.

There has always been a lot of emphasis on stopping the ball. This is an erroneous term used to describe controlling the ball. A beginning player who does not control a ball before she attempts to pass it may inadvertently send a dangerous and lofted ball.

The coördination between hand and eye is learned in childhood. As this learning is refined, it is possible for a person to use some implement which extends the hand and arm—in hockey, a stick. To achieve this coördination, it is necessary to watch the ball. Sometimes a player can assist the eye-stick accuracy by pointing to an oncoming loose ball with the toe of her stick. She also may find that feeling the ground with her stick will help her to become accustomed to the space and distance she can reach. No matter where she collects the ball, it should be close to her stick and not in a tangled mess of ball, feet, and stick.

As the fullback controls the ball, she surveys the game situation.

Often she can pass immediately using a drive, flick, scoop, or push-type pass. It should be unnecessary for a defense player to dribble up the field, although at times she may have to take a tap or two to lure the opponents toward her. Women seldom pass the ball backward, but Continental teams and men's teams seem to think this strategy will lure an opponent into a new position and then allow a space for a constructive pass.

If a short-toed stick is used, dexterity with the stick on both right and left sides of a player's body will permit greater variety of maneuvers. The ability to control the ball with the reversed-stick toe can be useful to a left fullback. A command of several basic strokes is preferable to a wide variety of carelessly executed strokes. If a reversed stick does not replace good footwork, it is a desirable and necessary part of a player's skills.

To gain control of the ball for her team, a defense player must learn to do a simple, straight tackle. Although this is the most basic tackle, it is probably the most difficult, and players should not expect to get the ball every time. Since the straight tackle is often used on a corner situation, the defense should practice in this situation as well as on a moving forward in midfield.

The lunge may be used with one or both hands gripping the stick. A strong left-hand lunge can be a valuable stroke to the right fullback, if her inner gains control of the ball upfield and temporarily gets past the fullback. A left fullback may have to use the lunge as an emergency tackle — on a center forward, on a center halfback, or on a right inner. The lunge should never be a wild slash at the ball; it should be a controlled stroke that is followed by a good pass.

Defense players on the left side should master a circular tackle. The ability to run quickly to overtake the forward, then to circle around to the right while taking and controlling the ball, will prevent the body contact and obstruction that lead to rough and poor play. The jab and reverse stick tackle can be used as emergency strokes by advanced players.

Wily dodges, which depend more on good timing than on complexity, are a joy to execute. A fullback can elude rushing opponents with a variation of a small pull to the left or push to the right dodge; the scoop dodge can be used against unsuspecting opponents. A dodge is used only to elude onrushing forwards and to give the defense player a chance to make an unobstructed pass. A defense player asks for trouble when she looks for people to dodge instead of immediately initiating the attack.

MIDFIELD PLAY

A current method of fullback play is the use of a "covering" fullback. One fullback plays "up" (offensively) when the ball is on her side of the field, and the other fullback covers the deeper (defensive) area by moving toward the center of the field. These two players work in a seesaw pattern, each balancing the other as they change from upfield to the deeper covering position. The angle of the ball, oncoming forwards, covering fullback, and goal should be studied so that the greatest area of ground can be made impenetrable to the attacking team.

The advisability of fullbacks supporting the team in the attacking half of the field (beyond the fifty-yard line) depends on individual speed, anticipation, and skill.

When a fullback is "up," she loses her identity as either a right or left side player. Her job now is to consider the angles through which the ball may be sent, and to prevent an opponent from gaining possession of the ball. For the defense to work as a unit, the fullback must cover the spaces that are not covered by her halfback. This offensive fullback must try to get the ball from the oncoming inner who is her immediate opponent. Because every tackle does not result in securing the ball, the tackle should be considered partially successful if it forces the forward to pass the ball. A teammate in the defense should be able to anticipate the direction of the pass and intercept the ball.

The covering fullback should not act impulsively. She often assumes a position in the middle of the field between the edge of the striking circle and the twenty-five yard line. If her team is stronger than the opposition, the covering fullback should keep alert, even though she sees little action. By concentrating on every play and adjusting her position even slightly, her body and mind will be ready for sudden action. She and the other fullback should agree to change on an occasional offensive corner so that each retains a sense of the game.

This latter type of inactivity is rare, and most fullbacks will not have to go looking for action. An intelligent fullback stays fairly deep in her covering area and watches in case the opposing team passes the other four defense players. She tries to stall, linger, and bait the oncoming forwards while her teammates are recovering. If no aid arrives and it is obvious that the opponents are going to get a shot at goal, this fullback must tackle the forward with the ball just before she gets to the edge of the circle. An opposing forward often makes a small, loose tap just to get the ball inside the circle; a good fullback will anticipate this move.

A fullback should never back up in the circle into the line of vision of the goalie or into the area where the goalie is expected to play the ball. The fullback should force the forward to commit herself; then the goalie will be able to judge and act.

Basic rules to remember:

1. There is always an "up" fullback and a "back" fullback. They should never play side by side in a parallel or square arrangement.
2. The "up" fullback moves quickly for interceptions and tackles.
3. The "covering" fullback tries to delay the play until the defense recovers and the forwards are marked.
4. An inner is the major opponent of the fullback. Balls that will be fielded by a wing or a wing who is dribbling down the field should be left to the side halfback, except under unusual circumstances.
5. A fullback should not hold onto the ball, but should control and pass quickly.

The responsibility of initiating the attack must be assumed by all members of the team. A fullback should practice hard cross-field drives so that she can send a ball to the wing or inner on the far side of the field. She should remember not to attempt this pass when she is deep in her defending circle, as a pass across the goal is dangerous.

PLAY IN THE DEFENSIVE END

There is satisfaction in coördinating defensive play inside the striking circle. Each defense player literally guards her own forward in a system called "marking."

A player learns to judge how close she can get without having her opponent elude her. Many coaches tell their players to stay "a stick's distance away." This general rule may help as a beginning guide. (You "mark" a player and you "cover" a space.)

A marked opponent is one who can neither receive a pass, nor shoot for goal if she has the ball. The fullback should prevent her inner from being available for a pass. By stationing herself between the girl and the goal, the fullback should be able to anticipate a possible cut and ensuing shot at goal. By keeping her back to her goal at all times, she can watch the possible spaces into which her forward may move. The fullback should be on an imaginary line between her inner and the goal. A left fullback should be positioned more to the right of her inner than the right fullback, because of the stick side of the inner and the angle on which a tackle must be made.

Constant attention to every move by the opponents and an awareness of teammates' positioning is vital to good play. Keeping her stick close to the ground gives a player the advantage of being ready to move out with the ball or to tackle instantly.

The key to tight marking and quick interchanges in the defensive circle is complete understanding and coöperation of the six players involved. The center halfback should mark the center forward closely and at all times. This will make it possible for the fullback to slide behind the center halfback and pick up a loose ball or free inner. For example, if a left inner dodges the right fullback, it might be predetermined that the left fullback will take this free player and the left halfback will leave her wing area and mark the dangerous right inner, rather than have the entire defense shift.

At no time should the defense players hesitate in their moves or tackles, or back up with a player who is controlling the ball. The defense player must force the play so that the rest of the defense, especially the goalkeeper, can adjust to the situation and expect a shot at goal.

The penalty corner and the long corner present another situation that calls for immediate marking. Each defense player should run out with her stick close to the ground to mark her opponent. She would like to gain possession of the ball and take it out of the circle area; but if her inner receives the ball, an immediate tackle must be made. If the inner does not receive the ball, she must be closely marked.

Regardless of the exact system used in the defensive circle, a basic "man to man" guarding system with a switch to mark the free player should be worked out. Most fullbacks like to rush out on their own inners on a corner situation, and rely on the side halfback to pick up the inner's dodge or pass. Some teams, however, have found that if the halfback follows the ball out and takes the receiver of this hit, the fullback is in an advantageous spot to take the dodge or pass. This is one example of how modifications can be made. A defensive system based on sound principles can be varied to suit any team.

HOW TO MAKE PLAY DIFFICULT FOR THE OPPONENTS

1. Constantly move with the play and adjust your position to block the path of your opponent.

2. Do not hesitate to start the offensive play.
3. Think of the entire game as you play; consider your teammates' positioning and your opponents' positioning. Be able to anticipate a series of plays and the possible solution to emergency situations.
4. Never give up, never let up; play your hardest and best during the entire game. Even when you are not immediately involved in the play, concentrate and get ready.

THE GOALKEEPER

by Jenepher Shillingford[3]

The goalkeeper position, like the fullback position, is not played by the largest, least able, or least energetic player on the team. There are few areas where the thrill of stopping a goal or the disappointment of allowing one are combined as intensely and vibrantly as in the goal. Goalkeeping is an area where one must retain utter composure in the face of the most extreme situations.

QUALITIES

All good goalkeepers have some basic qualities in common. Although it is difficult to find an *ideally* qualified player in any position, a goalkeeper should possess the following physical, mental, and emotional characteristics.

A goalie should have fast reaction time and movement time. Unfortunately, the specific instruments that measure these qualities are rarely available on a hockey field. However, a player's ability in other sports often indicates her reaction and movement time. For example, badminton demands both of these qualities. Many factors affect reaction time. A girl's ability to anticipate can assist her in reacting to the situation and move quickly. So, too, can her confidence in her own ability.

A goalie should be agile. Her ability to move with grace and precision will be directly proportional to her success in the goal.

Agility is intertwined with other factors. For instance, anticipation tends to place an individual in a ready position, thus increasing her ability to move quickly in any direction.

Good form is an efficient way of increasing a goalie's agility. A goalie with good form stands with her knees slightly bent and her weight directly over the balls of the feet (not toes), or in general, in a position of readiness.

Practicing the following drills can help an average player become an agile goalie.

1. Three players. Eighteen balls are placed in three groups of six along the edge of the circle. The three players shoot alternately from the right and left inner and center positions. By calling for rapid fire shots, the goalie is forced to move quickly around the goal area. To emphasize rapid clearing, the shots should be taken more slowly to allow the goalie time to concentrate and direct her clear.

2. One player—the goalie. Have the goalie practice clears against a wall with several tennis balls.

Speed is an essential quality of a good goalie. The skill of speed is really a composite of the above mentioned characteristics. A good reaction time coupled with agility and anticipation produces quickness. Drills designed to improve these skills will ultimately improve speed.

A goalie can become winded when playing against a strong opposing team. She therefore needs endurance. Whereas halfbacks need running endurance, a goalie needs stamina or "staying power." A good goalkeeper should possess the ability to "bounce back."

A goaltender should have good vision, including peripheral vision. Whereas basic eyesight cannot be improved without lenses, peripheral vision can be with practice.

A goalie who has imperfect vision should wear contact lenses or unbreakable lenses, or an eyeglass protector over her regular glasses.

In addition to being speedy and agile, a good goalie should have confidence in her own skills. Well-regulated goalie practices establish the confidence that comes with good timing. Once confidence is established, courage will develop.

Courage is the quality of mind that enables a goalie to encounter difficulties firmly, although she is aware of the danger involved. Goalies should be courageous, but some fear is not abnormal.

The greatest problem in goalkeeping is keeping the weight forward because it seems more natural and protective to move the head back and thus throw the weight on the heels.

A goalie can overcome much of her fear by (1) keeping her body weight forward, which will enable her to maneuver her head and shoulders quickly; (2) better than average protection; (3) knowing how to handle the aerial ball, which will be discussed later; and (4) regulated practice. The first few practice shots at a goalkeeper should be made from the edge of the circle, as eager line players must be reminded.

A goalie should be able to direct the play without producing resentment. Since she has full view of developing plays, she is in a better position than most players to offer defensive suggestions.

A team expects good, stable reactions from their goalie. A team often reflects the goalie's feelings. If a goalkeeper constantly criticizes her defense, little team unity will result. Every hockey player should possess the ability to laugh at herself and with others.

An intelligent player, who can study her opponents, analyze their moves, and then react with thought, is an asset to any team. Good placement of clears indicates an intelligent goalkeeper. Even though it usually is recommended that clears be made to the side of the goal, there are circumstances under which the goalie can clear directly up the middle. An intelligent goalie always will clear to the space or to her teammate.

The ability to anticipate the events that are about to occur is important for a goalkeeper. It depends upon experience, observation, and concentration. Anticipation can be improved by the following skills of observation. A goalie should keep her eye on the ball, check the ground area thoroughly, observe the position of the stick of the attacking player as she comes into the circle in an attempt to determine the type of shot that may result, and observe the opposing line players when they are not in the immediate area. She also should watch their drives, flicks, and how they move their bodies to shoot or dodge. A goalie should know whether a line player is capable of a reverse stick drive, as this shot makes both sides of her body potentially dangerous. A goalie should glance occasionally at the eyes of the opponent, as she may give her pass or shot away. (This technique should be reserved for advanced players and used only if the goalkeeper's concentration on the ball is not interrupted.)

Experience plays an important role in anticipation. A goalie who has successfully outsmarted a player will remember her technique. Unfortunately, the line player may also. Conversely, if the goalie has been scored upon by a certain unanticipated move, she will remember this move. The more a goalie plays, the more her experience will serve her. In this discussion of the qualities of a good goalie, it is important to note that a goalie must concentrate.

The final characteristic of a good goalie is sound judgment, which is a composite of intelligence and anticipation. If a goalie acts with confidence and sound judgment, her backfield as well as the opposing line will respect her.

Again, well-planned goalie practices are important. The easiest method of instructing a goalie in sound judgment is to place her in as many game situations as possible. For developing sound judgment, actual games and scrimmage situations surpass individual skill drills. Separate stickwork drills should not be minimized for the goalie, but game situations are more beneficial.

Certain specific situations, such as a single player advancing in the circle, can be outlined and the procedure to be followed can be indicated on a blackboard. The entire defense can be included in this discussion.

Players who try out for the position of goalie often are not always best suited for it. In that case, coaches should not hesitate to draft a player with greater potential for the position.

FOOTWORK AND STICKWORK

Before starting footwork or stickwork with a prospective goalie, the coach should examine her equipment. A sturdy, high shoe covered with kickers and firm leg pads should be worn to minimize pain.

The Clear

There are benefits to teaching a goalie to clear before teaching her to stop. This can be done by having the goalie run and clear a stationary ball. Follow this by slowly rolling the ball toward the player. These drills are valuable because they check the position of the goalie's body weight and emphasize the idea of clearing, or getting the ball out of the danger area. If a goalie's weight is back on her heels, tell her to clear a stationary ball and then to chase that same ball. This procedure places the goalie in a running position with her weight balanced over her feet.

A goalie's weight should be centered over her feet to enable her to change direction quickly and to clear with her weight behind the ball and thus with more strength, and for protection. A well-balanced goalie can duck and bob, and thus avoid being struck by a badly hit or lofted ball.

The ball should be cleared with the inside of the foot, using the toe joint. Generally, clears to the left are made with the right foot, and vice-versa, except along the end line, where the foot closest to the goal line should be used to keep the ball in play. A goalie should practice clearing with her weaker foot. When a goalie has learned to clear on the fly, she should be taught the stop. Whether a goalie stops and clears or clears on the fly depends on the situation. If a hard corner shot has been taken and the offense is off guard, it is safer to stop and place the clear carefully. However, the line often is rushing, thus limiting the amount of time. In this situation, it is wisest to clear immediately without stopping. The goalie should learn both skills of clearing.

Stop

When making a stop, the goalie should watch the ball, line up with it while charging, and then give when it strikes her pads so that it is placed in a good position for clearing. Faults to avoid are jumping at the ball, thus allowing a large rebound that can be easily seized by an opponent; stopping without giving, which indicates a lack of control; and bringing the ball to rest directly in front of the feet, where it is difficult to clear. To avoid the last fault, the goalie should step back, keeping her feet wide to avoid kicking the ball backwards, and then clear as usual. The exact position for a clear depends on the goalie's leg length and leg reach. A left-footed goalie would place the ball in front of her right foot.

The Lunge Stop

A goalkeeper often has to stop hard shots to the corner of the cage. If she is temporarily caught off guard, she cannot stop the ball with two feet (soccer stop). In this case, she should use a lunge stop and clear, or a one-footed stop. If the shot is hard and is not followed quickly by the forward, the goalie may want to stop and then clear. When this situation occurs, the goalkeeper should reach with her pad perpendicular to the ground and the knee slightly bent. This movement allows the ball to drop where she can easily clear it. If there is no time for this move, the goalie should place her pad so that the rebound also will be the clear. This move is not always safe, however, since the pad has a curved surface and the ball may rebound into the goal or into an easily accessible position for the line player. An experienced goalie should be able to place her leg in the proper position. In both cases, the weight should be brought forward as quickly as possible to insure both a powerful clear and control.

Aerial Balls

The key to handling a ball in the air is anticipating its being there. The ball should be fielded with the left hand, dropped in as nearly a perpendicular plane as possible (in accordance with the rules, goalies may advance the ball slightly), and then cleared. Either catching the ball momentarily or letting it rebound from the palm of the hand is acceptable as long as the ball is controlled. The ball must be placed legally in a good clearing position. The clear that follows is almost the same as a clear made on a ground ball. The goalkeeper should take care not to catch or control the ball too close to her body, as this will mean dropping the ball on or under her feet. Should this situation occur because of an extremely hard drive, the goalie should quickly move her feet back. The technique of clearing a dropped ball should be practiced often on all types of fields. Certain ground conditions, such as a hard, dry pitch, will cause the ball to bounce, and the goalie may find herself clearing under the ball. In this situation, the goalie can trail her stick so that it can be used if necessary.

The following drill can be used to teach goalies to field an aerial ball. Begin by gently throwing some balls in the air and gradually increase the strength of the throw. After about fifteen minutes, mix the throws, allowing some to hit the ground and others to remain in the air.

A goalie can increase her anticipation of an aerial ball by checking the turf at either end of the field so that she is aware of any ridges that may throw the ball into the air, by knowing the position of the stick for a scoop or a flick, and by knowing the incorrect position of a player who is about to undercut the ball. Balls that come from two sticks or from the goalie's own defense are most difficult to handle. In each situation, the goalie must depend upon her own reaction time and wits.

The Stick

Goalkeepers should hold their stick at all times, both in games and in practice, since it is mandatory to do so in a game. A goalie should grip her stick about nine inches from the top in her right hand. Because she rarely uses two hands on the stick, she has greater control if she shortens her grip on the stick. Using a short stick also gives better control.

A goalie can use her stick as a desperation measure for a hard shot to the corner of the goal and as a jabber when she is caught on the ground or on the wrong foot. For aerial balls, a goalie can practice a short hit with her stick as she drops the ball. Her foot can remain behind the play to clear the ball if the stick should miss contact. This type of hit can surprise the line player. A goalie should be careful to keep her stick below her shoulder, and also to keep the hit down to insure the safety of the forward.

The Bully

Penalty bullies are given for many reasons. Basically, if the goalie prevents a sure goal and fouls in the process, she will be penalized by a penalty bully. She may obstruct, "sit" on the ball, make sticks on the stop, throw the ball out of the goal area, or stop a shot with the rounded side of the stick, all of which are illegal. No matter how well a goalie knows the rules or how cautious she may be, sooner or later she will find herself taking a penalty bully. A well-trained and practiced goalie may have the upper hand in a penalty bully.

The goalie should play defensively in a penalty bully situation, since she is hampered by her pads which she may not remove. The goalie should take the bully slowly, forcing the line player to slow down and break her rhythm. After the final hit of the sticks, the goalie's stick should drop quickly to the ground, covering the ball as much as possible. Most line players will attempt to pull the ball to themselves and then push it into the goal, or play the ball towards the goalkeeper, or attempt to hop the ball over the goalie's stick. After the forward has made her move, the goalie will have a chance to push-pass the ball out of the circle. She should practice push-passes so that she has enough power to get the ball out of the circle. The stick should never be raised, since this gives the forward an opportunity to play under it.

The goalie should practice bullies in front of the goal with experienced forwards or bulliers.

POSITIONING

The goalie should wait about three or four feet in front of the goal with her weight over the balls of her feet, her knees slightly bent, and her stick in her right hand. The goalie need not remain in this position when the ball is in the other circle. This is a good time for her to size up the position of her defense and to anticipate offensive play.

Drill

A goalie can learn about angles of play from the following drill. Take a string and tie it to each of the goal posts and walk around the circle, asking the goalie to take her basic position in various angles.

A shot from one of the wing angles can more easily be protected against than a shot from the center. The angle of the shot often dictates when and how the goalkeeper should tackle a player.

All Players Marked

If all players are marked closely in the circle, the goalie becomes responsible for any player who breaks free and for the pass to the space in front of the goal. This is a good situation for a goalie who enjoys rushing and can reach the "through" pass. However, defending against strong forwards who frequently use a reverse stick drive is more difficult. This drive makes good forwards potentially dangerous on both sides of their body, greatly magnifying the goalkeeper's task. The goalie can no longer anticipate the play on just the right side of her body. This is a good reason for having a covering back in the circle.

Free Player Alone Approaching the Circle

When a forward approaches the circle alone and unhampered by any defense player, the goalkeeper should act with authority and good timing. When the goalie should rush depends on the speed of the forward, the relative position of the recovering defense, and the speed of the goalkeeper. A goalie always should rush in a one-on-one situation. She should practice the technique often so that she knows her speed and has had experience against many other players. The goalie should meet the forward as she comes into the circle. Many forwards take an additional hit as they cross the line or glance up to see the position of the goalkeeper. At this moment, the goalie hopes to have an advantage. A one-legged lunge at the end of a rush can be successful in a rush situation. The goalie should keep her weight forward, thus keeping the ball on the ground.

Free Player in the Circle

The most difficult situation for the goalie is when a player becomes free in the circle. Even with the covering fullback, a player may quickly spring free, leaving the goalie with half of the time to react. When a player approaches the circle and a fullback remains, it is wise for the defense to take the player at the edge of the circle, not before she enters and not after she has taken her shot. In this way, if the player gets by and the defense should err, the goalie still has time to rush and react while the forward is moving around the defensive player. This situation is ideal for the goalie. It can be easily manipulated, once the defense player and goalie understand each other. The words "I have it" are probably the most important ones a goalie can learn and are especially applicable in this case.

The hard shots across the goal or even back to the center of the circle are difficult for the defense. The hard shot from the wing across the goal (behind the defense) is used most frequently when all players are marked in the circle and a space appears behind the defense and in front of the goalie. The goalie can intercept the pass or play for the rebound against the line player. Intercepting a pass can be practiced by having players send the ball across the mouth of the goal.

The shot from the corner of the field back to the center of the circle also is difficult to defend against. Often this pass goes to a half-back, who must be defended by a line player tackling back. The halfback finds herself free to shoot and all of the forwards ready and available to rush. The goalie should position herself for the shot and hopefully clear on the fly.

These situations are best learned in actual game or scrimmage situations.

WHAT TO PRACTICE

Goalies should have substantial and regular practice sessions. During a regular scrimmage, a goalie does not have much contact with the ball. Therefore, she may need special drills, such as the following, to improve her ability and build her confidence. A goalie can take penalty bullies with sound line players. She can practice protection of the goal from the aerial ball by asking other players to throw the ball gently to her while she fields it. The speed of the toss can then be increased and finally mixed with some balls on the ground. Line players should be urged to allow the goalie to warm up with shots from the edge of the circle. Goalies also can have two players pass the ball flat across the goal. One player retrieving the ball and sending it back to the other gives practice to both the forward and the goalie. Lastly, the goalie can practice clearing to specific areas by setting up certain targets.

The following is a good daily regimen for a goalie:

1. Warm her up with hard shots from the edge of the circle.
2. Have the line player follow up the shot.

3. Pepper the goalie with various shots for about ten minutes before scrimmage, allowing her time to give directional clears.
4. Work with passes across (flat) the goal, having the goalie intercept some and wait for the rebound or "sweep" shot with others.
5. Have the goalie rush lone forwards as they approach the circle.

This practice can be accomplished in thirty minutes and can be absorbed as a stickwork period or a practice period for everyone.

The position of the goalie's weight should be checked constantly. Make sure that her weight is forward and that she is in a "ready" position at all times. Follow this with a good period of scrimmage and have goalies exchange ends if the play is one-sided. Asking for corner shots often keeps the ball in the circle for a period of time and allows the goalie practice. At the end of the scrimmage session, have the goalie take five penalty bullies. Select good opponents and switch them from day to day.

HOW TO MAKE SCORING DIFFICULT FOR THE OPPONENTS

The goalie can make scoring difficult for her opponents by demonstrating confidence in her skills and control of her defense. In a game, the first shot for goal is the most important one for the goalie. If she makes her first save with a sound directional clear, she can convince the opposing team of her strength and give her own team confidence in their goalie.

FOOTNOTES

1. Marilyn O'Neill holds a Bachelor's degree from Tufts College and a Master's degree from Villanova University. She is currently teaching at Conestoga High School, Berwyn, Pennsylvania. She has played for the Southeast, New Atlantic, and Philadelphia Sections and was a member of the United States Reserve Team in 1962 and the United States Team in 1965. She has coached high school teams as well as at hockey camps.

2. Adele Boyd played for the Philadelphia Section and was a member of the United States Team from 1959–1966. She was on the United States Touring Team to Great Britain and Denmark (1962), IFWHA Conference at Baltimore (1963), Jamaica (1965) and to Europe (1967). She has coached at Cheltenham High School, Pennsylvania, Ursinus College, and Merestead Hockey and Lacrosse Camp. She also is a National umpire.

She received her Bachelor's degree from Ursinus College and her Master's degree from Temple University. She is currently an assistant professor at Ursinus College.

3. A housewife and part time teacher-coach at Immaculate College, Pennsylvania, Jenepher Shillingford has a wealth of hockey knowledge. She played for the Philadelphia and Mideast Sections and was a member of the United States Team from 1955–1957. She served as president of the Philadelphia Field Hockey Association from 1964–1968. She is a National umpire. She holds a Bachelor's degree from Ursinus College and a Master's degree from Temple University.

VIII

SPECIAL SITUATIONS

Generally, the game of field hockey is one of continuous action. It is interrupted infrequently by an official's whistle. Skillful hockey is played with few fouls. Coaches at all levels should recognize the importance of developing proper footwork and stickwork so that advancing and obstruction fouls are minimized. In this way, players at all levels, including beginners, can enjoy the continuity of the game.

Even the most skillful players do commit occasional fouls, however. Then play is stopped momentarily to award a free hit or a corner to the opposing team. Another instance when play is stopped occurs when the ball crosses a boundary line of the field. Players should approach these foul and out-of-bounds situations with the intention of starting an offensive maneuver when awarded the ball. Each situation is an opportunity to start a scoring effort, not just a means of putting the ball back in play. Speed, accuracy, and good positioning are keys to success.

ROLL-IN

A roll-in is awarded to a team when an opponent hits the ball over the sideline. Usually, a halfback takes the roll-in. When the ball is near the attacking striking circle, the wing will take the roll-in so that the half is not drawn out of position. On rare occasions, when the opposing forwards are well up the field, a fullback may take the roll to conserve the energy of a half who is well upfield. This practice can be dangerous if the ball is intercepted, and perhaps this tactic should not be used by beginners.

The stick must be held by the player taking the roll-in, and her feet and stick must be outside the sideline. She uses the fundamental underhand throw to release the ball. Since the rules state that the ball must land on the ground within one yard of the sideline, the ball must be rolled. To roll the ball, the player should bend her knees to lower the height of her body so that her hand brushes along the ground at release. A forward stride position with knees bent also is conducive to good body balance. A player should never be permitted to enhance her balance by kneeling. Neither should her stride be so wide that her center of gravity remains within the base of support after the release. Once the ball is rolled, the player wants to return quickly within bounds. A transfer of weight helps the player to move her weight beyond the base of support and permits a rapid recovery. Figure 8:1 shows a left half using these principles.

Figure 8:1

The length of the backswing should be adjusted to the force of the roll desired. Obviously, more speed is necessary for a long roll. Velocity is built by increasing the length of the backswing, quickly contracting the muscles, and transferring the weight so that the hand is moving rapidly at release. To disguise the intention of the roll, the same length backswing as normally used is desirable, but the velocity and therefore the distance of the roll can be controlled by the speed with which the muscles contract. The reverse roll also can be concealed until the last instant by using this principle.

Direction is of the utmost importance for the success of the roll. For long rolls, an error in aim is magnified, since the ball has a longer time to veer from its intended direction. Shorter rolls also require precise direction because there is little space and time for players to maneuver. Desired direction is achieved by moving the arc of the arm in as straight a line as possible. At only one point along any arc can the ball be released and follow its desired direction. By transferring weight from the rear to the forward leg, the arc is flattened and the hand moves in a straighter line; thus, less divergency in direction is evident. Pointing the feet toward the end line helps square the hips and shoulders with the end line, and helps place the shoulder and hand in position for an accurate release.

To facilitate direction, the left half should roll the ball with her right hand and the right half with her left hand. This movement permits a natural arc to be followed so that adjustments on the downswing are unnecessary except for the reverse roll. By using the hand closer to the sideline, the player is not apt to violate the rule requiring the ball to enter within three feet of the point where it crossed the boundary line.

The ball should be rolled to the stick side of the receiver so that it can be fielded easily and is in a position for the player to pass in either direction. This procedure is easier for the right half than for the left half. Because of the position of the left wing along the alley line, she is on the non-stick side of the ball. Therefore, the roll to the left wing is difficult to execute well. The right half finds the right wing in a more favorable position to receive the ball, for it is already on her stick side. When the left half rolls to the left inner or left back, she can roll the ball ahead of them so that it is received on the stick side; this practice, of course, presumes good positioning on their part so that there is a space ahead into which the ball can be rolled. If the right half chooses to roll to the right inner or right back, the ball should be sent directly toward them or only slightly ahead so that they can receive it on their stick side. It is assumed that the ball is rolled in the desirable direction and that the players will cut to meet it. If the roll to the right inner or back is ahead of them, they are forced to receive it on their non-stick side and, therefore, are limited in their subsequent play.

For the reverse roll, the arc is altered in midstream and necessary adjustments must be made. The length of the backswing and the downswing remain identical. But, as the arm reaches a perpendicular position at the hip, it inwardly rotates so that the palm of the hand faces the opposite sideline. This position permits the ball to be rolled sideward or backward to the inner or back. Obvious direction problems arise, and players must practice so that they can roll the ball in any given direction with the straight or reverse roll.

Positioning for a Roll-in

As the ball goes out-of-bounds, the player taking the roll-in should recover it and take the roll-in as quickly as possible, waiting only for the players to clear the alley. If an opponent recovers the ball, she should be permitted the courtesy of awaiting her return to position. Simultaneous with the recovery of the ball, the player should evaluate the position of the opponents and her teammates so that a plan for action is theorized.

The selection of a teammate to whom the roll will be made is as important as the accuracy of the roll. Vital to the success of the roll-in is the responsibility that teammates accept in taking a good position. Players who always place themselves in the same position regardless of the situation minimize their effectiveness. First, players should consider the position of the roll-in (offensive or defensive end) and then the position of their opponents.

The wing, inner, fullback, and less often the center forward and center half are receivers for the roll-in. At times, it is more opportune for a half to roll to the wing. But all possible receivers should be in a position to receive the ball. Generally, the inner and the wing on the far side of the field position themselves the same distance from the goal as the center forward. All defense players on the team taking the roll position themselves closer to their own goal than to the ball.

Both the inner and the fullback receive the ball near the alley line or within the alley. Since they wish to receive the roll while they are free, they pull away from that space before the roll and cut toward the ball as it is rolled. A preliminary feint in another direction helps deceive

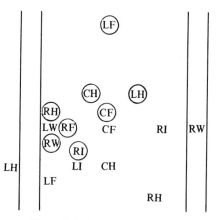

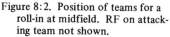

Figure 8:2. Position of teams for a roll-in at midfield. RF on attacking team not shown.

an opponent. The inner generally positions herself about on line with the roll, and the fullback is about five yards closer to her own goal (Figure 8:2).

Generally, the inners on the defensive team mark the opposing inners so that the defense players can position themselves for a roll that might be made into a space. The half marks the wing; the inner marks the opposing inner; the center forward marks the opposing center forward (or sometimes the half, in which case the center half must mark the center forward). The wing marks the opposing fullback, since she is a frequent receiver and otherwise would remain free. This leaves the fullback and center half to cover the spaces into which their opponents might cut.

In the defensive end. The halfback usually rolls the ball downfield for the wing. In this portion of the field, any other tactic is dangerous as an interception would place the team in a precarious position. Only rarely, and then only to vary play, should the half roll to the inner or back. Specifically, the half should:

1. Roll long down the alley to the wing.
   a. To the left wing, the ball is rolled midway in the alley so that the wing can field it on her stick side. The left wing is at a disadvantage, as the opposing halfback is in a more favorable position to field the ball since it is already on her stick side. The wing can minimize the effectiveness of the half by moving relatively close to the position where the roll-in will be made. By so doing and with the aid of a hard, fast roll, the ball will pass the right half before she can intercept it. Thus, the half is forced to overtake the ball or lunge to obtain it. This gives the wing an opportunity to cross the alley out near the sideline so that she can take the ball on her stick side.
   b. To the right wing, the ball is rolled as close to the sideline as possible; a roll directed further in the alley would help the opponents. A slow wing can minimize her deficiency by starting closer to the roll and drawing her opponent. A long roll will force the defensive half to overtake the ball before fielding it and make the circular tackle more difficult.
2. Roll directly to the stick of the wing if she is not marked closely.
   a. To the left wing, the ball is rolled just ahead of her on her stick side.
   b. To the right wing, the ball is rolled directly toward her.

3. Long roll down the alley to the inner, who interchanges with the wing. The inner feints toward the alley line and then cuts behind the halfback to receive the roll. The wing fakes toward the sideline and then cuts in to the inner's position. This play is useful only if the fullback is playing up for the roll.

A smart inner will draw back nearly opposite the roller-in to draw her opposing fullback. This move should eliminate the possibility of the back temporarily interchanging with the halfback to intercept the long roll. If the halfback does not mark the wing closely or if the back is disinterested in the inner, then the roll should be made directly to the space that is free.

If the defensive fullback persists in playing deep to help on the long rolls, the left wing can fake into the alley and the roll can be made into the space she just vacated. A quick pivot should enable the wing to receive the ball and leave the half behind (Figure 8:3). Because such a roll would be on the non-stick side of the right wing, this variation is less effective for her.

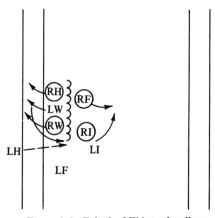

Figure 8:3. Fake by LW into the alley.
LW pivots and receives roll at space
she just vacated.

In midfield. More variation is afforded here, since the roll-in is not in such a dangerous position. Nevertheless, in the defensive portion of the field judicious use of any player but the wing should be exercised. Some examples follow:

1. The long roll down the alley to the wing (described above).
2. The roll directly to the wing if she is not marked closely (described above).
3. A roll to the inner who may:
   a. Pass to the wing. This is more effective on the left side of the field. The left wing has time to cut to the sideline, and then in toward the alley line to field the ball on her stick side (Figure 8:4). The right wing, on the other hand, must cut back in toward the alley line as the ball approaches from her non-stick side and on the stick side of her opponent.
   b. Pass to the stick side of the half, who just steps back onto the field and drives to the stick side of the wing.
   c. Continue down the alley and interchange with the wing.
   d. Pass ahead into the space between the wing and the center; on the left side, the wing will cut in for the ball because it is on her stick side and she interchanges with the inner; on the right side the center forward cuts for the ball (her stick side) and may interchange with the inner.
4. A reverse roll to the fullback who may (Figure 8:5):
   a. Pass to the wing (more effective on the left side than the right for reasons stated in 3a above).

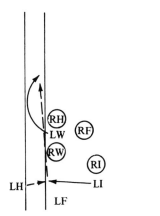

Figure 8:4. LH rolls to LI, who passes to stick side of LW.

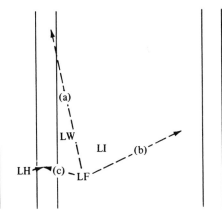

Figure 8:5. LH rolls to LF, who may hit to the LW (a); to the RI (b); or back to the LH (c).

     b. Pass to the inner or wing on the other side of the field (easier for the right back to hit to the left inner or left wing; more difficult for the left back to hit to the right inner, but a most effective plan when the inner is open).

     c. Pass back to the half (the halves should have their outside shoulder—left shoulder for left half and right shoulder for right half—turned forward so that the ball can be hit to their stick side); the half then hits cross field to the opposite inner.

    5. A roll to the center forward (to be used effectively, the inner should position herself on line with or slightly ahead of the ball so that the roll can go behind her and her opponent; this roll is more suitable for use from the right half to the stick side of the center).

    6. A reverse roll to the center half, who often is unmarked; the reception and subsequent hit is easier from the right half than from the left half.

When a long roll is sent to the wing, she should know that the inner is trailing her (if she pulled back on line with the wing taking the roll), and an immediate pass to this inner will be intercepted by a well-positioned back! As rolls are taken further upfield, a long roll down the alley is less desirable; therefore, the wing should position herself further downfield to allow more space for a roll-in to the inner.

In the attacking end, near the circle. If the halfback takes the roll from this portion of the field, she jeopardizes her defensive position because she is drawn so far downfield. This is true of the right half, who is vulnerable because a large area is opened on her non-stick side. For this reasons, wings take rolls-in near the offensive circle. Two options are available (Figure 8:6):

    1. A roll behind the opposing defense players and in front of the goal. (To create spaces, the inner and center pull back on line with or slightly behind the ball to draw their opponents away from goal.)

    2. A reverse roll to the halfback who may:
      a. Push pass into the circle.
      b. Drive to the opposite inner, wing, or halfback.
      c. Dribble to the edge of the circle and shoot.

The defending team can align their players differently at the last instant to confuse the attack or to overcome a weakness. For example, if the opposing wing receives the majority of the rolls and the halfback is unable to cope with her, the defending team may choose to have the wing mark the attacking wing closely while the halfback drops back to

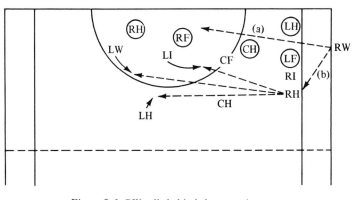

Figure 8:6. RW rolls behind the opposing
defense (a) or back to the RH (b) who
may pass to the LI, LW or LH; push
pass into the circle; dribble into the
circle and shoot.

intercept the long roll. Obviously, this leaves the attacking back free,
but this plan encourages a reverse roll and an additional pass to send
the ball forward. Possibly, the defending back will drop deep and let her
inner mark the opposing inner closely; if a long roll is sent to the wing,
she may interchange with the halfback.

Just as the defensive team attempts to conceal their weaknesses,
the attacking team tries to exploit them. The halfbacks should be
intelligent to find the free space for the roll, just as their teammates
should be smart in positioning themselves to create the spaces. Speed
in taking the roll-in, rolls to various players, and good positioning
enhance the success of rolls-in.

Drills

Time to practice rolls-in should be made available during every
practice session. While other players are practicing strokes, bullies, or
corners, the players involved can work on the roll.

    1. Targets are placed in the appropriate places—for long rolls
    near the alley line; and for rolls to the inner and back, near
    the alley line. Practice with the targets can be done individually
    by the side halfbacks.

2. Place the targets in the same fashion as for No. 1. The player to receive the roll positions herself so that the target serves as a point of aim. (This helps the half to aim for the correct spot so that the ball will be received on the stick side.)
3. Practice variations for use with rolls from the defensive end of the field.
4. Practice variations from midfield.
5. Practice wing rolls near the attacking striking circle.

FREE HITS

A free hit is awarded to the opponents whenever the attacking team fouls anywhere on the playing field and when the defense fouls outside of the striking circle. The free hit frequently is a frustrating reward, because often it becomes not a penalty for the offenders but only a temporary loss of the ball. Unless a free hit is taken quickly with forwards creating spaces, the free hit usually fails.

The free hit is taken where the foul occurred. If a player is unsure of the exact position, she need only look to the sideline. The umpire stands opposite that spot and holds one arm horizontal, pointing in the direction the free hit should be taken. The player taking the free hit should retrieve the ball, pick it up, and take it to the spot from which she will hit it; if the ball is no longer in the area of the foul, another player can retrieve it and roll it to the free hitter. Too often, players waste time by poking at the ball with the stick or driving it errantly to the free hitter with a resultant chase. When the free hit is taken quickly, the flow of the game is retained and the opposing team has little time to regain proper positioning.

Forwards make spaces, and the hitter looks for the freest player while the ball is retrieved. The hit should be made with thought and precision to the stick of a teammate. Hits should be sympathetic and stroked hard enough to clear the opponents, but not so hard as to make fielding difficult (or impossible) for a teammate.

Any player may take the free hit, although generally a halfback or fullback takes it so that the forwards can move ahead of the ball to receive it. When a foul occurs at the sideline and near the attacking circle, the wing usually takes the hit to prevent her halfback from being pulled out of position. When the halfbacks lag in the offensive end of the field, a forward may take the free hit occasionally as a surprise.

If the ball has been concentrated on one side of the field, an opportunity to change the direction is afforded. But the ball should not be hit across the center of the field if the player is near the goal she is defending. A free hit ahead into a space created by a forward is ideal. The free hit may be directed to a half or back if all angles for passes are closed, but the intent of the flat or backward pass should be concealed until the last instant. The defense player subsequently can pass the ball up to a forward through a space not available previously. In the offensive end of the field, wings may drop back, and if used immediately, a successful hit will result.

For proper positioning, forwards should make a space for themselves or for a teammate. Wings always move out to the sideline except when the ball is near or beyond the attacking twenty-five, at which time they begin to move in toward the circle. Possibly, the inners are the field generals for the success of the free hits, since their positioning in part determines whether the greatest spaces are toward the center of the field or toward the sidelines. Some suggestions follow for the placement of free hits. These suggestions can serve as a general pattern, but variation in positioning is important.

Defensive positions to combat the free hit are taken by the opponents. Forwards either mark the opposing forwards man-to-man, or the three forwards nearest the free hit form a semi-circle or ring before the hitter and the remaining two forwards play man-to-man. The defense players meanwhile cover the spaces into which the ball may be hit (Figure 8:7). It is for this reason that if the hit is not taken quickly, the ball may have to be directed to a defending teammate rather than immediately to a forward.

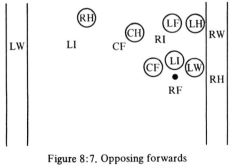

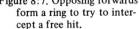

Figure 8:7. Opposing forwards form a ring to try to intercept a free hit.

Positioning for Free Hits

In the defensive end. Generally, the inners pull toward the center of the field to make spaces for the ball to be hit toward the sideline (Figure 8:8). The fullback or halfback should hit the ball hard upfield to the wing. If the wing is not free, an alternate choice is a pass to the half (or back) on that side of the field (Figure 8:9). The center half is never used this deep in her own territory for obvious reasons. If the foul occurs near the goal, the fullback need not bring the ball to the edge of the circle before hitting it. Although it is advisable to take the ball toward the side of the circle away from the goal, players should not give the opponents time to position themselves. A ten- to fifteen-yard sprint is unnecessary, as the ball can be put in play any place in the circle, and a hit ball travels faster than a player. If the opponents are out of position, take advantage by hitting the ball immediately. For fouls outside the circle and in the center of the field, the center half can hit to any player, although hitting to the sides of the field probably opens play more and places the ball in a less dangerous position.

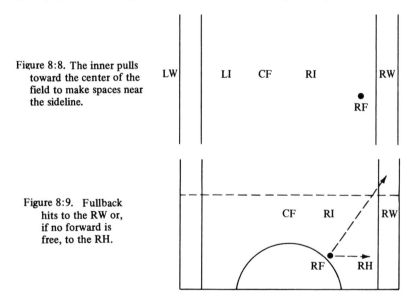

Figure 8:8. The inner pulls toward the center of the field to make spaces near the sideline.

Figure 8:9. Fullback hits to the RW or, if no forward is free, to the RH.

In midfield. More variety in passes is afforded between the twenty-five yard lines, and the inners and center are used more often. A side halfback usually passes to her wing or inner, less often to the center or center half. The fullback passes to the wing, inner, and center and less often to the side half or center half. The center half may pass to any forward or if necessary to one of her fullbacks.

Near the attacking twenty-five yard line. Generally, inners pull toward the sideline so that the spaces are in the center of the field nearer the goal. Halfbacks usually take free hits in this area. The side halfbacks pass to the inner, center or, if necessary, center half. Wings are used less frequently since the action is so near the circle (Figure 8:10). The center half can pass to either inner or the center forward. The inners pull toward the sideline, but the center forward decides where the pass will be sent by the direction toward which she pulls. If she moves toward the right inner, the greatest space is created for the pass to be sent to the center or left inner (Figure 8:11). Similarly, if she pulls toward the left inner, the space is made for the center and right inner. Finesse is important this close to a scoring opportunity.

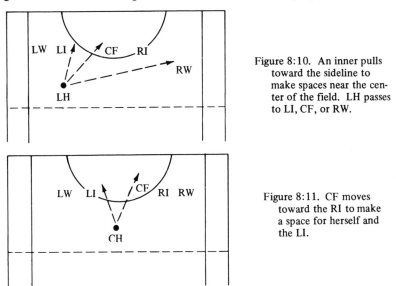

Figure 8:10. An inner pulls toward the sideline to make spaces near the center of the field. LH passes to LI, CF, or RW.

Figure 8:11. CF moves toward the RI to make a space for herself and the LI.

Near the attacking goal line. Wings take the free hit this far downfield so that the halves are not pulled out of position. The forward line pulls back from the line of the ball to create spaces in front of goal. The pass is placed across the goal mouth for the inner or center to shoot. The side halfback is free for a pass back if necessary; a pass to the center half is not helpful. The right wing passes the ball closer to the cutting forwards and the left wing passes ahead of them, so again the ball is received on the stick side (Figure 8:12).

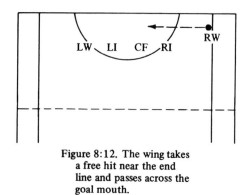

Figure 8:12. The wing takes
a free hit near the end
line and passes across the
goal mouth.

Drills

Players should pay more attention to practicing free hits. The fallibility of free hits presents strong testimony in this behalf. Too many free hits are intercepted due to poor positioning and lack of speed in getting organized. A coach would do well to spend more time on this aspect of the game.

1. All players on one team positioned on the field for a free hit by the right half near the team's defending goal line. Repeat from the left side.
2. Players from one team positioned for a free hit taken in the defending striking circle.
3. Take positions for a free hit by the right half at approximately the defending twenty-five yard line. Repeat for each of the other defense players.
4. The same directions as for No. 3, except take the free hit at midfield.
5. The same directions as for No. 3, except take the free hit near the attacking twenty-five yard line.
6. The same directions as for No. 3, except take the free hit just outside the attacking striking circle.
7. Take positions for a wing free hit near the attacking goal line (outside the circle). Try the free hit from both sides.
8. Try each of the above free hits with the defending team on the field. For the attack, emphasize: quickness, spaces; for the defense, emphasize: quickness and positioning.

CORNERS

A corner hit is awarded to the opponents whenever the defending team fouls in the striking circle or hits the ball over the end line.

Attacking Team Positioning and Play

The wing takes the free hit from the specified spot, and the remaining forwards line up along the edge of the striking circle, with the closer inner approximately opposite the near edge of the goal post. The other forwards space themselves accordingly, with the far inner opposite the other goal post. The halfbacks back up the forwards by spacing themselves to recover a forward's error in fielding or to block the angles for a defensive clear out of the circle (Figure 8:13).

The forwards make sure that the ground is level in front of them so that the ball will not bounce, place their feet in a stride position with the left foot forward and pointed toward the goal, and put their sticks on the ground in fielding position. The stick on the ground also serves as a target for the wing, much the same as a catcher in softball holds her glove as a target for the pitcher. This position assumed by the

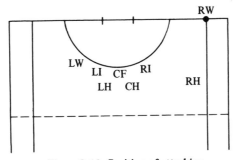

Figure 8:13. Position of attacking
forwards and halfbacks for a
long corner. Note: RH covers
space to her opposing LW in
case corner hit is intercepted.
CH backs up the RI; LH backs
up the CF for the hit.

forwards places their left shoulder toward the goal, so that they can stop the ball and hit for goal without any preliminary taps or adjustment of their feet before hitting.

The wing stands behind the end line to survey the position of her forwards, then steps up to the ball, keeps her eyes on it, and takes a stride onto the playing field toward the direction of the receiver as she hits the ball (Figure 8:14). She hits the ball hard and deftly without bounce or sideward spin to the stick of one of her forwards, usually the near inner. Immediately, the wing runs back to the edge of the circle to field clears made in that direction. This action also ensures that the wing will be onside.

Figure 8:14

The receiver should stop the hit cleanly, take a short backswing, and hit with great force and accuracy toward a corner of the goal. The receiver need not look up toward goal; she knows her relative position to the goal and to the goalkeeper. Frequent practice with the wing helps the inner or center forward in developing strong, quick hits and the necessary accuracy. It is essential that the receiver stop the ball cleanly. Taking just one more tap to place the ball in a more desirable position uses time and allows the defense opportunity to block or impede the shot. There is no defense for a perfectly executed corner play.

A corner hit is one of the few times a receiver is told to wait for the ball to arrive (Figure 8:15). The ball travels faster than a player. To cut for the ball only aids the defense by decreasing the distance the defense player must run to reach the receiver. Obviously, if the ball is hit slowly, the forward will have to cut to meet it and use her own resources thereafter. Either a dodge or a return pass to a wing may temporarily free one of them for a shot.

Figure 8:15

Rushing the shot at goal is productive. As always, the inside forwards are responsible for rushing. Because a shot from a corner hit
usually is directed toward the opposite corner of the goal, both corners
should be covered after the shot. Therefore, as the shooter takes her
backswing, the other two inside forwards rush a corner of the goal. The
left inner is always responsible for the left corner; the right inner, for the
right corner. If one of the inners is shooting, the center rushes the
corner normally covered by that player.

Following the corner hit, it may be necessary or desirable to return
a pass to the wing for a shot. In this instance, the two inners rush,

while the center can either rush or move midway into the circle to await deflections in that area.

Any player rushing has her stick on the ground and her left shoulder pointing toward the goal so that the ball can be immediately pushed, flicked, swept, or scooped into the goal without any preliminary dribbling (Figure 8:16). The wings move down toward the goal, but stay on the edge of the circle to field any clears in their direction.

Figure 8:16

A dodge may be necessary to evade a rushing defense player, particularly if the ball has not been fielded cleanly or if the wing has hit the ball poorly. A dodge also can be used occasionally to vary the play. A dodge is good to use when defense players keep running out to the receiver without stopping as the receiver is approached. The most effective dodge for the left inner is the pull to the left, because the ball is moved laterally. The dodge is less effective for other players because it pulls the ball toward the stick of another defender. The other dodges (scoop, dodge to the right) cause the ball to move forward and often toward the stick of a defender (Figure 8:17).

Too often, a player who improperly fields a corner hit tries to compensate for her error by immediately dashing for the ball. Whether she should recover it or let a teammate do so depends on whether the ball is on her stick side or non-stick side and whether it is in front or behind her. A ball that glances forward and to the right of the intended

Figure 8:17

receiver should be recovered by the player who has an immediate shot for goal with no taps prior to the shot. A ball that glances to the left should be recovered by a player on that side.

If the ball goes outside the striking circle, the forwards should move ahead toward goal and let one of the halfbacks field the ball. The half then can dribble to the edge of the circle and shoot. This should be done without delay before an opposing forward has time to tackle. If an opposing defense player tackles, the half may pass to the free forward. The forwards, by moving ahead, are in a better position to rush the goal and also to help screen the halfback's shot. The forwards should not move offside, and be certain that they do not interfere with the halfback's shot.

A gainful play may be initiated by the forwards when the opposing defense fails to run all the way out to the edge of the circle to mark. By intentionally permitting the ball to go beyond them, without any effort to field it, the forwards can move toward the goal to screen while a halfback fields the ball and shoots. This is an excellent play with sure-fielding halfbacks, but an unrewarding and dangerous plan with mediocre fielders.

On an inaccurate hit by the wing, the inner can be deceptive to thwart defensive efforts. If the ball is hit to the left of the right inner or to the right of the left inner, the inner may run forward as if to field the ball. This move may cause the defense players to brake before they reach the edge of the circle. The inner makes no attempt to field the ball, and the center is free momentarily for an unimpeded shot at goal.

Defensive Team Positioning and Play

Six players of the defending team must line up behind the end line until the ball is hit by the wing, and the rest of the team must line up behind the near twenty-five yard line until the ball is touched by a player other than the wing taking the hit or until the ball goes outside the striking circle. Although the rules do not stipulate precisely the position of players, there seems to be questionable value in having anyone but the defense players line up behind the end line and the attack players beyond the twenty-five.

The defense players should take a position behind the end line approximately opposite their opponent. Actually, more experienced players might alter this basic concept. If the corner is taken by the right wing, all of the defense players can move slightly to their left so that they are on the stick side of their opponent. The left full and center half know that the ball most likely will be hit to either of their players. Therefore, the right full and right half want to be goal side of their opponent for a subsequent pass. This positioning places them not only stick side but also goal side. When the corner is hit by the left wing the right half, the right full and center half move a step to their left to be on the stick side of their opponent. The right full and the right half usually stay approximately opposite their player so that they remain on the goal side (though not on the stick side) of their opponent for subsequent action.

As soon as the wing hits the ball, the defense players rush out toward their opponent. The halfback on whose side the hit is taken moves out quickly to intercept a poor hit. The center half and the fullback run out to the stick side of their opponent with their stick on the ground and try to impede the forward's hit for goal. Assuming the ball is well hit the center half and fullback should under no circumstances stop running until they get out to the forward or beyond her. Stopping before reaching the opponent's stick is not only poor defensive play but also dangerous. By rushing all of the way, the defense player has her stick in line with the opponent's stick and the ball. By rushing only part way, she is subject to being hit from more angles and is vulnerable to leg injuries. Furthermore, a rushing defense player is distracting to an attack player, who may take her eye off the ball and lose control of it. The defense players on the side opposite from where the hit is taken should run out to their opponents in a position to intercept any deflection or pass.

A team can decide to use a covering player to prevent an unimpeded shot at the goal if the rushing defense player is dodged. Generally, the fullback rushes out on her own inner and lets the halfback on her side stay to tackle the forward who successfully dodges. At this time, the half momentarily ignores her own wing who has just taken the hit because the wing must get back onside. The wing also is at the side of the circle and her shooting angle is difficult; if, however, the inner returns a pass to the wing, the halfback should hurry to mark her and impede her shot (Figure 8:18).

Whenever an attack player is ready to shoot unimpeded, a defense

Figure 8:18

Figure 8:18 continued

player on her stick side should tackle her; for example, left fullback
tackles the opposing center half. A jabbing type stroke is most often
used to spoil the shot and yet not force the defense player to leave her
own opponent entirely free. It is the responsibility of the defending team's
inside forwards to retreat over the twenty-five as soon as ·possible to
prevent the opposing halves from shooting. The center tackles the
center half, and the inners tackle the halfbacks, thus allowing the wings
to be in a position for clears from the defense. This action by the inside
forwards is important against teams whose halfbacks take every opportunity to shoot. Five defense players cannot be expected to defend
against eight potential shooters. On the other hand, if halfbacks fail to
attempt shots, it is undesirable for the forwards to play defensively, for
they are in a more advantageous position to start the attack if they
can stay at the twenty-five or further upfield.

Long Corners

A long corner is taken when the defensive team unintentionally
hits the ball over the end line. The corner hit must be taken within
five yards of the corner of the field on the side where the ball crossed
the goal line. The corner hit can be taken at the intersection of the alley
line and the goal line, or on a spot on the sideline five yards from the
goal line. The option of hitting the ball from the sideline seems to lack
merit. Fielding a ball approaching from the side is more difficult than
fielding a ball from in front.

Although the closer inner should stand opposite the near goal post, some inners edge toward the wing for the long corner. An adjustment of this sort is questionable since it takes the inner to the side edge of the circle. This move not only decreases the distance the fullback must run but also decreases the angle at which she will shoot (Figure 8:19). If the wing lacks a strong hit or if the intention is to hit to the center rather than to the inner, such positioning may be essential.

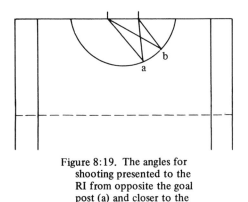

Figure 8:19. The angles for shooting presented to the RI from opposite the goal post (a) and closer to the wing (b).

Figure 8:13 showed the position of the attacking halfbacks when the corner is taken by the right wing. The right half remains out toward the side of the field to prevent a clear resulting from a defense interception; the center half backs up the inner and the left half backs up the center. The left halfback plays closer to the alley line than the right half when the corner is taken by the left wing to protect her non-stick side.

Penalty (Short) Corners

A penalty corner is awarded when the defensive team fouls in the striking circle or intentionally hits the ball over the end line. The corner hit is taken ten yards from the near goal post, and the attacking team may select on which side of the field it will be taken. The attacking team considers the position of their strongest hitter and weakness of the defense, the fact that the reception is easier from the right side (stick side), and the fact that the clear of the defense (by the right half, right back and center half) is more difficult from the left side. Teams usually choose the right wing to hit the corner, presumably because the ball is easier to field from that direction.

The half on whose side the corner is taken can move in closer to the circle on short corners, because the ball is played from within the circle and the angles for defense clears are less acute.

Drills

Each of the following drills can be used for either a corner or penalty corner:

1. Groups of three—wing, inner, and goalie. The wing hits to the inner who stops the ball and shoots. Repeat several times.
2. Same directions as for No. 1, but use a stop watch to ascertain the time it takes from the instant the ball is struck by the wing until the ball is contacted on the shot for goal. Further refine the timing to learn how long it takes the ball to reach the inner, and how long it takes her to drive for goal after she initially contacts the ball in her fielding effort. Compute the average time it takes in five attempts. Also recognize the fastest time. Keep a chart so that improvement can be shown.
3. Groups of five—one wing, two inners, the center, and the goalie. The wing drives the ball to one of her forwards who shoots, and the three inside players immediately rush the goalie. Repeat from the other side.
4. Five forwards and their halfbacks opposed by the other defense. Take corners from both sides. Alternate defense players as this practice is exhausting for them.

THE BULLY

The importance of the bully has been minimized substantially because of the advent of the defense hit when the attack hits the ball over the end line. Essentially, bullies are taken at the start of each half and following the scoring of a goal. Infrequently, on-the-spot bullies and penalty bullies are taken.

Nevertheless, any player on the field may be forced to bully, and so all players should familiarize themselves with the technique involved. It is imperative, however, that the center forward and goalkeeper become extremely proficient in executing a bully. The center takes the bully at the start of each half and after a goal is scored, and the center is the most likely choice of the attack to participate in the penalty bully. The defense player most often penalized for preventing a "most probable score" is the goalkeeper. Poor bullying by her results in a score by the opponents. For this reason, she should practice with full equipment until she is proficient.

Center Bully

The ball is placed on the center line, and all players must be on sides, that is, closer to their own goal than are the opponents. The centers stand squarely astride the center line, face one another with knees bent, head down, and head as nearly over the ball as possible. Each center places her right hand several inches down the stick, and extends it in front of her so that the ball is between the two sticks. Sliding the hand down the stick gives better control and shortens the lever, thus increasing the speed with which it can be moved.

The bully is started by the centers simultaneously striking the ground and the flat surface of the opponent's stick alternately three times (ground, stick, ground, stick, ground, stick). This action completes the bully and each player is free to hit the ball. Skillfull bulliers recognize the importance of lifting the stick above the ball only as high as necessary to strike the opponent's stick. The center who completes the bully quickest is able to hit the ball sooner. For this reason, speed in completing the bully is important. A less skillful player may attempt to alter the timing of a more proficient bullier. By bullying at a slower rate than the opponent prefers, a player may offset the opponent's advantage.

Positioning for the bully. The inners start approximately five to seven yards from the centers and the wings remain in (or outside) the alley. As soon as the bully is completed, the forwards dart across the center line to receive a pass. The center half backs up the bully one to two steps to the right of the centers. From this position, she can intercept a pass in that direction. The left fullback plays up to protect the non-stick side of the center half. The left half plays out near the alley. The right fullback plays deep and in the center of the field, and the right half plays on the stick side of the left wing. If the ball constantly is hit toward the left inner, it may be desirable to have the right back play up for the bully. This action would eliminate the need for the backs

switching positions if the center half failed to intercept. When the right
back plays up, the center half moves slightly to the left of the centers
to protect her non-stick side.

Means of securing the ball.

1. Pass to the right inner by pushing the ball between the opposing
   center's right foot and stick.
2. Reverse the stick and hit the ball back about three feet; take a
   step backward with the right foot and hit the ball behind the
   opposing center to the right inner (Figure 8:20).

Figure 8:20

3. Reverse the stick and hit the ball back to the center half, who may pass to either inner or wing.

4. Lift the stick (against an inexperienced player) and the opponent may inadvertently hit to the center half or fullback.

5. Pull the ball toward yourself and at the same time move the left foot sideward. Immediately get behind the ball and pass to the left inner or left wing; if the player fails to move her feet, she will obstruct by imposing her shoulder between her opponent and the ball (Figure 8:21).

6. Push the ball hard against the opponent's stick and force the ball away from her. If the ball becomes wedged, the player moves her feet behind the ball for better leverage and lifts the ball over her opponent's stick.

Figure 8:21

On-the-Spot Bully

A bully is taken on a spot selected by the umpire when a double foul occurs (very rare), when an injury occurs (not as the result of a foul), or when action is suspended for some other reason. Although this type of bully is relatively infrequent, it may be called in any game. The spot selected by the umpire will be in the area of action prior to the suspension of play. Because of this, any forward may be called upon to bully.

Penalty Bully

A penalty bully is awarded when a defense player willfully violates the rules, fouls repeatedly, or commits a foul when a goal would most probably have been scored. Any defense player may be the offender, but the goalkeeper is the most likely candidate.

The bully is taken five yards in front of the goal by the defense player who committed the foul and by any player selected by the attack. All other players stand behind the nearer twenty-five yard line and observe play until the umpires invite them to participate again. If the goalkeeper is the offender, she suffers a distinct disadvantage since she cannot remove her equipment.

Following the bully, the attack player tries to score while the defense player tries to hit the ball out of the circle. The attack player usually pushes the ball forward and to the non-stick side of the goalie. The goalie, due to her bulky equipment, finds it difficult to retreat quickly to play the ball legally; and if she turns to reach the ball, she fouls and the opponents are awarded a penalty goal. The center also can pull the ball toward her and flick it immediately into the goal before the goalie can move toward her.

The goalie may apply some psychology to gain an advantage over her opponent. During the bully, the sticks must be contacted simultaneously. By bullying more slowly than the center, the goalie might cause repeated bullies until one is completed legally. By forcing the center to change her rhythm, the center may be less proficient than usual. The goalie may then surprise the center and quickly hit the ball out of the circle. The loss of the penalty bully by the attacking team is demoralizing; the winning of the bully by the defense is inspiring.

Drills

1. Centers, inners, and wings try each of the bullies suggested.
2. Defense players bully against their opposing forward.
3. Goalies bully against each other.
4. Goalies bully against a center forward.
5. Centers bully against other members of the team to gain experience in bullying at different tempos.
6. Using a stop watch, clock the time it takes from the whistle for the bully until it is completed (or until the ball is hit).

IX

TEACHING BEGINNERS

Teaching field hockey to beginners is a challenge, particularly if they have not been exposed to a field game previously. Their ability to understand the concepts of hockey and to progress beyond the basic fundamentals depends on their age, strength, and previous experience. So, in terms of planning a sequential progression, these items must be considered, and certain adjustments may become desirable. For example, it would be wise to decrease the size of the field for young children who lack the strength and endurance that come with maturity. With the size of the field decreased, it may become necessary to decrease the number of players on the field to prevent crowding. Therefore, playing six aside (without a goalie) or seven aside with a goalie is common practice with very young children.

SAFETY

When starting hockey, children and adults should wear shinguards. They should become as much a part of the player's equipment as her stick. Shinguards make play safer for the student and also aid psychologically in giving her more courage to oppose a player who drives the ball with force. Safety on the field also should be considered. All extra balls should be off the field whenever drills or a game are in progress. Hazardous conditions exist when the fields are wet and slippery due to dew, frost, or rain. Some youngsters enjoy sliding on the muddy surface to attract attention, but a comment by the instructor about the ground conditions and the fact that players with good body control will not fall will deter many intentional slips. With muddy ground, it is wise to pay close attention to sticks that tend to go above shoulder level and to uncontrolled body speed. Placing flags in the corner of the fields can serve as a point of aim on hits to the wings, and can identify the limitations of the field boundaries.

INTRODUCING HOCKEY

When game play is started, it is beneficial to form permanent teams. Later, students who are dissatisfied with their positions can change with a teammate. Hockey is too complicated a game to expect students to be able to change positions daily or even frequently. The duties of each position are so varied that no beginner can learn to play a number of positions with any degree of skill. Frequent change of positions also forces the instructor to repeat the same information as a player moves into a new position. This tends to keep play at an elementary level, with little progress evident toward teamwork. Later in the unit, teams can be changed to allow different players to work with one another. Basically, however, players should be encouraged to stay in the same position. Later in the unit, it is good to have forwards and defense players exchange positions for a short time so that they may understand the positioning of their opponent.

There are two other advantages to the formation of permanent teams. First, a few minutes can be saved at the beginning of each class hour, because roll taking is unnecessary. Absentees are immediately apparent as teams take the field. Secondly, learning names of new students is facilitated. Names of the outstanding left wing, the out-of-position right fullback, and the lazy center forward are learned quickly.

The instructor can help students select suitable positions. She can deter the slow student from playing left wing and suggest a more suitable position for her. All players on the left side of the field need better footwork than those on the right side. Defense players on the left side find interceptions relatively easy, but tackles more difficult. Defense players on the right side find the tackles easy, but interceptions more difficult. Forwards on the left side probably have greater difficulty in both passing and receiving. As teams are formed, the instructor should attempt to see that opposing teams have overall equal ability, that both teams have at least one strong player on the left and right side of the forward line and the left and right side of the defensive unit, and that inexperienced players oppose each other. This is no easy task, and adjustments of personnel may be necessary after the initial selection of teams.

Until team play is developed, it seems unnecessary to play with a goalkeeper. An individual selecting that position would probably benefit more from the stickwork and movement that are necessary in the other positions. As game play improves, the goalkeeper may be added. If, however, teams have too few players, a piece of plywood can be cut out in the shape of a goalkeeper, painted realistically, and placed in the goal to encourage greater accuracy of shots by forwards.

In large classes, experienced players from upper grades can be selected to come to a class during a free period to help with the instruction. These students can be trained by the instructor so that they can conduct meaningful practice sessions and coach during game play. If upperclassmen are unavailable, the instructor can use team captains or experienced players within the class. Although this opportunity provides these students with leadership opportunities, it does not give them a chance to improve their own skills and reactions in game situations.

In teaching hockey, the progression should allow students to learn a few skills well each season and annually build on whatever has been learned previously. Proficiency in a great number of skills by beginners is impossible. The students will benefit by an introduction and practice in a few strokes one year, to be followed the next year by a quick review of those strokes and practice on additional strokes. In this way, greater skill is achieved initially, and students are not confronted with units in subsequent years that appear identical to those already experienced. Failure to adopt this type of philosophy in constructing units encourages mediocrity. It may be the reason why play of students in their fourth unit of hockey is not significantly different from their play in the second unit. A math student cannot do calculus well without being proficient in adding and subtracting. Similarly, hockey players cannot perform the advanced skills well without a thorough grounding in the fundamentals.

Students will gain a more meaningful concept of hockey if the game form is introduced early in the unit. Participating in a game helps players see the need for additional practice in which drills become more meaningful. Boundaries for the playing area can be determined by the number of players per team. The fewer players per team, the smaller the area needed and the more contests that can be conducted simultaneously.

In the early stages of play, students should have a chance to play the ball frequently and apply whatever strategy they know. Therefore, at the onset, one-player teams can be established, with each player assuming both offensive and defensive responsibilities. Shortly, the addition of a partner is desirable so that some teamwork can be developed. Initially, the two players on each team serve as both forwards and defense players. Then the two player teams can be retained, but one player becomes a forward and her teammate a defense player. Now, the beginning strategy of who marks whom and the position of the forward when her team does not have the ball can be introduced. Other than this, little strategy can be taught because basically it is one attack player vs. one defense player. Later, additional players are added so that a team has two attack and two defense players.

Now, the basic elements of where and when the forwards should pass and the adherence to a man-to-man defense become important. When these concepts are learned, six-player teams can be formed. For the first time, players pass to and receive from two directions. The positioning of the two fullbacks is introduced (the one on the ball side plays up and the other one plays back), and the center halfback is instructed to stay with the center forward. By this time, players have increased the force of their passes so that the ball can be hit from inner to inner or right back to left inner. These tactics can be encouraged, and forwards should become convinced quickly that the inner to inner pass is an effective tactic since one back is in a covering position. In this modified game, one inner will always be free, and the defense will be forced to change the position of their backs repeatedly. This situation should give the forwards an advantage over the defense, and forwards should have many opportunities for scoring. Following the six-a-side contest, the regulation game should be played. During the first unit of hockey play, the game might be limited to the seven player game, including a goalie. Thereafter, the regulation game should be played.

A goalkeeper was not used in any of the contests discussed above. If a goalie is needed, an additional player should be assigned to each team. Many teachers advocate the game of six player hockey. With beginning players, small classes, or a small playing area, this technique is fine provided that each team has three forwards and three defense players. At no time, however, should a game be organized with an even number of players on a team (2, 4, 6) with one player serving as a goalie. If this is done in a six player game, for instance, a team would have three forwards, two defense players, and a goalkeeper. Selection of this type of game constitutes a danger of negative transfer if the students advance to the parent game later. The defense is forced to become a zone and switch from one player to another because they always are one player short. Therefore, correct defensive tactics are negated and the corresponding means for defeating them by the attack is also lost. If goalkeepers are desired, teams should be composed of an odd number of players (3, 5, 7) so that proper defensive tactics can be taught.

FOULS

Fouls usually occur because players are not proficient in executing skills or because they do not understand the rules. Rough play commonly is caused by players with poor body control. All of these faults can be reduced, if not eliminated, early in play with emphasis on proper footwork and stickwork. This emphasis, combined with encouraging open play, should practically eliminate obstruction, which is the principal violation.

The teacher should insist on perfection as skills are being practiced. Laziness or improper footwork, as evidenced by stopping the ball with the foot or the rounded side of the stick, should not be accepted. Similarly, emphasis should be placed on the correct method of obtaining force for a drive, so that students do not commit sticks in an effort to increase power. Attention should be devoted to the manner of receiving a pass and retrieving one that is missed. Thus, the bad habit of turning incorrectly is never formed. Players should be encouraged to use their speed and to develop ball control to accompany it. If students learn correct techniques early, there will be few whistles during a game and play will be more enjoyable for all players.

IMPROVING STICKWORK

Establishing stations on the field, to which students of different abilities can advance, enables students to develop their stickwork at a rate commensurate with their individual ability. Many stations can be established, and all students start at station No. 1. As a player can perform the task at the desired level of proficiency, she moves on to station No. 2. The process is repeated at each station, until the student completes the circuit.

The teacher can give instructions in the execution of many skills during the beginning stages of a unit and then use the station concept as a self-testing device. This is the more traditional approach. At each station, directions are given for the execution of the task and the time limit and/or the percentage of success that is required before a player may advance to the next station.

The instructor also can use the stations for programmed learning. This is a newer concept that has received extensive attention in theory courses, particularly in mathematics and sciences. It can be equally effective in the gymnasium or on the practice field. Using this method, no instruction is given on the execution of skill before the students are assigned to the first station. There the students are provided instructions in performing the skill and are given a series of drills that they perform to help them learn the skill. Each student works with a partner, who helps evaluate the performance in terms of the cues that are mentioned on the cue sheet. When the student has performed the lead-up drills correctly, she may attempt the task at the station. If she and her partner judged performance well, she should be successful at the required task. If she cannot complete the task at the stated level of proficiency, she will return to the lead-up drills for more practice.

Before returning to the lead-up drills, the student looks at the cue sheet and answers the questions that the teacher has prepared. For example, at a station on dribbling the questions might be: "Did you lack control because the ball was too far off your stick?" "Did you lose the ball when you were turning to your left?" "Did you lose the ball when you turned to your right?," or "Did you keep the ball close to the stake when you turned to your right?" After each question, the teacher cites a drill that will help the student improve her dribbling technique if she answers "yes" to the question. After practicing again with the assistance of a partner, the player may return to attempt the task a second time. She repeats the process until she can execute the task as described, and then proceeds to the next station.

Repeated unsuccessful attempts at the task itself are undesirable. It indicates that the suggestions (cues) for the partners to look for are deficient in any/all of three areas:

1. The description of the skill itself is incomplete so that a clear concept is not gained by the student.
2. The lead-up drills are not in a progressive sequence or are not sufficiently demanding to breed proficiency.
3. The cues given for the partner to observe are not sufficiently declarative.

As a teacher observes students attempting the drills and the tasks, it should become apparent if revisions in any of the three areas are necessary. Refinement of a program takes considerable time, so it may undergo several revisions before the teacher is satisfied that the program represents a proper sequential development.

Some suggestions follow for tasks to be accomplished at a number of stations. As proficiency improves, the difficulty of the tasks can be increased by decreasing the time requirement or by increasing the percentage of success, or by a combination of both. Figure 9:1 shows stations that can be developed, and directions for each station follow:

1. Dribble around five posts (18″ in diameter), the centers of which are two yards apart. (Hoops or discs made out of plywood can be substituted for the posts.) Dribble to the right of the first post, left of the second, and return to the starting line. This must be done in 20 seconds, in three out of five attempts.

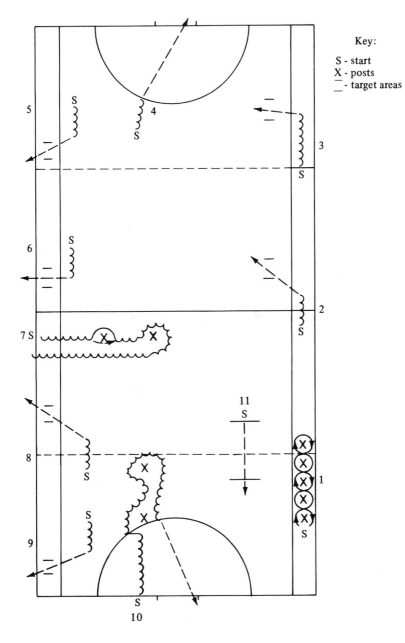

Key:

S - start
X - posts
— - target areas

Figure 9:1. Stations for stickwork practice.

2. Dribble to the restraining line and drive diagonally to the left between two stakes that are one yard apart and three yards to the left of the restraining line. Students must be successful in three out of five attempts.

3. Dribble to the restraining line and drive directly left (flat pass) between two stakes that are one yard apart and three yards directly left of the restraining line. Students must be successful in three out of five attempts.

4. Dribble to the edge of the circle and shoot. The ball must go into the goal, the middle two and one-half yards of which have been blocked by cardboard boxes. Students must be successful in three out of five attempts.

5. Dribble to the restraining line and drive diagonally to the right between two stakes one yard apart and three yards to the right of the restraining line. Students must be successful in three out of five attempts.

6. Dribble to the restraining line and drive directly to the right (flat pass) between two stakes one yard apart and three yards to the right of the restraining line. Students must be successful in three out of five attempts.

7. Place a post five yards from the starting line and another post ten yards beyond. Place a line 10 yards from the starting line and parallel to it called line A. Place a line perpendicular to the starting line and extending to line A, called the restraining line. The player dribbles toward the first post and must remain to the left of the restraining line until line A is reached. She then pushes the ball to the right of the post and runs to the left of the post (dodge to the non-stick side), dribbles to the second post, passes it with her right shoulder close to it and dribbles back to the starting line. Students must complete the drill in 18 seconds, timed until the player crosses the starting line. They must be successful in three out of five attempts.

8. Dribble to the restraining line and push pass diagonally to the left between two stakes one yard apart and three yards from the restraining line. Students must be successful in three out of five attempts.

9. Dribble to the restraining line, and push pass diagonally to the right between two stakes one yard apart and three yards to the right of the restraining line. Students must be successful in three out of five attempts.

10. Place a post 15 yards from the starting line and another post 10 yards beyond. Place a line perpendicular to the starting line and extending to the second post, called the restraining line. Place a line 10 yards from the starting line and parallel to it, called line A. Place another line 20 yards from the starting line and parallel to it, called line B. The player dribbles to the right of the re-

straining line until she reaches line A, then does a dodge to the left around the post and continues to dribble toward the second post. She must return to the right of the restraining line by the time she reaches line B. She dribbles around the second post with her right shoulder close to it, dribbles to the circle and drives for goal, the middle two and one-half yards of which are blocked by cardboard boxes. She must score a goal and have the ball cross the goal line in 15 seconds, in three out of five attempts.

11. The player starts with the ball stationary, and flicks it across a gap of 12 yards successfully in three out of five attempts.

For more highly skilled players, the success in eight out of ten attempts may be required. The time limit can be adjusted upwards or downwards, depending upon the level of skill.

STARTING THE GAME

When students have acquired minimal skill of dribbling, passing, and fielding, they should be introduced to the game form. A brief introduction can be made to the positions so that players can select the position they wish to play. Students who like to play forward in basketball or soccer may prefer a forward position in hockey; similarly, those who like to defend in basketball or soccer may desire a defensive position in hockey. If students have not played either sport, then those students who like to score probably will favor forward positions, and those who prefer to prevent scoring probably will like defense positions. Students can be told that the wings and halfbacks need more speed than the other positions.

With that introduction, players will have an idea of what position they might like. The instructor can ask, "Who would like to play left wing?" and give a pinnie to a player and name the other left wing to the non-pinnie team. The remaining positions are named and two teams (or more) are formed. Teams are requested to sit down facing each other about one yard apart, with all defense players sitting just behind their own attack players. The instructor checks to see that they are seated properly—forwards in position from left wing to right wing, and the correct defense player behind each of the attack players. At this point, players should recognize that they line up facing the goal they are attacking; hence, the left wing is opposite the right wing. Each defense player can be introduced to the player she marks—left back to right inner—and each defense player can get up and shake the hand of her opponent. In this way, the instructor will recognize whether halfbacks shake each other's hand and can assist them in finding the correct opponent. Forwards should be told that they do not mark the opposing forward and that only the defense player behind her attempts to get the ball from that player. The only player the forward tries to get the ball from is the player who shook her hand. Frequent reminders of this fact will be needed during play.

The concept of the forward line proceeding down the field on line with one another can be introduced. Each forward should think of her section of the field as railroad tracks. She must stay within them or she will be derailed. This concept may help keep forwards spaced at the beginning. Forwards of one team can be placed on the field and permitted to pass the ball down the field starting from the center line. They can return to the center line and proceed again with their halfbacks trailing about ten yards behind. Halfbacks think in terms of being extra attack players to make it more difficult for the opposing defense. The fullbacks and goalkeeper can be added, with the concept introduced of one fullback playing up and the other one back.

That team may sit on the field and the other team may repeat the process by passing around the seated players. This procedure is followed by the attack of one team playing against the defense of the other team. Finally, both teams are ready to play. Chaos is likely to occur if students have not played a modified game with fewer players previously. This confusion is natural, and the instructor frequently must stop the game whenever the concepts that have been introduced are not applied by the students.

The game can start by players lining up at the center line, with the teacher rolling the ball into a space out toward the alley instead of starting with a bully. This makes the position of wing more desirable, and at least starts with the ball in a less cluttered area. The teacher should devote careful attention to forwards staying in their railroad tracks, forwards not tackling other forwards, and defense players only tackling the player for whom they are responsible. No more than two people should be permitted near the ball. It is likely that players will not be able to hit the ball from one side of the field to the other, so that as play is concentrated on one side the instructor may intercede and roll or hit the ball to the other side of the field.

When the forwards of one team do not have the ball, they should be encouraged to move about ten yards ahead of the ball toward the goal they are attacking. Then, when a defensive teammate gets the ball, she has someone to whom the ball can be hit. Start immediately in striving to have the forwards get their feet facing the way they are attacking. Do not permit the forwards to stand facing their own defense players while waiting for the ball.

As the ball moves up and down the field, the attack players will inquire how far down the field they go on defense. At the beginning, they can be informed to return to the twenty-five yard line. They will tend to stay upfield nearer the center line, but an inquiry as to whether the defense can hit the ball that far probably will make them realize that they must get back near the twenty-five. The halfbacks will wonder how far they go on attack, and they must be discouraged from going any farther than the edge of the striking circle. At least one fullback should stay on the defensive side of the center line.

Little attention should be given to the advancing foul at this time. It is more important for play to be continuous. It may be unnecessary to be concerned about any fouls at the beginning unless they are dangerous. The danger of sticks can be demonstrated humorously. Soon, however, concern should be given to obstruction, at least to the extent that players face the correct direction and receive a pass to avoid obstruction. Hitting the ball on the fly should be prohibited from the start.

As play is in progress, players should be encouraged to hold the stick away from their bodies. Hockey is a reaching game. From the beginning, forwards should be discouraged from hitting the ball straight ahead and then running after it. The only time a forward hits the ball straight ahead is on a shot for goal. If the defense players know only the straight tackle, they are informed to recover and face their opponent before tackling again, if their previous tackle or attempted interception was unsuccessful.

Once these basic concepts have been learned, the instructor can begin to focus on the development of team play. The forwards are given suggestions for making spaces so that there is a space through which the ball can pass to reach them, and so that one defense player cannot mark two forwards at the same time. When an attack player has the ball, forwards pull away from her to give her more space and also to create a space into which a pass can be made. After passing the ball, the forward pulls in the opposite direction. When a defense player has the ball, spaces are created by the attack player pulling to the side and back toward the defensive player. On this move, the inners are the key to where the spaces will exist, as they pull either toward the center of the field or toward the sideline. With players of both teams on the field, they can practice positioning as the instructor identifies the player who has an imaginary ball. The forwards make spaces accordingly and look over the proper shoulder to receive the pass when it comes from a defensive player.

As forwards begin to make spaces better, their passing will improve. At this time, the covering position of the defense should be emphasized to prevent the long through passes. Previously, the defense players probably have been marking their opponent or been positioned relatively close to her. They should be made aware of the fallacy of this system in midfield, and therefore should recognize the need for covering positions. If it has not been introduced earlier, the halfbacks can be brought in on the inner. Emphasis should be placed on the diagonal line that should exist if all defensive players are in the proper covering position. One fullback plays deeper toward goal. Attack players now should become aware of whether the space is open for a flat pass or a through pass. Many drills as well as game experience are necessary for them to become aware of where openings for passes exist. This awareness takes considerable practice, and without it the defense dominates the game. Emphasis on the fact that defenders cannot mark and cover at the same time should help.

If the attack is experiencing success, a defensive player who has little opposition can drift away from her opponent and aid a teammate. This should make the forwards more aware of which player has not been used, so that her opponent cannot take such liberties. Attack players should remember, too, that if they are being tackled by two opponents, one of their teammates must be free.

It is this technique of helping the forwards to defeat the defense and then assisting the defense to get back on a par with the attack that improves play. Then the process is repeated.

IMPROVING POSITIONING AND STRATEGY

As concepts for the attack and defense are added, it may be necessary to use different methods to stress particular points. The teacher should remember that only the most vital points should be emphasized. The points for emphasis will depend upon the skill level of the players at a particular time. Some suggestions follow.

1. Pass the ball whenever the whistle sounds. Used to discourage dribbling and encourage quick passes to keep the defense off balance.
2. Tie a wandering center halfback to her opposing center forward. This is an old technique that teaches a lesson quickly.
3. Play on half the field with forwards of one team against the opposing defense. The halfbacks of the attacking team may be added. This may be used for:
   a. Forwards learning to pull away from another forward with the ball.
   b. Forwards spacing to receive a pass from their halfbacks.

    c. Forwards not retreating when the ball is intercepted, but re-positioning and waiting for a halfback to return it to them.

    d. Halfbacks backing up their forwards.

    e. Fullback up and back positioning.

    f. Halfback moving in on the inner when the ball is on the other side of the field.

    g. Covering position of defense in midfield; players on a diagonal.

4. Take one defense player off the field during play. Encourage attack players to find the free player.

5. Occasionally have forwards and their opponents exchange places for a short time to gain insight into the demands of the opposing position. The information thus gleaned should be used by players as they return to their regular position.

6. Practice corners—again and again and again. Emphasize that if the ball goes outside the circle, the halfback will retrieve it. Forwards should then re-position to allow the halfback to shoot, or if tackled, a space into which to pass. Also emphasize stop and shoot immediately.

7. Practice circle play. Forwards must score more. Emphasize moving toward goal and backing up, rushing again and backing up, as the ball is sent toward the edge of the circle. Emphasize marking on the part of the defense. Players will see a need for superior stickwork if circle play is emphasized.

8. Bonus point games. After a new technique or skill has been introduced, give a point during game play to any player who attempts the particular skill and two points if she does it successfully. The team with the most number of points wins. Examples of techniques that may be used in bonus games include: a specific dodge, triangular pass, wing-to-wing or inner-to-inner pass, and halfback who shoots.

9. Rainy day technique. Cut out triangular pieces of paper in sufficient quantity and in different colors to give each student one or two teams of "players." Each student finds some space on the gymnasium floor for her hockey field. The instructor then gives situations, and each student places her players on the field in appropriate positions. Examples:

    a. Line up for a center bully.

    b. The right inner has the ball at the offensive twenty-five yard line.

    c. The left halfback has the ball just outside the attacking striking circle.

    d. The right back has the ball just outside the defensive striking circle.

e. The left wing has the ball near the center line.
f. The left wing (above) passes to the right inner.
g. The right halfback takes a roll-in at the defensive twenty-five yard line (or at midfield or near the attacking twenty-five).
h. The left back has a free hit outside the offensive striking circle.
i. The left wing is taking a penalty corner hit (or a long corner).

SQUAD PRACTICE

A coach generally discovers that all of the players on her squad do not possess comparable ability. There are always a few players who have less potential than others. With this in mind, it is advisable to compensate for any deficiencies in the best manner possible. Weaker players can be hidden to some degree by placing a less able forward in front of a strong defense player, or by placing an attack player who tackles back in front of a weak defense player.

A few other considerations are worthy of mention. Although all of the halfbacks should have speed, the left halfback probably needs the greatest speed because she must overtake her opponent to execute the circular tackle. The right half needs speed because she has a greater distance to run to get into covering position. Perhaps she can compensate for a lack of speed by good anticipation. The right back should be faster than the left back for the same reason as the right halfback. The left wing needs greater speed than the right wing so that she can get ahead of the ball to field it. The center forward should be one of the better forwards so that she can keep the opposing center halfback alert and prevent her from wandering to assist her teammates.

Once teams are selected, it is wise to have the best line of forwards practice against the best defense players. Part of the time, the coach will want to have the halfbacks back up their own forward line so that they become accustomed to the speed and positioning of their teammates. At this time, the fullbacks for each team should play against their teammates to provide better opposition. Occasionally, the first team should play against the second team so that each team can refine its teamwork. The frequency of teams opposing one another probably depends on the relative ability of the two squads. If the teams are very close in ability, a coach may use this method more often. Two teams that are vastly different in ability gain little benefit, however.

In special situations, it is possible to exploit the weaknesses of the opponents. As they line up to take a roll-in or free hit, the opponents can force them to use their weakest players by leaving them relatively unmarked. By carefully marking the better players and covering the spaces for passes to them, a team may effectively force a pass to a less skilled player. Immediate harassment of this player may result in the defending team gaining the ball.

X

COMPETITION

The question is not whether to compete but how. It is an intransigent fact that when one plays hockey, one competes. No one can play by herself or play in a vacuum. Competition in and of itself cannot be dramatized as good or bad. Competition is what the teacher or coach makes of it. Developing desirable competitive attitudes is as important for the teacher in the physical education class as for the coach of the interscholastic team. Clear manifestations of poor sportsmanship are sometimes more visible in class games than in inter-school games. Fortunately, these games are witnessed by few viewers. Nevertheless, the development of desirable attitudes toward competition should be given its rightful priority at all levels of play.

The game of hockey has a proud heritage. It is played by thousands of young women, from beginners to international players, for the sheer joy of matching wits and skill against others. It is an amateur sport, completely free of any professionalism. It is the only sport under international supervision that is governed by women and devoid of paid personnel. Devoted hockey enthusiasts volunteer many hours of their time to promote hockey at the local, sectional, and national levels. Their only remuneration is the thanks from the players they serve.

DEVELOPING ATTITUDES AND STANDARDS

The teacher should prepare students for each contest and should schedule opponents against whom they can compete on equitable terms. She should demand that the players play hard, but most important, that they play fairly. There is no place in women's athletics for the "win at any cost" philosophy. Roughness and circumvention of rules cannot be tolerated. A premium should be placed on finesse and skill and the desire to play within the limitations of the rules. On the hockey field, the player who loses her temper—throws her hockey stick, kicks at the ground, pushes, trips an evasive opponent, challenges an official, or yells at a teammate to "hit it"—is an undesirable team player and a detriment to hockey.

In contrast is the team that plays in relative silence and saves its breath for the challenge at hand. An occasional "with you," "Susie is free," or "I'm back" may be heard, but the constant yelling of directions is absent. (Not only does the continuous banter cost energy, but it also advertises the player's position on the field.)

The years ahead are critical for interscholastic and intercollegiate competition. The coaches during this period will be on trial during each contest. They will be judged by some observers on their ability to teach, and by others on their ability to develop desirable attitudes and conduct of players, both on and off the field. The jury is well aware that the attitude and character of the coach is reflected in the actions of the players. It might be advisable for all of us to take an objective look at our players and decide whether we like what we see! With the increased emphasis on competition for women, more of the general public are becoming aware of it. Their attitude toward it will, in large measure, determine the future role of athletics for women. Let us do our part to ensure that hockey is "for the good of those who play."

As pre-requisites for an interscholastic or intercollegiate program, DGWS recommends:

For the best welfare of the participants, it is essential that the program be conducted by qualified leaders, be supported by budgeted funds, be representative of approved objectives and standards for girls' and women's sports, including acceptable conditions of travel, protective insurance, appropriate facilities, proper equipment, and desirable practices in the conduct of the events.[1]

Recognizing the importance of minimum standards in women's competition, the Division for Girls' and Women's Sports has documented guidelines for the conduct of interscholastic and intercollegiate athletic programs. Clearly stated are general principles and standards for participants, leadership and administration. DGWS strongly urges that

. . . no individual and/or school attempt the establishment of interscholastic programs if these minimal requirements cannot be adequately met . . . a thorough understanding and knowledge of these recommendations is essential for women physical educators desirous of developing such programs as well as for the school administrators ultimately responsible for such programs.[2]

Presented below are the Guidelines for Interscholastic Athletic Programs for Junior High School and High School girls and Guidelines for Intercollegiate Athletic Programs.

During the junior high school years, girls should have the time and opportunity to explore a great variety of sports. Because of growth and development patterns, this is an age when many goals can be accomplished through team sports, and a time when skills of individual sports should also be sampled and developed. Therefore, the junior high school sports program for girls should involve opportunities to participate in many kinds of sports and in a variety of sports situations.

It is also recognized that some girls with high skill potential will wish to extend their training and competitive experiences under competent leadership outside the jurisdiction of the school.

A wide variety of activities should be offered and made available to all students in the school instructional and intramural programs. Opportunities for interschool competition may be provided in the form of a limited number of sports days at the end of the intramural season. The following guidelines are recommended:

1. Competitive sports opportunities for junior high school girls should be planned as a program separate and different from the program of competitive athletics for senior high school girls, whether or not the state high school athletic organization includes the junior high school level.

2. Sports competition should be planned for the values offered to the participant rather than as a spectator sport or as a training program for senior high school teams.

3. Extramural programs should not be organized until there are broad instructional and intramural programs and a sufficient allotment of time, facilities, and personnel for new programs.

4. One or two sports days following the end of the intramural season will, in most cases, give enough breadth to the opportunity for student competition in sports at this age. If a more extensive schedule is planned, individual participation should not exceed more than one contest per week and three contests per sport season.

5. The wide variation in growth and development within this age grouping necessitates equating of competitors with reference to skill level, age, and/or size.

6. Travel should be kept to a minimum by competing only with other schools in the vicinity. Travel should be in school buses or with bonded carriers.[3]

Competitive sports are an important part of the total physical education program for high school girls. A program of intramural and extramural participation should be arranged to augment a sound and inclusive instructional program in physical education. The interscholastic program should not be promoted at the expense of the instructional or intramural programs.

As the interscholastic program is expanded, the State High School Athletic Association will be the regulatory body for its member schools. For schools that are not members, a regulatory body may need to be formed. The State Department of Education should be involved.

1. Existing legislative and administrative bodies for interscholastic athletic programs will retain ultimate control of the total program for girls within the state. However, a women's advisory board composed mainly of women high school physical educators will be formed to propose policies to these administrative and legislative groups and to review policies approved by them.

2. Total responsibility for the administration and supervision of the local interscholastic athletic program is vested in the local school administration and the appropriate persons designated by the administration.[4]

GUIDELINES COMMON TO JUNIOR HIGH
AND HIGH SCHOOL

1. The responsibility for leadership of the local girls' interscholastic program should be delegated to the women physical education teachers. The school administration should delegate to them the major responsibility for planning, organizing, coaching, and supervising the program, with the understanding that the ultimate authority remains in the hands of the administration.

2. The program, based on the needs and interests of the girls, should include those individual and team activities for which qualified leadership, financial support, and adequate facilities are available.

3. The entire financing of the girls' sports program should be included in the total school budget. Any monies collected should go into the general fund.

4. DGWS approved standards should be used in all sports. It is strongly recommended that DGWS rules be used in those sports in which DGWS publishes rules.

5. The administration should provide a healthful, safe, and sanitary environment for all participants.

STANDARDS FOR THE PARTICIPANT:

1. Participants must be bona fide students of the school which they represent. They shall not have attended high school for more than eight semesters after entering the ninth grade.* They must be successfully carrying full academic loads.* Students under temporary suspension or probation for disciplinary reasons should not be allowed to participate.

2. Participants must have amateur standing in the interscholastic sports in which they participate.

3. Written permission of the parent or guardian is required for all participants.

4. A physician's certification of girls' fitness for participation shall be filed with the administration prior to the first practice in a sport. The examination must have been made within the time specified by local regulations. Written permission by a physician should be required for participation after a serious illness, injury or surgery.

* Omitted from Junior High School Guidelines.

5. Participants should carry some type of accident insurance coverage that protects them during athletic competition.

LEADERSHIP:

1. The interscholastic program should be directed, coached and officiated by women whenever and wherever possible. No program should be expanded past the ability of the girls' department of physical education to direct it.

2. All coaches should be certified teachers employed by the local board of education. If teachers other than trained women physical educators are used to coach, they should work closely with the girls' department.

3. A woman faculty member appointed by the principal shall accompany and supervise girls' teams at all contests.

4. Officials should hold a current DGWS rating or its equivalent rating in the specific sport, and should be registered with the appropriate administrative or regulatory bodies.

5. A doctor should be on call for all contests, and someone who is qualified in first aid should be in attendance.

6. In case of question as to fitness for play, the official has the right to overrule the coach for the protection of the welfare of the girl.

ADMINISTRATION:

1. All games and contests in which school teams participate must be under the direct sponsorship and supervision of the schools involved. No post-season games for teams or individuals should be permitted.

2. Girls may participate on only one interscholastic team during a season. They may not take part in a contest on any out-of-school team until the school sport season is completed. A girl is considered a member of a team when she participates in her first contest.

3.* Competition should be limited to a geographical area which will permit players to return at reasonable hours. Safe transportation should be assured.

4.* The maximum length of a sport season should be twelve weeks, with the first three weeks devoted to training and conditioning. The participant should take part in no more than five participation periods per week including games or contests. There should be no more than two games per week, which should not be played on consecutive days. Standards for specific sports are listed in the current DGWS guides.

5. Interscholastic competition should be limited to those sports for which DGWS publishes rules and standards, and they should be used in the administration of the program.

6. Awards when given should be of a symbolic type, such as ribbons, letters, and small pins. The giving of other types of awards, as well as fund raising for expansive or elaborate awards, is considered a violation of this guideline.[5, 6]

* Omitted from Junior High School Guidelines.

ADMINISTRATION

The intercollegiate athletic program should be specifically designed for women, and its administration and organization should be the responsibility of the department of physical education for women. It is also the responsibility of the physical education faculty women to recommend and formulate policy for the expanded program to be submitted to the appropriate policy-approving authority of the institution.

BUDGET

The budget for women's intercollegiate athletics should be part of the budget of the institution so that the program is assured. A separate budget item should be specifically designated for this program. (This does not preclude the use of state monies, student fees, gate receipts, and other sources of income, but the program should not depend solely on fluctuating sources of income.) The budget should be administered by the women's physical education department as part of overall administration.

SCHEDULING

Contests should be scheduled among schools having players of comparable ability in order to equate competition. In order to make this possible, scheduling in each sport need not be done with the same institutions each season.

Scheduling with college institutions is recommended. However, when budget is inadequate for travel, limited scheduling with outside organizations (i.e., church, industrial leagues, etc.) in the local area may be desirable. Scheduling should allow opportunities for participants of intercollegiate teams to meet on an informal social basis.

HEALTH AND SAFETY

Adequate health and insurance protection should be provided by the institution for all members of athletic teams. First aid services and emergency medical care should be available during all scheduled intercollegiate athletic events.

LEADERSHIP (TEACHERS, COACHES AND OFFICIALS)

1. Good leadership is essential to a desirable sports program. The qualified leader meets the standard set by the profession through an understanding of (a) the place and purpose of sports in education, (b) the growth and development of children and youth, (c) the effects of exercise on the human organism, (d) first aid and accident prevention, (e) understanding of specific skills, and (f) sound teaching methods. It is desirable that, when possible, leaders of women's sports have personal experience in organized extramural competition. The leader should demonstrate personal integrity and a primary concern for the welfare of the participant.

2. The program should be under the direct supervision of the women's physical education department. Qualified women should teach, coach and officiate wherever and whenever possible, and in all cases the professional background and experience of the leader must meet establishd standards of the physical education profession.

3. It is strongly recommended that an official's rating be considered a prerequisite for coaching in order to enhance the coach's understanding of the official's role.

4. Intercollegiate events should be officiated by DGWS nationally rated officials. In those sports where DGWS does not rate officials, an equivalent rating is acceptable.

5. If a non-staff member is teaching or coaching, a woman member of the physical education faculty should supervise and chaperone the participants. Cooperative institutional efforts should be devoted toward pre-service and in-service programs, and clinics for teachers and leaders.

6. DGWS approved rules should be used in the conduct of all intercollegiate sports events.

PARTICIPATION

1. Intercollegiate participation should not interfere with primary educational objectives.
   a. A student may not participate as a member of an intercollegiate athletic team and at the same time be a member of a team in the same sport outside her institution.
   b. Local policy-making groups may wish to qualify this policy for occasional students.

2. The athletic schedule should not jeopardize the student's class and study time.
   a. The length of the season and the number of games should be established and agreed upon by the participating schools.
   b. The length of the season will vary according to the locale and sport but should not exceed twelve weeks, including at least three weeks of preliminary conditioning and instruction.
   c. Standards for specific sports concerning number of practices and/or contests per week are found in the DGWS guides.

3. Women should be prohibited from participating
   a. On a men's intercollegiate team.
   b. Against a men's intercollegiate team.
   c. Against a man in a scheduled intercollegiate contest.

4. To be eligible to participate in intercollegiate athletics, the individual must be a full-time student of the institution and maintain the academic average required for participation in all other major activities. Undergraduate students only are eligible to participate in the intercollegiate athletic program. For the purpose of eligibility, an undergraduate student is defined as one who has not received the B.A. degree or its equivalent.

5. Transfer students are immediately eligible for participation following enrollment in the institution.

6. A medical examination is a prerequisite to participation in intercollegiate athletics. This examination should be given within the six-month period prior to the start of the sports season each year. Where health examinations are done by the family physician, a covering letter explaining the program of activities and an examination which would include the information needed are suggested. Written permission by the physician should be required for participation after serious illness, injury, or surgery.

7. A participant in intercollegiate athletics maintains amateur status if she has not received money other than expenses as a player, instructor, or official in any sport.

8. There should be no scholarships or financial assistance specifically designated for women athletes. This does not preclude women who participate in the intercollegiate athletic program from holding scholarships or grants-in-aid obtained through normal scholarship programs of the institution.[7]

COMMISSION ON INTERCOLLEGIATE ATHLETICS FOR WOMEN

Because of the increased expansion of intercollegiate athletics, DGWS formed a Commission on Intercollegiate Athletics. Its purpose, as stated in the Operating Code (January, 1967), shall be to encourage and promote philosophically sound, educationally oriented, and physically satisfying intercollegiate athletic contests for college women by:

1. Developing and publishing guidelines and standards for the conduct of such events.

2. Providing assistance in the planning of intercollegiate events.

3. Sanctioning (approval) of organizational plans for all statewide or larger intercollegiate championships.

4. Providing leadership in the development of DGWS national championships, as the need for these becomes apparent.

5. Evaluating intercollegiate championships in terms of desired outcomes.

6. Encouraging the development of organizational patterns to deal with the conduct of intercollegiate athletic opportunities for college women.[8]

Members and their duties

The Commission shall be composed of four members who are appointed on a rotating basis for three-year terms. Two Commissioners divide the responsibilities for national championships; one is in charge of sanctioning (approving) intercollegiate events, and one Commissioner is in charge of postal tournaments and assists in regional development.

The following criteria should be met before anyone sponsoring a district, state, or regional intercollegiate field hockey tournament for five or more schools contacts the Commissioner in charge to request a sanction:

1. Teams invited are made up of highly selected, well coached individuals who play together throughout a season against similar units from other colleges.

2. Undergraduate college students are the only competitors invited.

3. Five or more colleges are being invited.

4. Team competition is *not primarily* for the purpose of selecting individuals for the formation of an "all star team" to compete in higher level competition.

5. The primary purpose is not a clinic or rating session for officials, and the competition is merely a tool.

When an event is sanctioned, all institutions attending are assured that DGWS standards will be followed in the conduct of the tournament.[9]

PREPARATIONS FOR THE SEASON

Scheduling

One important factor in interschool competition is ensuring equitable competition. Unequal competition is not educationally sound for either team. When the opponents are superior in skill, players do not have the opportunity to use their own skills or to demonstrate strategic maneuvers at their own level. Nor are poise or self-confidence (and many of the other desirable objectives) gained when whatever one does proves ineffective.

For a team that schedules inferior opponents, many of the values of competition go unchallenged. The better team may defeat the inferior team, but the joy of competition—of matching one's intelligence and skill—is lost. It is analogous to a simple mathematics problem. A student may be asked to add two and two. She may get the right answer, but will not gain much satisfaction from her success! For this reason, league organization should be avoided if the regulations stipulate that the identical schools must be scheduled for all sports. If this is true, in no way can equal competition be assured. This is why in many league standings one team may be undefeated and another may not have won a game. In a sense, the coach who proudly proclaims that her teams have not lost a game in three years may be doing a disservice to her players. The playing schedule should be carefully evaluated to determine whether her teams are playing the best opposition in the locale. Although every team and its coach would like to experience undefeated seasons, there is merit in winning some games and losing some.

Constructing the schedule so that the stronger opponents are met near the end of the season enables a team to gain experience and build its confidence against less experienced teams. Ideally, each successive rival would be a more difficult opponent, but constructing this type of schedule is indeed difficult. Scheduling problems can be reduced to a minimum if the same teams are scheduled annually on corresponding dates. Pre-season scrimmages with neighboring teams are beneficial to provide game experience prior to the first regularly scheduled contest. Experienced coaches generally complete scheduling details in the preceding spring.

When scheduled games are finalized, a written agreement between coaches should be made. Whether it be in the form of a contractual agreement or a letter to confirm an earlier phone conversation, the information should include: the time, date, and location of the game; number of games to be played; whether games are scheduled consecutively or simultaneously (if more than one is scheduled); location of dressing facilities; the type and location of parking facilities for cars and/or buses; and designation of responsibility for hiring officials.

Officials

The responsibility for enforcing the rules and seeing that the game moves along smoothly lies with the officials. It is their task to call the game so that the team committing a foul or engaging in rough play does not gain the immediate advantage. Holding the whistle to see which team gains the advantage following a foul requires experience and concentration. Good officials aid good teams; similarly, poor officials aid poor teams. A skilled and experienced official can discern the subtle fouls and know when to blow the whistle. She is able to detect offsides and obstruction that block an opponent from playing the ball. These are common fouls that frequently remain undetected by the inexperienced official. For this reason, teams that are well trained benefit from good officiating.

Early hiring of officials will improve a team's success in obtaining good officials. When hired, officials should be notified of the time, date, and location of the game; the number of games scheduled; and the telephone number of the school that is hiring (for contact in case of inclement weather). The official should supply the coach with the telephone number at which she can be reached on the day of the game.

Uniform and equipment

Undoubtedly, a feeling of unity permeates a team that is dressed uniformly. A team attired in their regulation "gym outfit" has an advantage over a team in motley disarray. A team outfitted in a tunic, kilt, or other special uniform has a decided psychological advantage over a team dressed otherwise. Since a team may gape in awe at their opponents' beautiful outfits, it is advisable for a team to select a uniform of which they will be proud.

Equipment in good repair, an ample supply of balls for practice, a goalie dressed in durable, protective equipment, and precise execution of pre-planned warm-up drills help provide the air of sophistication that accompanies a confident team. A sense of inadequacy or loss of confidence can overcome a team less well prepared. To this extent, if the opponents can establish an attacking pattern quickly and score first, a demoralizing effect on the team scored upon may become apparent. However, whatever psychological advantage is gained through smart appearance and well executed pre-game drills quickly evaporates if skillful play during the game is not evident.

Team preparation

Practice sessions should be conducted in such a manner that the coach gains the respect of her players. This is achieved by her actions, words, appearance and knowledge of the game. Discipline is an important aspect. Whatever rules and regulations are established should be strictly enforced. Tolerance of individual forgetfulness or lack of regard for rules breeds ill-feeling among those who adhere to the regulations set forth. If rules cannot be enforced, they should not be enacted. The rules that do exist must be respected by all players on the squad. Permissiveness for even one player brings resentment on the part of others. A simple matter of being late for practice, wearing the wrong colored socks to a game or failing to attend practice all tend to spread discontent and the dissolution of what might have been a promising team is near. For building a feeling of unity, there is no substitute for treating all players equally—what is fair for one is fair for all.

Discipline on the field is equally important. Demanding an optimum performance by each player trains players to perform to the best of their ability, regardless of the circumstances. Permitting a lackadaisical effort in drills or in play against a reserve squad or against weaker opponents helps cement bad habits that are difficult to correct later. It is reasonably common to see a good team that is playing a weaker opponent adopt their poor habits; whereas, against a better team, a team often rises to their level of play. It is too bad that coaches are unable to bring out the best in their players all of the time.

Prior to or at least at the start of the season, the managers should be selected and each provided with a job analysis so that their duties are clearly identified. Close supervision of the managers at the beginning of the season will help them establish the desired pattern for the entire season. The captain of the squad can provide desirable leadership during the early stages of the season as well as when games commence. If the captain is not elected until after practice is under way, it is helpful to hold the elections far enough in advance of the first match so that she can help establish an *esprit de corps.*

One objective of the early season practices should be to prepare the team both physically and mentally. A well-conducted conditioning program enables a team to maintain stamina in the last few minutes of each half. During this time, many a game is won or lost. As fatigue sets in, stickwork disintegrates and positioning deteriorates. Telltale signs of fatigue occur when the opposing halfbacks fail to back up their forward line or fail to get back on defense, or when the forwards straggle back only as far as the center line. When this occurs, every effort should be made to break through the opponent's defense for a score. What a lift the scoring team experiences and what a letdown for the opponents, particularly if they have been outplaying the other team during most of the half!

It is helpful if a coach knows the style of play of each opponent. Do they tend to crowd? Do they play one side of the field more than another? Who are the most skillful players? Who is the best defense player, the best attack player? How do the fullbacks play? In what direction does the defense tend to clear the ball? Does the attack play down one side of the field or do they swing the ball? Is the attack accustomed to being closely marked? Does the defense mark closely or loosely? Having the answers to these questions, the coach can establish intrasquad scrimmages before each match, in which one team enacts the same style of play as the opponents. In this way, both the attack and defense players become acquainted with what their opponents might do. Therefore, they may counteract their tactics more quickly once the match is under way. Football coaches have done this for years.

During the season, the squad should experience scrimmages under all types of weather and ground conditions. Fortunate is the team that has a smooth field, but their beautiful fielding may be transformed to a novice's when they play on a bumpy field with a ball that bounces rather than rolls. A pre-season scrimmage on another field might help alleviate this situation. Game play on wet fields or fields with long or heavy grass is different from play on dry and closely cut fields. Players learn several lessons as they experience these ground conditions. On bumpy fields, dribbling and fielding drives particularly may be erratic. Therefore, dribbling should be limited, and push passes should be employed to aid fielding. On long or wet grass, dribbling, dodging, and push passing should be kept to a minimum. Drives are used in passing, and the ball must be hit harder in order for it to travel the desired distance.

In summary, early season practices should prepare players to perform skills well and provide them with sufficient intrasquad practice so that they can execute stratagems during the stress of a game and under many and varied conditions.

ROLE OF THE CAPTAIN

Being named captain of the team is a high honor for any hockey player. It also is a position of great responsibility. The captain need not be the best player on the team and often is not. She is, however, the best leader. This is demonstrated by her influence on her teammates, her unselfishness, and her dedication to the game. By her actions and attitude, a team is inspired to perform at its optimum level of ability. Her friendly manner toward all and her words of praise and encouragement both during and after the game help the team achieve the togetherness that is so important for outstanding teams. She has the ability to keep team morale high. By having different players work together on committees and other tasks, she can be influential in preventing the formation of cliques, which may eventually have a negative influence on the team's play.

While participating in pre-game warm-up, the captain surveys the condition of the field in terms of bumpiness, bare spots, wet turf, and sloping ground. The information thus gained can be transmitted to the team before the game starts. These conditions and the position of the sun may influence her decision in attacking a particular goal if she wins the toss of the coin. If these factors do not seem to be detrimental to either team, she may choose to attack her team's favorite goal.

RESPONSIBILITIES—GAME DAY

When playing at home, the hostess school should attempt to make their guests feel welcome and at ease in the unfamiliar surroundings. Similarly, when a team is playing away, they should be the perfect guests (except for winning the game) and respect the hospitality and property of their hostesses. Inasmuch as several people are responsible for carrying out the details, each will be discussed separately.

Coach

For home games, the coach will check to see that the playing field is in good repair, is mowed, and lined. Prior to the game, she ascertains the current health status of the players and accordingly designates the starting lineup. She checks to see that the managers have all of the equipment needed and have carried out the rest of their responsibilities. For away games, the coach counts the number of personnel who board the bus and does a recount after the game prior to returning home. Embarrassing it is to have a student running after the bus as it pulls out of the parking lot! For home games, the coach greets the opposing coach and officials. She introduces them, directs them to dressing rooms, and invites them for refreshments after the game.

Managers

A managerial system by which the physically handicapped or unskilled but interested students can be of assistance to the squad is a valuable asset. The number of managers selected will be determined in part by the size of the squad, the number of teams that participate in competitive matches, and the number of duties assigned to the managers. Generally, two to four managers are needed.

The managers can be elected by the squad or appointed by the coach or captain. Once a manager, the individual may automatically retain her job each year or she may have to prove her merit for re-election or re-appointment the following year. Regardless, the system for advancement should be clearly delineated.

Job analyses for each manager should be formulated. Managers should maintain the equipment in good repair, including cleaning and painting balls. For home games, they should take to the field a table, chairs, set of pinnies (in case both teams wear the same color uniforms), first aid kit, game clocks and scorebook, practice balls (enough for the visitors, if needed), and at least four game balls for each game (one for each half and one for each umpire). If desired, oranges should be cut, taken to the field and served at half time to players and umpires. While waiting the arrival of the opponents, the manager(s) should stake out the door(s) through which they are most likely to enter, greet them on their arrival, and show them to the locker room. The opposing coaches and umpires are taken to the home coach for introductions. Lockers, locks, and towels are available for the visiting team.

During the game, the managers are responsible for scoring, timing, and recording statistics. The data should be compiled and collated later and posted, if desired. Following games and practices, the locker room is checked to see that all equipment is stored. For away games, the managers are responsible for taking all of the necessary equipment and returning with the same supplies. It is helpful if a number of practice balls is designated to take to each away game.

Players—pre-game

As the opponents appear on the field, the home team gives them practice balls, if needed, and half of the field for practice. Prior to the start of the game, the traditional cheer of welcome is given and as the players move to their starting positions, they shake hands with their opponents and introduce themselves.

Players and coach—during the game

Once the game is under way, it is in the hands of the players under the leadership of the captain. The manner in which the team can adjust to varying circumstances is a valuable criterion for the coach to evaluate her own teaching. How well a team is prepared in stickwork, strategy, and endurance is easily discernible.

As the game progresses, the coach can explain to players sitting beside her how particular strategy is working and how errors committed by players can be corrected. This should be done in a constructive manner for the benefit of those not playing. The coach refrains from coaching while the game is in progress, but she may find it impossible not to give words of encouragement.

Meanwhile, the players quietly challenge their opponents and try to outplay them. At half time, the players are permitted time to catch their breath before a review of the first half is made. Data are analyzed, and the players evaluate their opponents and tactics used. Finally, a review of the game plan is made and tactics altered, if indicated.

Players and coach—post-game

At the expiration of playing time, the players shake their opponent's hand and give a final cheer. Both players and coach thank the umpires for calling the game and remind them that they are invited for refreshments. The home team escorts the visiting players to the locker room, lets them shower first, and then accompanies them for refreshments. The captains or managers serve the coaches and umpires. Then each of the home team players escorts her opponent to the refreshment table. When it is time for the visiting team to depart, the home team players escort them to the door and thank them for coming. At the same time, the visitors thank their hostesses for the hospitality.

Evaluation

An objective evaluation of a player's ability (or that of a team as a whole) provides supplementary information to the coach's overall analysis of an individual's (team) play. There are numerous methods for collecting data, some of which are applicable for practices and others for both practice sessions and games.

Skill charts probably are used extensively, but they have limited value. Perhaps their greatest benefit is as a motivating device, particularly at the secondary level. On a skill chart, all of the skills are listed. As a player performs each skill adequately—not only in drills but also under game conditions—a check (✔) or other means is used to signify acceptable performance. "Passing" skills may provide added incentive for extra practice.

An incidence chart, in which all of the skills are listed, can be drawn up for each player. During a scrimmage or game, players on the sideline can be responsible for tallying the number of times each stroke is used by a player. By tallying a zero (0) for a poor performance, an estimate can be made of a player's ability with each stroke. Few tallies indicate that a player has played the ball infrequently, and the reason for this should be determined. The chart should indicate what strokes a player fails to use at all and those strokes that need improvement.

A more simple means of ascertaining whether a player is in the game can be made by tallying the number of times she plays the ball.

This technique supplies little other information and does not indicate whether the player is out of position to play the ball or what she does with it once she obtains it.

To chart team tactics and individual play as well, either of two charts can be used. The first method indicates which players are involved in each offensive movement. Each player on the team is given a number, LW-1, LI-2, CF-3, RI-4, RW-5, LH-6, LF-7, CH-8, RF-9, RH-10, and G-11. The technique used is similar to scoring in softball, in which 6–3 indicates a putout was made by the shortstop throwing to first base.

Figure 10:1 shows a chart prepared for this purpose and recordings for a portion of the first half of a game. The chart indicates that at the opening center bully, the visitor's center half intercepted and passed to her right wing (8–5). The left half of the home team intercepted and passed to the left wing. She passed to the center forward, who passed

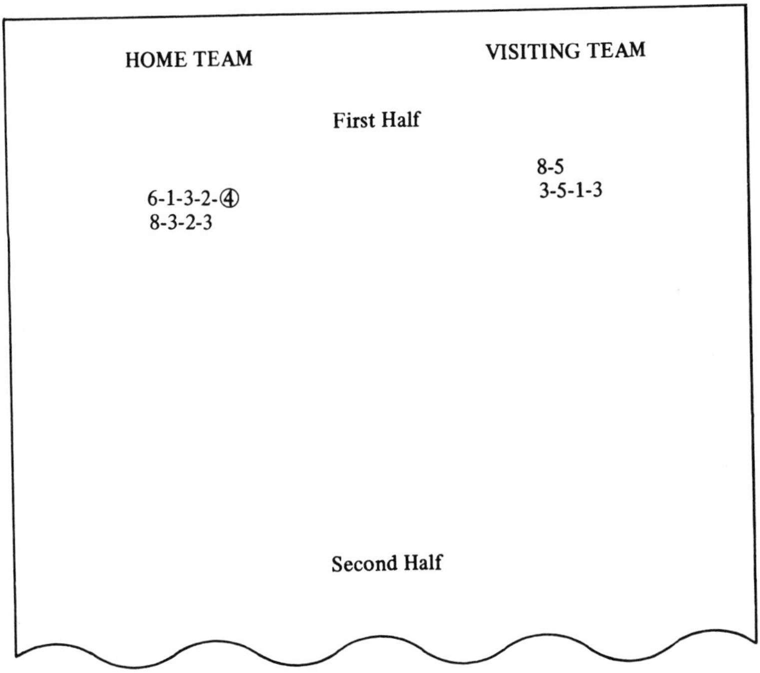

HOME TEAM	VISITING TEAM

First Half

	8-5
6-1-3-2-④	3-5-1-3
8-3-2-3	

Second Half

Figure 10:1. Play-by-play recording of game action.

to the right inner for a shot and score. (A circle around a number designates a goal is scored.) At the center bully which followed, the center passed to her right wing, who passed to her left wing, who centered the ball to the center forward. This pass was deployed by the center half, who passed to her center, who passed to her left inner, and a triangular pass was completed as the ball was returned to the center. A complete play-by-play account of the game can be recorded in this manner. Recorders need extensive practice in using this chart because the ball changes direction so quickly. It may be advisable to work in partners, with one person verbalizing the play-by-play and the other one recording; or one person may record for the home team while another person does the same for the visitors. This technique loses some of its value when play is muddled and more than two opponents attempt to play the ball at a time.

A less complicated means of recording can be done by diagramming a field and designating the direction of the offensive maneuvers as shown in Figure 10:2. This charting clearly shows whether the ball swings from one side of the field to the other and which defense player is most effective in gaining the ball. Where the offense stops also indicates at what position the turnover of the ball occurred.

Again, one person may chart for the home team and another for the visitors. Only a few offensive efforts should be recorded on each sheet; otherwise, the lines tend to blend. Each recorder should be equipped with a supply of diagrams. Colored pencils can be used to further identify each offensive maneuver. This chart also can be used for diagramming where opponents stand for free hits and rolls-in in various portions of the field.

Analysis of either of these charts at half time should provide valuable information both offensively and defensively. The team will benefit from the data collected to the extent that the coach can provide an accurate prognosis for the second half. Data gathered for an entire game can be used to compare a player's performance in a game versus that in a scrimmage or intrasquad game. Some players play much better under game conditions than in practice, whereas others tend to be influenced adversely by game pressures and play more poorly.

Evaluating the opponent's style of play and the individual ability of each player provides valuable information in preparation for a game against them the following year. Information should be collected on the players for all of the teams, including varsity and junior varsity, for members of the non-varsity squad will replace some of the varsity players in another year. Indication of the style of play is particularly important in planning game tactics. Storing the information on each

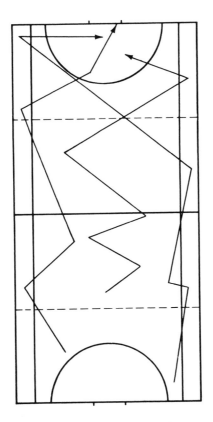

Figure 10:2. Direction of
offensive maneuvers.

team in a card file provides easy reference the following fall. Scouting a team during the season is beneficial, if time permits.

FOOTNOTES

1. "Statement of Policies for Competition in Girls and Women's Sports" (Washington: American Association for Health, Physical Education and Recreation, 1201 Sixteenth St., N.W.).

2. "Guidelines for Interscholastic Athletic Programs for High School Girls" (Washington: American Association for Health, Physical Education and Recreation, 1201 Sixteenth St. N.W.). Reprinted by permission.

3. "Guidelines for Interscholastic Athletic Programs for Junior High School Girls" (Washington: American Association for Health, Physical Education and Recreation, 1201 Sixteenth St., N.W.). Reprinted by permission.

4. Guidelines for High School Girls, *op. cit.*

5. Guidelines for Junior High School Girls, *op. cit.*

6. *Ibid.*

7. "Guidelines for Intercollegiate Athletic Programs for Women (Washington: American Association for Health, Physical Education and Recreation, 1201 Sixteenth St., N.W.). Reprinted by permission.

8. "Commission on Intercollegiate Athletics for Women: Operating Code" (Washington: American Association for Health, Physical Education and Recreation, 1201 Sixteenth St., N.W.). Reprinted by permission.

9. Ley, Katherine, "DGWS National Intercollegiate Athletic Championships for Women," *Journal of Health, Physical Education and Recreation* (Washington: 1201 Sixteenth St., N.W.), 39:2:26–28 (Feb., 1968).

XI

COACHING

by Libby Williams[1]

It is important to establish the responsibilities and philosophy of coaching before attempting to give details and suggestions for successful coaching. The coach is responsible for selecting, training, and teaching a group of hockey players to compete against other teams.

The philosophy of coaching is simple. The best trained, the best disciplined, the most skillful, and the most highly competitive team will be successful on the hockey field. Success is measured in terms of applying individual skills and cohesive team play to defeat opponents of equal experience. The goal of the coach is to produce teams that play better hockey than their opponents. Without competition, a coach is unnecessary. Teachers do an excellent job of introducing the game to classes and working with interested players in preparation for intramurals and play days. They present the opportunity for developing skills and playing the game without the emphasis on player selection and training for the purpose of winning games. But, even though there are many fine teachers, there are few experienced coaches. In many areas, players benefit from the knowledge and skill of outstanding teachers while in school or college, but never have the opportunity to advance to the national level because of a lack of competition and competent coaching. The excellent teacher often shies away from competitive coaching; without experience to rely on, she feels insecure in a coaching situation. But if the level of play is ever to improve in the United States, more teachers and experienced players will have to accept the challenge of coaching.

The coach is an individual who is striving to mold a large number of individuals into a strong, efficient unit. Her personality, knowledge, experience, and skill all play important roles in developing strong teams. Each coach must work with the individuals and the squad as a whole within the framework of her own personality and experience. No two coaches use the same approach to individuals or groups, and it is impossible to pattern your own methods after that of a "successful coach."

Qualities that are common to all successful coaches are a love of the game, a love of competition, the pleasure received from working with people, and the thrill and challenge of taking a group of individuals and molding them into a highly skilled and united team.

In hockey, as in all women's sports, coaching is not a full time job nor is it financially rewarding. Even in areas where coaches are paid, they receive less for their time and efforts than do the umpires. Coaching is hard work, but it is a thoroughly rewarding experience.

HIGH SCHOOL COACHING

The high school coach is faced with the problem of starting from scratch. Possibly some of the players reporting for practice have played on junior high school teams, whereas others have never seen a hockey stick.

Selecting the Squad

Selecting the squad members is one of the most difficult and probably the most important tasks a coach faces. She is selecting players not just for one year, but for the coming years as well. Coaching is not a one-year job; it is a building process. A strong team is not put together on the spot; it is a result of careful selection, teaching, and planning for the future.

It is a sound policy to carry a squad of from 35 to 40 players. The first two teams will be experienced and skilled players. The rest will be future teams. Selecting the first group is not difficult because a coach can judge these girls by the way they play. Selecting the future teams is a true test of judgment. There are no valid tests to determine who will develop into a good hockey player and who will not. But by careful planning and hard work, a coach tries to make as few judgment errors as possible. There are a few hints that may prove useful.

Do not make snap judgments. Have as many practices as possible before selecting the squad. Organize practices so that every girl has an opportunity to learn basic skills and to demonstrate her ability.

Even beginners will show signs of future promise. Look for speed, endurance, coördination, willingness to work, and ability to learn. Do not be blinded by speed. Look for "balance" in natural abilities. Quickness is as valuable as speed. Speed without coördination is hopeless.

Take a long second look at the physically immature girl. By comparison, the more mature girl will seem the overwhelming choice.

Remember that she may have reached the limits of her ability and by her senior year will be an also-ran. Give a physically immature girl a chance to put growth and coördination together and she may become a superb athlete.

Hockey is a full-time activity. Therefore, a team cannot develop if girls are not at practice. A girl who has violin lessons on Monday, cheerleading on Wednesday, and Dramatic Club every other Thursday will never be a hockey player.

Will this girl turn into a first team player or not? A coach will keep from 15 to 20 beginners, only six to eight of whom will ever play on the varsity team. The end of a player's first year is a better opportunity to evaluate her potential fairly. Coaches more often overestimate the potential of youngsters than underestimate. By keeping a future squad, a coach will reduce the number of judgment errors.

Before posting the list of squad members, take a good look at the girls out there on the field. There may be a girl who needs hockey more than the squad needs her. If belonging to the hockey squad will keep her in school, if it will give her the companionship, leadership, and discipline she needs, then add her name to the list.

Practice Sessions

Hockey squads are built on the practice fields. Games are won by hours of hard work in practice. Skills require hours of repetitive practice, and a sound team can only be developed through hours of scrimmage.

Each coach will have her own method of working with the squad, and few have ever tried to analyze reasons for success or mediocrity. No matter what the method used to build a strong squad, there must be hours of work, fair but clearly defined discipline, and pleasure and pride in accomplishment.

Fun and fellowship are part of any game, but they should come naturally and should take a back seat to discipline and work.

The self-confidence, self-control, and reliability of the individual and the unity of the team depend on squad discipline. Discipline is not punishment; it is a pattern of behavior that permits the individual and the group to make maximum use of practice time, gives the team the backbone it needs under game pressure, and is basic to pride of self, team, and the school represented. It takes a year or two for a coach to establish the standards. After that time, discipline is a matter of passing on the standards to each new group. The returning players easily accept the discipline as part of the game.

Long lists of rules are unnecessary. Regular attendance, promptness, paying close attention to instruction, common politeness, and respect for each other, for coaches, and for officials, and pride in conduct and appearance will be sufficient to insure squad discipline.

A coach should beware of making rules she cannot enforce. A common mistake made by coaches is to make a no-smoking rule with threat of dismissal from the squad for breaking training. All the turmoil that results when someone tells on a smoker only destroys team morale and unity. It is more effective to let hard practice sessions and wind sprints point out the inadvisability of smoking. A coach may find that the girls who smoke naturally assume that smoking is responsible for the torture of wind sprints and will give it up of their own accord. Extra wind sprints will convince any of the more persistent smokers on the squad.

Early sessions. From the first practice session until the final selection of the squad, the coach fights a losing battle of too much to do and too little time to do it. Beginners and less experienced players must receive basic instruction, and the more advanced players must be prepared for the scheduled games. Careful screening of new players must go on at the same time as replacements are found for players lost by graduation. It is not easy; but with planning and hard work, both jobs can be done.

Each practice should consist of a brief warm-up period, stickwork fundamentals, and a scrimmage period. Much time is saved if a routine is established that will last throughout the season. When practice starts, have the girls line up four deep with lines about five yards apart. Have no more than one senior girl and one junior in each line. This arrangement will put experienced players where they can help beginners and will eliminate the uncontrollable urge for socializing and fooling around. Use of these short lines has several advantages. Each girl has frequent opportunities to work. The last two in line can about face and work away from the lines, thus giving two girls a chance to work at the same time. It is not difficult to combine lines into workable groups of eight when desired. Warm-up exercises and all stickwork fundamentals can be taught and reviewed daily with this simple but expedient system of organization.

Warming up with normal calisthenics loosens kinks from previous practices, prepares muscles for the hard work ahead, and generally adds to the physical condition of the girl. A period of ten minutes is sufficient; any more is a waste of valuable time.

Running is the best all around conditioner for an athlete, and a good practice session will give any girl all the running she needs. Wind sprints of 25, 50, and 75 yards should be included at the end of the warm-up period, but aimlessly jogging laps around the field is a tradition and a waste of time. Time spent running while dribbling, receiving, and passing is time spent mastering fundamentals, whereas running laps is drudgery. Daily wind sprints (sprint 25, jog 25, sprint 50, jog 50, sprint 75, jog 75) serve as a conditioner, gives the coach an idea of each girl's speed and endurance, and impress each girl with her own need to improve both speed and physical condition. Sprints and jogging more closely approach the running during a game than do long stretches of jogging. A coach who feels that tradition must be honored, should tell her squad that they must report to the first practice ready to play and that daily running will be the best preparation. Those who ignore the advice will suffer a bit, but they soon will catch up with the help of organized sprints and hard practice sessions.

Because of the beginners in the group, stickwork must be carefully taught, and sufficient time for practice and correction allowed. By combining skills and adding new ones each day, beginners catch on rapidly and returning players have the opportunity to review and improve their stickwork. The basis of this organizational method is daily review of all skills previously learned and then the addition of one or more new skills. Since most skills can be easily combined with others, variety in the drills relieves monotony. After the second or third practice, the group can go from one drill straight into another with no time lost for reorganizing.

By mid-season, most fundamentals can be practiced effectively in a fifteen-minute stickwork session, and there will be more time for specialized practice such as corners, shooting, and rolls-in. Brief daily repetition of skills is more effective than long sessions devoted to a particular skill once or twice a season.

Dribbling, dodges, tackles, push passing, and flicks fit quite well into this organizational set-up. The one problem encountered is teaching the drive. Rather than starting beginners off with instruction on driving hard to the right and left, try giving basic instruction on hitting and stopping a ball and have the line use it for passing the ball short distances in drills combined with dribbling. Stress accuracy and control. Using a shuttle formation and drives of no more than ten yards, the drive can be introduced and combined with little difficulty. As ball control gradually improves, two lines can combine to form shuttle formations to practice longer drives to both the right and left. The stress is still on accuracy and control in driving and stopping while on the move. Long hard drives from one stationary person to another wastes time spent chasing wild drives, and also quickly destroys the confidence of a player who misses one uncontrolled drive after another.

Early practices should end with short scrimmages. Thirty minutes of scrimmage should be ample time to give all returning players an opportunity to play. It will serve to get players back into the feel of the game, relieve the monotony of stickwork drills, and give the beginners a chance to see hockey played.

These scrimmages should be coached. Beginners will benefit if explanations accompany the play. Each beginner can be assigned a specific position to watch. Through association, she will begin to pick up an idea of the game. After the second practice, choose five or six of the beginners who have shown ability and put them into the scrimmage for a short time. After the fourth practice, dismiss the advanced squad fifteen minutes early and put all of the beginners into a scrimmage. This will do little for the coach's morale, but it will be a thrill for the beginners.

Sample of early practices.

Practice I

Work from lines of 4
1. Exercises and sprints.
2. Teach the grip.
3. Teach and practice dribble—use posts and variations.
4. Teach drive and stop—use short drives for accuracy and control.
5. Combine dribble and drive in drills.
6. Teach non-stick side dodge.
7. Combine non-stick side dodge and dribble in drill.

Short scrimmage for experienced players. Teach beginners the positions and explain the rules.

Practice II

Work from lines of 4
1. Exercises and sprints.
2. Review correct grip.
3. Review dribble and practice.
4. Review drive and stop—combine with dribble in drill.
5. Review non-stick side dodge and combine with dribble in drill.
6. Teach push pass—drill.
7. Teach receiving ball from right and left—practice; combine with push pass in drill.
8. Teach stick side dodge—practice; combine with dribble and non-stick side dodge in drill.

Scrimmage—put a few of the beginning players in for a short time.

Practice III

Work in lines of 4
1. Exercises and sprints.
2. Practice dribble; then add dodges.
3. Review push pass and receiving from left and right; combine in a practice drill.
4. Teach straight tackle—practice.
5. Teach left hand lunge—practice.
6. Use lines of 8 (4 on each side) for shuttle formation to practice longer drives—stress control and accuracy.

Scrimmage—include some beginners for a few minutes.

The first two weeks of practice are demanding and tedious for a coach. She repeats and corrects until she is saying "keep two hands on that stick" in her sleep. No youngster will concentrate for two hours, and gentle reminders like a lap around the field for a varsity player will snap the others back on the ball. A coach is both teacher and selector. Her teams for the next three years need the best in teaching and judgment. She will be anxious to get rid of the "dead wood" and begin serious work with her squad. She should not be tempted to spend more time with her first two teams!

All coaches have pet idiosyncrasies that should be communicated to the players. A coach who is bothered by gum chewing should tell the girls. After two or three laps, the gum chewers will get the message and the teams will look better in practice and in games.

Squad Practices

It is a great day when the selected players report and the coach can begin to dream of the potential of this squad. A coach should let the squad in on her dreams and tell them that they are going to work longer and harder than any of their rivals. Put the new members of the squad to work making posters for each of the games and start talking hockey to the players. From now until the last whistle in November, a coach's interest, drive, and enthusiasm will set the pace for the squad.

Practice sessions are now more interesting for both players and coach. The organization remains much the same for the first part of each practice. A few exercises and wind sprints start the practice and are followed by fifteen or twenty minutes of stickwork drills. Hockey is based on stickwork, and it is important to stress needed improvement in all skills. After stickwork, the squad can be broken up into practice groups for special work. Each day this will have a new stress, but basically forwards practice receiving passes, shooting, corners, rushing, and moving on a line with the ball being centered for a shot. The halves work on tackles, passing to forwards, rolls-in, shooting, and backing up corners. The backs work on tackles, dodges, passing, and quick, hard drives. Goalies are kept busy by the shooting and corner practice.

When practicing corners against defense players, have mercy on the defense. Nothing is as exhausting or as bruising as one corner after another. Use two defensive units and have them alternate sprinting out. That will save their energy. To save their shins, teach them to go straight out with their sticks opposite the stick of their opponent and have them go on past her without stopping. The forwards will have their practice against a rushing defense, and the defense will learn to go out fast without stopping. The player who stops before she reaches the forward is the one who is badly bruised.

The scrimmage session is now longer and is the most popular part of practice for both players and coach. The teams must be molded into the strongest units possible. There are always open positions and weak positions that need help. The problem is to find the right girls for the open positions and to try to put beginners in positions that best suit their abilities.

When looking for a player to strengthen a weak position or to fill a vacancy, a coach should be open-minded and try any player if the change will improve the team. She should not hesitate to move an established player or to move a forward to defense or a defense player to forward. Players often can be outstanding in a position they never thought of trying. A line player who is a sixth forward or who has beautiful stickwork but lacks the finishing rush for goal may be a good back to strengthen the defense. Many trials will not succeed, but they are not a waste of time. When a girl tries a new position, she learns more about the game and also learns to appreciate the work being done by other players on the field.

Placing beginners in positions is not a permanent assignment. They may be moved several times before the coach decides where they best fit into positions. There are usually two or three who seem to be outstanding, and they should be tried in positions that will be open the following year. By moving these girls up to the JV, they will gain more experience and will be ready for the varsity when needed. New players are placed in accordance with their abilities and with the needs of the squad. The majority of the future group should play several positions while learning the game. They all should learn to play on both the right and the left. They should work on fundamental skills, such as receiving from left and right, and passing right and left, without regard to position.

Many school players go on to play for colleges and clubs, and their hockey experience should not be limited to one position or to one side of the field.

All of these scrimmages should be coached. They should be teaching situations. Play should be stopped whenever necessary to correct errors in judgment or in positioning. Explain both the "why" and "how" and point out the possibilities on the play. The play should be run and re-run until the players have mastered the move. They must learn positioning and the moves possible in situations, even though they have not mastered the ball control necessary to be successful each time. Through practice, ball control will improve. Do not stop play for every foul or misplay. Point out the fouls, but let play continue unless a player or the team as a whole can gain more knowledge by stopping at that point. If players on the sidelines are not working on stickwork, they should watch the play and listen to corrections.

As games approach, it is best to use the last ten or fifteen minutes of scrimmage as a game situation. Call fouls and, if corrections are necessary, make them without stopping play. Although a coach has to give her team opportunity to work together as a unit, it is important to give both the forwards and defense hard workouts against each other. The halves should be used with the forwards so that the attack will be sustained and so that the backs and goalie will be under constant pressure.

It is advisable to arrange at least one practice game against another school before regular games. Stage fright is common to inexperienced young players, and the sight of strange faces and uniforms may make them forget which way they are going. Both teams will benefit from the experience of having played a full game under game conditions, including good officiating. It will give players needed experience and it will give the coach the opportunity to see her players against equal competition. It is hard to judge a team realistically when they play against less talented players every day. The practice game may show both the strengths and weaknesses that the coach has overlooked.

When preparing the team for a game, the coach should tell the players all that she knows about the team from previous years. Invariably, the style will be the same, unless a coaching change has been made. Some teams hang back on defense, some have backs that play square, some forward lines depend on one player, and some teams have extraordinary speed and power but lack stickwork. Tell them what they will face and possible solutions. Above all, be sure that they respect the abilities of their opponents and have confidence in their own team.

The day before the game should vary from other practice sessions.

There should be stickwork as a warm-up and then a short period of specialized practice, such as corners and shooting for goal. Scrimmage should be hard but shorter than usual. Dismiss practice early. Before the first game, it is wise to call a brief meeting after practice has been stopped. Remind the players that they represent the school and that they should display the highest standards of sportsmanship and conduct. They must fulfill their obligations as hostesses or guests, as the case may be. Explain that it is equally important to be as gracious in victory as in defeat. It is not easy to control the excitement, tension, and fatigue, but that is part of the game and the coach wants to be as proud of their behavior as she is of their hockey ability.

On game day, try to stay out of the way of the managers (no coach should be without them) and have faith that the team will remember some of the hockey they have been taught. Concentrate on watching positioning and over-all play. Look for the strengths and weaknesses of both teams and give this information to the team at half time. Tell individual players the mistakes they must correct and commend them for good play. Talk to the attack as a whole and to the defense, reviewing basic theories and pointing out opportunities that are presented. Show your confidence in their ability to play the game, prod them if they need it, and then leave them to talk it over among themselves. If they win the game, start them thinking of their next opponent. If they lose, point out the over-all weaknesses that can be corrected in preparation for the next game. Once the game is over, win or lose, the coach and her players take what they have learned and go to work preparing for future games. Rehashing mistakes and causes for a loss destroys both individual confidence and team morale. Prolonged congratulations and celebrations give any team an overrated opinion of its ability and lessens their striving for improvement and their eagerness to work. The whole season is an uphill pull. A coach is always striving for a higher degree of individual skill and teamwork. The team should never become satisfied. They always should see the need for work and improvement. A loss or two indicates the need for work. It is harder for a coach to keep prodding an unbeaten team with an emphasis on continued improvement.

While playing out the season, continue to build for the future. Keep a close watch on the younger players, and constantly evaluate the progress shown by the individual in comparison with others in the group. Work hard on possible replacements for the seniors on the squad. Always prepare for the future while working with the present team. Do not overestimate the importance of the won and lost record of the junior varsity. The purpose of that team is to give players as much instruction and experience as possible in the short season. Do not limit this team to eleven or twelve players. Give all those who show promise a chance to play. What really counts is the development of the skills of these younger players, not the number of games won.

COLLEGE COACHING

College coaches are faced with the same problems as the high school coach, but they deal with more mature girls.

The coach must face a mixed group of beginners and advanced players and try to attain even a higher level of skill than is reached by school teams. The selection and development of a strong squad, the organization of practice and building for the future are still the keys to success. Although more advanced hockey often can be taught, the system of coaching does not vary sufficiently to warrant repetition.

COACHING ASSOCIATION PRACTICES

Each year, hockey associations are faced with the problem of finding someone to coach their teams. Associations often have school or college coaches as members, but these people are reluctant to accept the responsibility of coaching adults. Former players are willing to help at one or two practices, but do not want to give up every weekend. Active players cannot play and coach and be successful at both. The United States Field Hockey Association will send an excellent coach upon request, but she will be available for only a short period of time.

Faced with these problems, association officers try to plan their schedule using the volunteers and visiting coaches whenever possible. Sometimes each member of the selection committee is asked to coach one practice. When no outside help is available, the officers must organize the practices.

The obvious need is for a coach who is willing to work all season. A sounder coaching program is possible when there is carry-over in the instruction from week to week. A regular coach has the definite advantage of knowing the players and of working for the progressive improvement of individuals and the group.

Each association has members who are quite capable of assuming the responsibilities of a coach. These members are experienced hockey players, some of whom have taught hockey for years in schools or colleges. Many have attended hockey camps and have had the opportunity to observe fine coaches. It is a shame to waste this valuable experience. Associations should encourage these members to try coaching. Coaching is a rewarding experience; it is a way to make a definite contribution to the association when playing days are over.

The association can help their prospective coach by sending her to hockey camp. The established camps have always been interested in helping coaches, and many of the staff members are willing to give detailed assistance to a new coach. Hockey camps also will bring the coach up to date on the style of hockey (theories of attack and defense) that is now being used by sectional and national teams.

The coaching situation will vary in different associations. The following suggestions for schedules, games, and practices will have to be adapted to meet the particular needs of the group that is to be coached.

The Schedule

The hockey season is short, and the demands on the limited time are great. Games, umpiring clinics, selection, and rain can greatly reduce the number of practices. A coach cannot do much about the rain, but it may be possible to arrange practices along with the games and the clinics. It also may be possible to use games and the final weeks of selection for coaching. The purpose is to improve the hockey, and a coach should take advantage of every opportunity.

Games

Scheduled games with other associations should be used to develop interest, to give the better players equal competition, and to build the strongest team for later tournaments.

On game days, try to schedule two or three games so that everyone will have the opportunity to play. The association will lose players if they come out and sit. If there are players who will not play in the games, schedule an hour of practice for them before the game, ask the more skilled players to come and fill in if needed. A coached scrimmage and a hard session of drills will help these inexperienced players. If two teams are scheduled to play away, be sure to plan a full afternoon of stickwork, coached play, and a squad game for those not selected to go. This is one of the few opportunities that a coach has to concentrate her attention on these players. It will help their hockey and, equally important, will demonstrate that they are part of the program and not just leftovers.

When visiting teams come to play, be sure to analyze the play of both teams carefully. A team will need to know the weaknesses and strength of their opponents as well as their own. Half time is not long enough to teach hockey but weaknesses in positioning, over-use of players, and halfback support of the line can be pointed out. These games should be learning situations. They are an opportunity for a coach to watch her players under pressure of equal competition. Have the team meet briefly after the game to go over weaknesses of the attack and defense. If individuals have shown weaknesses in particular skills, suggest that they try to put in several hours of practice on their own during the week. Usually the fault is poor technique, and it will help to take the time to demonstrate and have the player do it correctly several times so that she will not practice doing it wrong.

Ask the visiting team to play one period (after the game) with players from the first and second team equally mixed. This will give the second team players a chance to play a better level of hockey. It also will give them incentive to keep working. To know that "once a second team player, always a second team player" makes hockey a much less attractive pastime for many girls.

Practices. Association practices are like high school practices in that players will range from beginners to experienced players. But unlike high school or college, the personnel may vary greatly from practice to practice. Encouraging players to attend regularly and pointing out the advantages of regular attendance to the individual and to the group may improve attendance. If the sessions are challenging and if all players have equal opportunity to participate, a coach's chances of seeing the same faces greatly improve.

The practices can be conducted like any school practice, but much more must be presented and hopefully accomplished because of the limited number of practices available.

To expedite learning, divide the groups into lines of four across the field. Have experienced players and beginners in each line. Ask two of the better players to help several of the lines.

Assume nothing! Teach, demonstrate, practice, and review. Insist on proper grip, good footwork, and ball control. So many players have established poor habits and are reluctant to change. Ball control is a must!

The drills need not be fancy or complicated. One half hour spent reviewing all the fundamentals by combining them in drills should be sufficient after the first practice. The next half hour can well be spent on specialized practice for forwards, halves, backs, and goalies. Show each group the work they are expected to do and then leave the most capable member to assist the others while moving from group to group.

The emphasis for each group can be changed several times during this practice period to relieve monotony and to cover more skills.

During the first practice, it is wise to take the entire group to one goal for a demonstration of corners, explaining fundamentals for both defense and forwards. Stress accurate, hard hits by the wings, controlled stops and quick drives by inside forwards, and the absolute necessity of a rushing forward line supported by the halves. Stress the importance and the safety factor of the defense players going out fast with the stick down opposite the opponent's stick and the importance of going all the way out. Experienced players are generally guilty of going three quarters of the way out and stopping dead in their tracks. Have the demonstration group take repeated corners while pointing out necessary corrections. Then send half the players to the other goal to practice, giving each player a chance to work.

After the first session, a short time should be given to corner practice each week. Have beginners and experienced players in each group, as the beginners will learn more rapidly this way.

For the first two or three practices, the majority of the scrimmages should be coached play. Without officials, and with play continuing as much as possible, corrections in positioning and judgment can be made. When you stop play, be sure to offer corrections and possibilities to all players and not just to one girl.

Quickly check the positioning of all players on the field; check the marking and covering of the defense; be sure that the forwards without the ball have come back quickly to help; show the forwards on attack where they would be most useful at that moment. It sounds like a lot of ground to cover, but a coach who knows the game will be aware of all these points and can quickly make the corrections. All players on the field should feel that the coach knows exactly where they are and where they should be at every moment. There will be 100 percent effort and concentration by all players, even those far out of play, if they know that the entire field is under scrutiny. Do not concentrate corrections or advice on one player. Let the entire group know what should have happened and their responsibility at the moment. Individual help can be given as play goes on or after the scrimmage. Keep the entire group working, thinking hockey, and on their toes.

Do not let selectors enter into these early practice sessions. Try to combine teams so that beginners will have the opportunity to play with better players at least part of the time. It is an impossible chore to meet all the needs, but remember that the coach is there to teach the game to all the players who come out to practice. She is not going to perform miracles, but if each girl has an equal opportunity to practice and learn, a coach has done her best.

As the season progresses, the practices should devote less time to organized stickwork and more time to coached play and actual periods of officiated game play. The stickwork will be a review and a warm-up; the specialized practice will be used to meet obvious needs of the attack and the defense; the coached play will be primarily the same but with greater demands for fewer mechanical errors and the emphasis on achieving a higher standard of play; the game periods will be longer and will be used to find the best combinations and to develop teamwork.

Selection must now be faced. Once again, a compromise must be made. The selectors will select, and the coach will coach. Have the selectors divide the players into teams, and coach these teams for twenty-minute periods. They will have hundreds of things to try, but insist on twenty-minute periods without substitutions. Nothing is accomplished by either coach or selectors when players are shuttled in and out. They will want to see uninterrupted play, so use half of the practice for coaching their dream teams and then let them use game play for the rest of the practice. Keep a close watch to see that all of the players have a fair opportunity. A coach has worked hard on the less talented, and this is no time to have them discouraged or humiliated. If a second field is available, continue coached sessions with players not being used at the moment. If some players are obviously on the "out" list, try to schedule a game for them before the regular season starts. Ask players from the "in" group to fill in where needed. Ask one or two of the selectors to come an hour early to watch. They may not see anything, but they will be seen and that is what counts.

It helps to show the association officers the wisdom of having the coach serve as a member of the Selection Committee. The coach attends every practice, has worked with every player, and her ultimate goals are much the same. A coach can evenly divide the talent for the coached session on the first day the Committee meets. Let the Committee pick the players from the group. It should keep them busy and will give every girl at least one good chance to demonstrate her ability.

Selections are a necessary evil. They open the door to great opportunities for some players and they completely destroy the pleasure of the game for others. No matter how carefully and wisely the teams are selected, there will be players who feel slighted. This is unavoidable. The coach can help by pointing out the skills that need improvement and by emphasizing the pleasures received from playing the game. Not everyone is cut out to move up to Sectional hockey. If players feel that they have received good coaching, have improved their skills, have had an equal opportunity, and have enjoyed the hours spent at hockey, they will not drop out because of selections. Realistic self-appraisal is never easy, but the coach is in the best position to help with suggestions for improvement, a fair evaluation, and encouragement.

SUMMARY

Coaching on any level is a great challenge and a thrill. It requires hours of thought, careful planning and a fair amount of worrying. Discouraging moments come often, but one beautifully executed play makes them worthwhile. There are long hours of hard work and there are exhausting games when a coach mentally and physically seems to be playing all eleven positions. Above all, there is the thrill of watching the team that you have built play with skill, finesse, and heart.

FOOTNOTE

1. Libby Williams is recognized as one of the outstanding coaches of our time. She has coached at the high school level, at hockey camps, and most recently was selected to coach the 1967 United States Touring Team. She also has organized and directed an invitational hockey camp for advanced players. She gained playing experience as a member of the Philadelphia Sectional team, the United States and Reserve teams, and the Touring Team to South Africa (1950) and to Australia and New Zealand (1956). She received her B.S. and M.S. degrees from the University of Pennsylvania and currently is teaching at the Plymouth Whitemarsh High School in Pennsylvania.

XII

EQUIPMENT AND THE FIELD

Quality equipment can be purchased through suppliers specializing in hockey equipment. Purchasing equipment through local sporting goods stores is not alway good economy unless, of course, they stock quality merchandise. Most topflight players prefer imported equipment, which is found infrequently in general sporting goods stores.

STICKS

Probably the two most important features of a stick are the length and the "feel" of the stick to the player. At the secondary level and higher, 35–38 inch sticks are common, with the 35- and 36-inch sticks in greatest demand. For junior players (upper elementary grades), 30–34-inch sticks should be purchased.

The "feel" of the stick is determined by its weight and balance. Sticks can be purchased in 17, 18, or 19 ounces. Some sticks are evenly balanced, whereas others have more of the weight in the head of the stick. In selecting a stick, a player should take her grip and swing the stick back and forth. The stick should feel comfortable to her and just brush the grass. Too long a stick causes a player to hit behind the ball, and too short a stick causes topping, limits a player's reach, and causes her to bend considerably.

When purchasing hockey sticks, 35- and 36-inch sticks should be ordered in approximately equal numbers. Very few 37- and 38-inch sticks are needed. For an initial purchase of twenty-four sticks, about ten 35-inch, ten 36-inch, three 37-inch, and one 38-inch stick should be purchased. If students are unusually tall, the proportion of 37- and 38-inch sticks should be increased. An equal number of 17- and 18-ounce sticks should be purchased for the 35- and 36-inch sticks, and 19 ounces may be preferred for the 37- and 38-inch sticks. When expanding the hockey program, sticks should be purchased in about the same proportion unless knowledge suggests otherwise.

In quality sticks, the grain of the wood follows the line of the toe, the handle is made of cane identified by the large number of little holes at the top of the handle, and there are three rubber inserts in the handle. Cheaper sticks have only one or two inserts that limit the flexibility of the stick and also absorb less of the vibration from hard drives. This is particularly noticeable on cold days.

Sticks come with either an English toe, which is rather long, or the Indian toe, which is short and chubby. Although the English toe was preferred by most players 10–15 years ago, more recently the Indian toe has gained favor because of the better control it provides. Good players contact the ball at the heel of the stick, and the extra length provided by the English toe is unnecessary and often cumbersome. The only disadvantage to the Indian toe is that the reach is limited on a reverse stick stop.

Care

Hockey wax (beeswax) should be applied to the stick at the start of the season and periodically during the season to prevent moisture from penetrating the grain. Whenever the stick becomes damp, it should be wiped dry. Towels should be provided near the storage area for this purpose. Dampness causes the stick to fray. If this happens, the stick should be sandpapered immediately. If repair is delayed, the stick may splinter and it may be necessary to shave the splintered end with a knife. The shaving motion must be done toward the open end to prevent further splintering. After the splinter is trimmed, the stick should be sanded. Warm weather causes the rubber grips to dry out and disintegrate. The rubber grips and a grip applicator may be purchased inexpensively and new grips applied when necessary. Waxed string applied to the top of the grip prevents the grip from sliding down the stick. The string is similar to that used on golf clubs and can be purchased at local sporting goods stores.

Storage

Both during the season and following, the sticks should be stored so that they are separated. Storage in a barrel so that students have to tug to pull one out is uneconomical, as the grips and toe of the stick become damaged during the rough handling. If possible, a rack should be constructed so that the sticks may stand upright and be separated by nails (or other means) at the top and bottom. The place for each stick can be numbered, the sticks numbered and each set in the appropriate place. Students in each class then can sign up for the stick they want and locate it easily.

At the end of the season, steel wool should be applied to remove dirt and grass stains. The sticks should be sanded, waxed, and stored in a cool, dry place.

BALLS

Various quality balls are available. The lowest grade are practice balls, which tend to chip easily and do not have the "feel" of a regulation ball. If purchased, they should be painted red or orange to distinguish them from other types of balls so that they are not used during game play or goalie practice because of their tendency to bounce abnormally. The Chingford ball is a highly economical ball. It may be used during practice sessions or for game play. Because of its plastic cover, it does not absorb moisture and therefore is good on damp or wet grounds. The ball is inexpensive and easily cleaned with soap and water. It should not be painted, as the paint chips off. The leather covered ball or Tugite ball (chrome leather) are both official balls. From a player's point of view, they are the most desirable kind, but they are expensive and need constant upkeep. After each use, they need an application of a quick drying lacquer paint. Only a light coat should be applied, and frequent use of a paint remover helps to retain the normal shape of the ball. Otherwise, the paint chips unevenly and the shape of the ball is distorted. A ball painting rack can be constructed out of a piece of wood with three nails angled into it for the placement of each ball to dry. To expedite the painting process, paint can be poured into a pail, and a coat hanger (or stronger metal) can be bent so that the ball can be grasped at the end. In this way, the ball can be dipped into the paint, permitted to drip, and then placed on the rack to dry. Pudding balls may be purchased for indoor use or old balls may be covered with a cloth material or sock.

Storage

Balls can be stored in ball bags or metal baskets. The latter provides easier access for student use. Leather balls tend to crack if stored in a hot place. For this reason, only enough leather balls to last through the season should be purchased annually.

SHIN GUARDS

The use of shin guards by all players is psychologically sound. They reduce or eliminate fear and prevent serious leg injuries. Shin guards are made of canvas with cane or reed rib inserts. They fasten snugly around the ankle and leg with leather straps. The buckles should go on the outside of the leg to prevent snagging. Plastic shin guards to insert under knee socks also are available, but are seldom used. A high quality shin guard will give good service.

Care

A whisk broom can be used to keep shin guards free of mud. They should be dried thoroughly before storing. The leather straps can be re-stitched if they become unsewn. When the canvas becomes worn, there is little that can be done to improve it. Before discarding unusable shin guards, remove the straps for future repairs.

Storage

Shin guards can be stored on a flat surface. Mates should be buckled together so that pairs can be distinguished. Keep in a cool, dry place.

SHOES

A cleated shoe provides good traction and permits a player to change direction, stop, and start quickly. Cleats are particularly advantageous when the field is damp, as they prevent or at least decrease the amount of slipping. Black canvas shoes with rubber cleats molded to the sole are common. Recently, a lightweight leather shoe with leather cleats has become popular among United States players. They offer greater support of the foot and can be waterproofed.

Care

Use of a whisk broom will remove dirt from the canvas shoe. Shoe soap and polish will keep the leather shoe clean and waterproof. The cleats should be kept clean of mud and grass for both styles of shoes.

DRESS

Neat, feminine costumes such as kilts, tunics, double knit nylon blouses, and shorts are popular on the hockey field. Not only do they give the players freedom of movement, but they also are attractive in appearance. During cold weather, players should be dressed appropriately—gloves (not mittens), knee socks or tights, sweaters, and if the ground is frozen, tennis shoes may provide better traction than the cleated shoe. Water repellent jackets may be worn in wet weather.

PINNIES

Pinnies of distinctive colors to distinguish teams should be available for every practice session and game. They should be long enough—extending below the waistline in front and back—so that they do not blow up into a player's face. When teaching beginners, it may be desirable to use pinnies with lettered positions to better identify players on the field. The letters can be placed on the pinnies with a marking pen, iron-on tape, or other means.

FIRST AID

Emergency first aid supplies should be on hand for every practice session and game. The teacher/coach would be wise to investigate carefully the laws in her state relative to first aid treatment and the care of injured students. The teacher should have immediate access to a telephone, and in the public schools should have a list of the home and business telephone of the parents and the name of each student's family physician. The name and number of the school doctor should be available. At the college level, the teacher should be familiar with the policies of the college and her department in giving first aid and the services that are available through student health. Every teacher should know where emergency ambulance service can be obtained. Although hockey is not a dangerous game, accidents do occur sometimes, and teachers must be aware of the proper procedures to follow.

GOALKEEPER EQUIPMENT

Goal pads are available in various sizes to outfit the junior and the adult player. Care is needed to order the appropriate size. The goalkeeper's pads cover her thigh, leg, and instep. There are two or three rolls at the knee to permit mobility. The pads should be fastened snugly to the leg with the buckles on the outside. Kicking pads or kickers may be purchased to give added protection to the instep and ankle. The more expensive styles have a partial sole, and the others fit over the instep and ankle of the shoe. A sturdy, leather shoe with cleats and a boxed toe is worn. The shoe should be large enough to allow an extra pair of wool socks. Sponge rubber may be inserted in the shoe to give added protection at the ankle and instep. The goalkeeper should be dressed warmly. Slacks or a warm-up suit may be appropriate for her throughout the season. Reaction times of players who are cold are slower than those who are warm. Goalies may wish to investigate the use of the battery-warmed socks and gloves.

Care

Proper care of the goalkeeper's equipment is similar to that of the other players' equipment. Her pads and shoes should be kept clean. The goalie may even wish to paint her pads white occasionally during the season to draw the attention of the opposing forwards. It may keep them from looking for other parts of the goal!

THE FIELD

A field hockey field is 100 yards long and 60 yards wide. The longer lines are the *sidelines* and the shorter lines, the *goal lines*. The center line should be a solid line, dividing the field into two equal parts. The 25-yard lines (always placed 25 yards from the goal lines) should be dotted throughout their length. A similar dotted line should be marked five yards from and parallel to the sidelines. It is to be known as the *five yard line;* the area it and the sideline enclose is called the *alley*. A mark not to exceed twelve inches in length should be placed on each five yard line parallel to the goal line and fifteen yards from its inner edge. The field also is marked on each goal line five and ten yards from each goal post. The ten-yard mark identifies the spot from which penalty corner hits are taken. The five-yard mark identifies the distance that the defense players must remain from the player taking the corner hit.

Striking circles are marked at each goal line. A line is drawn four yards long and three inches wide, parallel to and sixteen yards from the goal line. The line is continued each way to meet the goal line by quarter circles having the goal posts as the center.

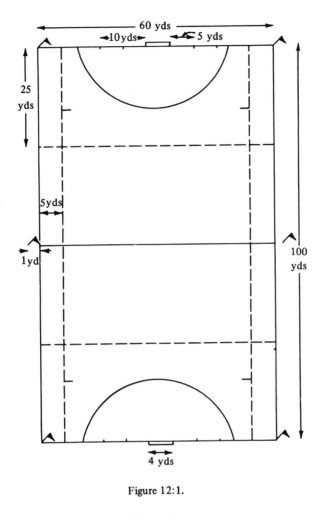

Figure 12:1.

The Field

The hockey field should be free of holes, stones, glass, and other obstructions, and it should be level. The grass should be clipped short, and the field marked often enough to keep the lines visible.

Flags

Flags made from a bright colored cloth and attached to dowels (at least four feet high) should be placed at each corner of the field. They help players and umpires in locating the corners. Also, a flag should be placed at the center of each sideline at least one yard outside the sideline.

GOALS

A *goal* consists of two perpendicular posts four yards apart joined together by a horizontal bar seven feet from the ground (inside measurement). It is placed in the center of each goal line. The front of the goal posts touch the outer edge of the goal line. The goal posts must not extend beyond the crossbar nor the crossbar beyond the goal posts. Nets are attached firmly to the goal posts and crossbar and to the ground behind the goals.

Goals and nets can be purchased from a hockey equipment supplier, but they are expensive. They can be constructed more cheaply by using 2″ × 3″'s to make the frame. Two uprights 7′ high and a horizontal crossbar 4′ wide are attached. Four to six feet back, two other uprights and crossbar are attached and connected to the front posts by horizontal bars along the ground and level with the top of the uprights. A horizontal bar along the ground is attached to the two rear uprights. The front uprights and horizontal bar are painted white, and the frame is enclosed with tarred golf nets, fish nets, tennis nets, or metal fencing.

The goals can be constructed so that they rest on the surface of the ground and are movable, or the front uprights may be 6″–8″ longer so that they may be lowered into the ground. The extension of the uprights should be treated with tar or wood conditioner to prevent the wood lowered in the ground from rotting. For better protection, the frame can be lowered into metal tubing inserted in the ground. Metal caps can be placed over the tubing when the goals are stored during the winter.

XIII

RAINY DAY SUGGESTIONS

Every teacher/coach welcomes an occasional rainy day during the season. It provides an opportunity to reinforce information presented out-of-doors, a chance to introduce new rules and strategy, and time to practice stickwork. Time spent indoors can be time well spent, if planned and used wisely. Nonetheless, frequent rainy days do tax one's ingenuity!

STICKWORK

If stickwork practice is desired, a regulation gymnasium will accommodate approximately 40 students rather easily. Students should be cautioned to move at a moderate speed, and drills should be planned with care so that they are safe. Columns, rows, and shuttle formations probably offer maximum use of space and safety when drills involve much running. Old balls can be covered with a cloth material to decrease their speed and to protect the gymnasium floor. Some suggestions follow.

Footwork

1. Scattered; no balls necessary. Players move as the instructor points left, right, forward, or back. Emphasize sticks held away from the body and close to the floor.
2. Scattered. Each player has a ball. Players tap the ball to the left and back to the right. The feet move constantly, and the ball is never permitted to the side of the feet. Prohibit use of the reverse stick.
3. Columns; no balls necessary. Run forward and swerve to the left as if to receive a pass from the right or to start a circular tackle.
4. Columns; each player with a ball. Dribble a few times, pull the ball to the left, dribble forward, and repeat. Emphasize the quick pull to the left. Players in each column may start as soon as there is space ahead.

Dribble

1. Columns. Placing the left hand only on the stick, dribble to the other end of the gym.
2. Columns; place four or five Indian clubs in front of each column. With the left hand only on the stick, players dribble around the Indian clubs.
3. Same as No. 2 above, except players dribble around Indian clubs with both hands on the stick.
4. Circles of eight players. Individually, players dribble clockwise in and around the players forming the circle. Substitute Indian clubs or tin cans for the players, so that more students can perform at the same time.
5. Scattered. Each player with a ball. Players make circles by dribbling clockwise in a limited space. Emphasize making a small circle with the ball and a larger one with the feet.
6. Two columns four to five feet apart. Last players in each line alternate and dribble between the columns to the head of the group; next player starts as soon as there is space. (This drill teaches players to keep the ball in front of the body rather than to the side.)
7. Scattered; each player with a ball. Players side-step to the left and back to the right and keep the ball at all times between their feet. Do not permit use of the reverse stick.
8. Scattered; each player with a ball. Players dribble in any direction they wish. Discourage everyone moving in the same direction. (Teaches ball control and improves dodging ability.)

Passing and Receiving

1. Circle or line of six players with a leader. The leader starts with a ball and pushes a pass to each player in turn. Change leaders.
2. Circle of six players with a leader. Players in circle pass (push) to one another and the leader attempts to intercept. When successful, she exchanges places with the passer.
3. Shuttle formation with one column to the right of the other one. Players use push pass. Emphasize stop and push; no dribbling. Change, so passes are made both to the right and to the left.
4. Shuttle; start groups as far apart as possible. Player dribbles and then drives to teammate. Continue. Change so that drives are hit both to the right and to the left.

5. Columns with a retriever. Place two Indian clubs a designated distance apart. Each player in turn dribbles and pushes the ball between the Indian clubs. Pass to the right and left.

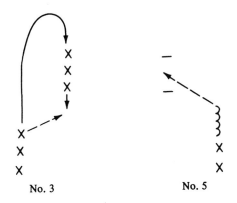

No. 3   No. 5

6. Columns with a retriever. Place an Indian club or tin can in front or to the side of the column. How many times can each player hit the object?

7. Line on each side of the gym; one ball for every member of one line. Players drive to the stick side of the person opposite them. Later drive to the non-stick side. Emphasize moving behind the ball to field it.

8. Partners; one ball per couple. Players pass to each other while moving the length of the gym. Later have each partner intentionally pass behind her teammate, causing her to go back to field the pass. Emphasize correct fielding and eliminating obstruction. Later pass ahead of partner so that she must accelerate and reach for the pass.

9. Partners, with one player standing several yards in front of her partner and facing the same direction. One player serves as a defense player and the other as an attack; both are on the same team. The defense player starts with the ball and passes to the forward, who runs back to receive the pass. Have the attack player practice fielding from the left and right sides.

10. Two lines 20 yards apart; five or six players in each line. Place an Indian club in the center. Each player may have a ball, or fewer balls may be used. On signal, every player with a ball attempts to knock down the Indian club. One point is awarded to the team that is successful. Play a game of ten points.

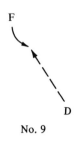

No. 9

11. Two lines 20 yards apart; five or six players in each line. Place a ball in the center. Players in each line number off for a game similar to Steal the Bacon. As the instructor calls a number, one player from each team goes to the center and attempts to push the ball over the opponent's goal line (where the other players are standing).

12. Same description and formation as No. 11 above except place the lines farther apart and call out two to four numbers so that players can use teamwork to advance the ball. Permit players to get into groups to discuss strategy before starting, if desired.

13. Columns with a leader to the left and facing the same direction. Supply the leader with several balls. The leader passes the ball diagonally ahead to the first player in the column. She fields it, dribbles a few times, turns to her right, and dribbles back to the end of the column. Change leaders and repeat with the leader to the right of the column.

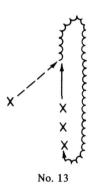

No. 13

14. Columns of three or four players stand behind a line 10–15 feet from a wall. Each player in turn counts the number of hits made against the wall in 30 seconds.

15. Same description as No. 14 above, except a vertical line is placed on the wall at the intersection of the floor and wall. Players start to the right of the vertical line and hit the ball to the left of it, retrieve the ball and hit to the right of the line. Players must remain behind the starting line throughout. Each player counts the number of hits made in 30 seconds.

Dodges

1. Circles of five or six players with a shallow box in the center. Each player has a ball and attempts to scoop it into the box. The first circle with 10 successful scoops wins.
2. Shuttle formation with groups separated as far as possible. Place a chair in the center of the gym. First player dribbles up to the chair and does a right dodge around it and drives to the first person in the opposite group. She dribbles to the chair and does a left dodge around the chair and drives to the opposite column. Players go to the end of the other group. In this way, players attempt both dodges.

Tackles

1. Pairs. The player with the ball dribbles toward her partner, who attempts a straight tackle. Exchange places. Later, let the attack player attempt a dodge or quick acceleration to evade the tackler.
2. Scattered; each player with a ball. Each player dribbles clockwise in a circular pattern. Emphasize a large circle with the feet and a small one with the ball. (This is a lead-up to and practice for the circular tackle.)

GAMES

1. Teams of five to seven players. Play a game lengthwise in the gymnasium, designating an area to represent the striking circle (keyhole area or the free throw line on the basketball court).
2. Two teams are formed (any number of players), and each team stands on one sideline and the end line to its right (around a basketball court). The entire end line can serve as the goal or it can be limited to the keyhole or other designated area. Four to six players from each team start on the court and play. When a goal is scored or after a certain time period, new teams go onto the court. (Use rules similar to line soccer.)

RULES

An explanation, interpretation, and demonstration of fouls can give students an understanding of how they can be avoided. Use of a blackboard or magnetic board is helpful in explaining the boundaries of the field, out-of-bounds plays, and penalties for fouls. A thorough explanation of the rules with time for questions and discussion may take several class periods.

Explain and demonstrate

(using students, if desired).

1. Sticks and method of fielding the ball above the shoulder.
2. Obstruction and how to avoid the foul.
   a. How a forward should receive a pass from another forward.
   b. How a forward should receive a pass from one of her defense players.
   c. Defensive tackling—when a circular tackle is necessary.

Explain and discuss

(using blackboard or magnetic board).

1. Offsides.
   a. At midfield and approaching the striking circle.
   b. Hazards in the striking circle.
2. Penalties for fouls.
   a. Free hit.
   b. Corner.
   c. Penalty corner.
3. Out-of-bounds plays.
   a. Rolls-in.
   b. Defense hits.
   c. Corners.
4. Penalty bully

Rule bee

Divide students into two teams (or more). Alternate teams and ask a question of each player. A correct answer by a player scores a goal for her team.

STRATEGY

In terms of strategy, there is a myriad of ideas that can be formulated. The reason for forwards to remain in their "railroad tracks" and defense players to mark or cover their own opponent should be clearly demonstrated with the use of the blackboard or magnetic board. Marking, covering, square, and flat passes, the coöperation between the two fullbacks, the shifting of the halves in on the inner when the ball is on the opposite side of the field, and other aspects of the game can be shown. If students then have an opportunity to try to use the information, their chance of gaining a clear understanding of it is improved. For this purpose, the following technique may be helpful.

A table is used and each student is supplied with an object to serve as a player, such as a toy soldier, chess piece, domino, or piece of paper. The students form two teams, and each student, preferably, plays her own position. The instructor identifies a specific situation, and each student places her player on the table in the correct position. The positioning of each player on both teams is evaluated and corrected, if necessary, before the teacher cites the next situation. The students reposition the players, and the process continues.

In more advanced classes, each student can be given objects for players of two teams. Each student then finds a spot on the floor (in the gymnasium, classroom, or locker room) and maps out her field. She places players of both teams on the field as the teacher indicates the situation. After each student has had time to arrange her players, all should have the opportunity to see how they *should* be placed. They can gather around one student as the teacher (or students) evaluates the position of the players and corrects, if necessary. Then each student should be given time to go back to her own players and place them in the correct position. A new situation can be identified and the process repeated.

Explain, with the use of a magnetic board or blackboard, followed by students placing players (objects provided) in position for each of the following:

1. Beginning forwards staying in their own area—analogy with railroad tracks.
2. The covering position of the fullbacks and halfbacks in midfield.
3. Positioning of the halfbacks backing up near the attacking striking circle.

4. Positioning of the defense marking in the circle.
5. Positioning of the defense when a free forward approaches the striking circle.
6. Positioning of the forwards in relation to the ball when the opponents have the ball—show what happens when forwards tackle back on opposing forwards.
7. How forwards can make spaces.
   a. For the center and inners.
   b. For the wings.
8. The placement of passes.
   a. Giving a square pass if the opponents are covering the space.
   b. Giving a through pass if the opponents are marking.
9. Positioning of forwards in circle play—rushing the goal and pulling back on sides.
10. Positioning on free hits for attack and defense players.
    a. In the defensive end.
    b. In midfield.
    c. Near the attacking striking circle.
11. Positioning on corners.
    a. Attack players.
    b. Defense players.
12. Positioning on a roll-in for attack and defense players.
    a. In the defensive end.
    b. In midfield.
    c. Near the circle.

If, after all of this, it is still raining—lots of luck!

APPENDIX
OUTSTANDING PLAYERS IN
UNITED STATES FIELD HOCKEY

UNITED STATES TEAM PLAYERS

As in any sport in which "all-star" teams are selected, there are certain players who demonstrate their outstanding ability over the years. Baseball has had Babe Ruth, Lou Gehrig, Ted Williams, Mickey Mantle, and Stan Musial. Hockey has had women who have dominated United States teams. Listed below are the names of players who have been named to the United States Teams five, ten, fifteen or more years: [1,2]

Members of a United States Team 15 Years or More
Betty Richey (10*10')
Betty Shellenberger (15*2')
Anne Townsend (16*1')

Members of a United States Team 10–14 Years
Gertrude Dunn (6*6')
Joan Edenborn (7*3')
Frances Elliott (8*5')
Vonnie Gros (11*1')
Mary Ann Leight Harris (10*1')
Alison Hersey (6*5')
Patricia Kenworthy Nuckols (10*1')
Elenore Pepper (6*4')
Nancy Sawin (7*4')
Barbara Strebeigh (10*3')
Ann McConaghie Volp (13*1')
Alice Putnam Willets (10*)

Members of a United States Team 5–9 Years
Ruth Heller Aucott (7*1')
Jean Graham Bingham (3*3')
Agnes Rodgers Bixler (3*2')
Rosemary Deniken Blankley (5*1')
Virginia Bourquardez (3*3')
Adele Boyd (8*)
Elizabeth Burger (5*3')

* Number of times on United States team, including 1968 teams.
' Number of times on United States Reserve team, including 1968 teams.

255

Members of a United States Team 5–9 Years, continued

Betty Cadbury (7*1')
Barbara Stobhar Clement (4*2')
Suzanne Cross (5*2')
Barbara Crowe (3*4')
Margot Cunningham (5*4')
Anne Delano (5*2')
Jean Chapin Dolat (2*3')
Betty White Drobac (4*3')
Katherine Weiner DuBois (5*)
Betty Tausig Flershem (6*3')
Helen Tomlinsen Gibson (3*4')
Priscilla Bartol Grace (3*2')
Marjorie Harrowell (3*5')
Barbara Heylmun Longstreth (2*5')
Kitty McLean (7*1')
Betty Miller (6*2')
Dorothy Moffet (4*2')
Barbara Newhall Newlin (3*2')
Anne Page (5*2')
Frances Pierce (4*5')
Angela Geraci Poisson (7*2')
Anne Pugh (6*3')
Beth Ralph (2*4')
Geraldine Thaete Shipley (5*)
Selina Silleck (1*6')
Jean Siterlet (1*4')
Judy Smiley (1*4')
Jane Adair Cameron Smith (1*4')
Phyllis Stadler (8*1')
Ann Parry Tillman (2*4')
Harriet Walton (1*8')
Barbara Black Ware (4*3')
Helena Wheeler (2*6')
Sally Wilkins (2*7')
Patricia Zelley (5*2')
Patricia Zimmerman (5*2')

TOURING TEAMS

Since 1948, the USFHA has sponsored an increased number of touring teams. Almost biennally, a team has gone on tour. Touring has provided many hockey players with the opportunity to become world

* Number of times on United States team, including 1968 teams.
' Number of times on United States Reserve team, including 1968 teams.

travelers, as tours have traveled to every continent. Tours have included the following:

1924	Great Britain
1933	Europe—IFWHA Conference at Copenhagen
1938	Australia
1939	British Guiana
1948	Great Britain and Holland
1950	South Africa—IFWHA Conference at Johannesburg
1953	Great Britain and Ireland—IFWHA Conference at Folkestone
1955	England
1956	Australia and New Zealand—IFWHA Conference at Sydney
1958	South Africa
1959	Europe—IFWHA Conference at Amsterdam
1962	Great Britain and Denmark
*1963	IFWHA Conference at Baltimore
1965	Jamaica
1967	Europe—IFWHA Conference at Leverkusen, Germany
1969	Guyana

Members of the United States team have the first option of representing this country on a touring team. When members of that team are unable to go, the Reserve team has the next option, followed by Sectional players. Because players must finance their own transportation costs and because some players are unable to obtain a leave of absence from school if they are students, from teaching positions, or other jobs, there are occasions when United States first team players cannot go.

Several players have played on more than one touring team. Their names and the year they toured are included below.

Members of 5 or More Touring Teams

Vonnie Gros ('58, '59, '62, '63, '65, '67)
Alison Hersey ('58, '59, '62, '63, '67)
Elenore Pepper ('48, '50, '53, '55, '63)
Angela Geraci Poisson ('56, '58, '59, '62, '63)
Betty Shellenberger ('48, '50, '53, '55, '56, '59)
Phyllis Stadler ('58, '59, '62, '63, '65)

Members of 2–4 Touring Teams

Helen Allen ('48, '53)
Ruth Heller Aucott ('56, '59, '63)

* IFWHA Conference held in the United States

Members of 2–4 Touring Teams, continued

Adele Boyd ('62, '63, '65, '67)
Elizabeth Burger ('39, '50, '53, '56)
Betty Cadbury ('24, '33)
Suzanne Cross ('33, '38)
Margot Cunningham ('53, '55, '59, '62)
Anne Delano ('48, '67)
Gertrude Dunn ('59, '62, '63)
Joan Edenborn ('55, '56, '58, '59)
Frances Elliott ('33, '38, '48)
Jean Graham ('48, '50)
Betty Fehr Gribbel ('38, '48, '50)
Mary Ann Leight Harris ('59, '62, '63, '67)
Caroline Haussermann ('58, '59, '62)
Eleanor Keady ('59, '62)
Jane Kenworthy ('39, '50)
Anne Le Duc ('50, '53, '56, '58)
Barbara Heylmun Longstreth ('62, '63)
Margaret McVey ('48, '50)
Betty Miller ('63, '65, '67)
Dorothy Moffet ('48, '50, '53)
Patricia Kenworthy Nuckols ('48, '53)
Frances Pierce ('33, '39)
Beth Ralph ('50, '53, '56)
Nancy Sawin ('48, '55, '56, '62)
Judy Smiley ('65, '67)
Sue Day Stahl ('65, '67)
Barbara Strebeigh ('33, '38)
Anne Townsend ('24, '33)
Harriet Walton ('38, '48, '50)
Anne Westervelt ('59, '63)
Sally Wilkins ('62, '67)
Elizabeth Williams ('50, '56, '67)
Patricia Zimmerman ('58, '59, '63)

FOOTNOTES

1. BOTTARO, MARY, *USFHA—Past and Present* (Detroit: 19984 Whitcomb Ave., n.d.), pp. 15–38 and supplement.

2. *DGWS Field Hockey—Lacrosse Guides* (Washington, D.C.: American Association for Health, Physical Education and Recreation, 1201 Sixteenth St., N.W.), all publications.

INDEX